CLASSICAL ARCHITECTURE

By the same author:

Victorian Architecture: its Practical Aspects (David & Charles (Holdings) Ltd, Newton Abbot, 1973)

The Erosion of Oxford (Oxford Illustrated Press Ltd, Oxford, 1977)

English Architecture: an Illustrated Glossary (David & Charles (Publishers) Ltd, Newton Abbot, 1977 and 1987)

Mausolea in Ulster (Ulster Architectural Heritage Society, Belfast, 1978)

Moneymore and Draperstown. The Architecture and Planning of the Ulster Estates of the Drapers' Company (Ulster Architectural Society, Belfast, 1979)

A Celebration of Death. An introduction to some of the buildings, monuments, and settings of funerary architecture in the Western European tradition (Constable & Co. Ltd, London, and Scribners, New York, 1980)

The History, Architecture, and Planning of the Estates of the Fishmongers' Company in Ulster (Ulster Architectural Heritage Society, Belfast, 1981)

The Life and Work of Henry Roberts (1803–76), Architect (Phillimore & Co. Ltd, Chichester, 1983)

The Londonderry Plantation 1609–1914. The History, Architecture, and Planning of the Estates of the City of London and its Livery Companies in Ulster (Phillimore & Co. Ltd, Chichester, 1986)

Victorian Architecture (David & Charles Publishers plc, Newton Abbot, 1990)

The Art and Architecture of Freemasonry (B.T. Batsford Ltd, London, 1991)

Encyclopedia of Architectural Terms (Donhead Publishing Ltd, London, 1993, and Shaftesbury, 1997)

Georgian Architecture (David & Charles Publishers plc, Newton Abbot, 1993)

Egyptomania. The Egyptian Revival as a recurring theme in the History of Taste (Manchester University Press, Manchester, 1994)

The English Heritage Book of Victorian Churches (B.T. Batsford Ltd, London, 1995)

Oxford Dictionary of Architecture (Oxford University Press, Oxford, 1999 and 2000)

The Honourable The Irish Society and the Plantation of Ulster, 1608–2000: The City of London and the Colonisation of County Londonderry in the Province of Ulster in Ireland. A History and Critique (Phillimore & Co. Ltd, Chichester, 2000)

The Victorian Celebration of Death (Sutton Publishing Ltd, Thrupp, Stroud, 2000)

Contributor to: *The Encyclopedia of Urban Planning* (McGraw-Hill, New York, 1974); *The Survey of London* (Athlone Press for the GLC, London, 1973, 1975, and 1983); *Transactions* of the Ancient Monuments Society (Ancient Monuments Society, London, 1977); *National Trust Studies* (Sotheby Parke Bernet, London, 1980); *Contemporary Architects* (Macmillan Press, London, 1980 and St James Press, Chicago and London, 1987); a new edition of J.C. Loudon's *On the Laying Out, Planting, and Managing of Cemeteries, and on the Improvement of Churchyards* (Ivelet Books, Redhill, Surrey, 1981); the *Macmillan Encyclopedia of Architects* (Macmillan, London, 1982); *Charles Sargeant Jagger. War and Peace Sculpture* (Imperial War Museum, London, 1985); *Influences in Victorian Art and Architecture* (Society of Antiquaries of London, London, 1985); *O Ewich is so Lanck. Die historischen Friedhöfe in Berlin-Kreuzberg* (Beuermann, Berlin, 1987); *The Book of London* (Weidenfeld & Nicolson, London, 1989); *The Victorian Façade: The work of William Watkins and his Son* (Lincolnshire College of Art & Design, Lincoln, 1990); *Louis Visconti 1791–1853* (Délégation à l'Action Artistique de la Ville de Paris, Paris, 1991); *L'Egitto fuori dell'Egitto* (Editrice CLUEB, Bologna, 1991); *Contemporary Masterworks* (St James Press, Chicago and London, 1991); *The Rattle of the North* (Blackstaff Press, Belfast, 1992); *Companion to Contemporary Architectural Thought* (Routledge, London and New York, 1993); *International Dictionary of Architects and Architecture* (St James Press, Detroit, London, and Washington DC, 1993); *Una Arquitectura para la Muerte* (Junta de Andalucía, Seville, 1993); *Contemporary Architects* (St James Press, Detroit and London, 1994); *L Égyptomanie à l'épreuve de l'archéologie* (Éditions du Gram, Brussels, and Musée du Louvre, Paris, 1996); *The Dictionary of Art* (Macmillan, London and New York, 1996); *Culture and Identity in Late 20th Century Scotland* (Tuckwell Press, Phantassie, 1998); *A Republic for the Ages: the United States Capitol and the Political Culture of the Early Republic* (University Press of Virginia, Charlottesville, Va, 1999); *Een Introductie tot de zorg voor het Funerair Erfgoed. Verlagsboek* (Vlaamse Contactcommissie Monumentenzorg, Brussels, 1999); and sundry journals (including *Country Life, The Journal of Garden History, Architectural History, The Literary Review, Connaissance des Arts, The Architects' Journal, The Times Higher Education Supplement,* and many others).

CLASSICAL ARCHITECTURE

An Introduction to its Vocabulary and Essentials,
with a Select Glossary of Terms

JAMES STEVENS CURL

W. W. Norton & Company
New York • London

For
DAVID WATKIN
with affection and gratitude

For information about permission to reproduce selections from this book, write to Permissions,
W. W. Norton & Company, Inc., 500 Fifth Avenue, New York, NY 10110

Library of Congress Cataloging-in-Publication Data

Curl, James Stevens, 1937–
Classical architecture : an introduction to its vocabulary and essentials, with a select glossary of terms /
James Stevens Curl. — [2nd ed.]
p. cm.
"1st American pbk. ed."—T.p. verso.
First published in 1992; 2nd ed. originally published in London by B. T. Batsford.
Includes bibliographical references and index.
ISBN 0-393-73119-7 (pbk.)
1. Architecture, Classical. 2. Classicism in architecture. I. Title

NA260 .C87 2003

720'.9—dc21   2002041073

W. W. Norton & Company, Inc., 500 Fifth Avenue, New York, NY 10110
www.wwnorton.com

W. W. Norton & Company Ltd., Castle House, 75/76 Wells Street, London W1T 3QT

2 4 6 8 0 9 7 5 3 1

CONTENTS

ILLUSTRATION SOURCES

6

PREFACE TO THE SECOND EDITION

7

PREFACE TO THE FIRST EDITION

9

I INTRODUCTION

What is Classical Architecture? A few definitions

11

II THE ORDERS OF ARCHITECTURE AND THEIR APPLICATION

Introduction; the Greek Orders; the Greek Doric Order; the Greek Ionic Order; the Greek Corinthian Order; the Roman Orders; the Tuscan Order; the Roman Doric Order; the Roman Ionic Order; the Roman Corinthian Order; the Roman Composite Order; application of the Orders

15

III THE GRAECO-ROMAN ROOTS OF CLASSICAL ARCHITECTURE

The main sources of Classicism: Greek Architecture; Roman Architecture; concluding comparative remarks

55

IV THE RENAISSANCE PERIOD

Columns, pilasters, antae, and piers; key buildings of the Early Renaissance; later *Palazzi*; Venetian *Palazzi*, Sansovino, and Alberti; centralized and circular plans; Michelangelo; Serlio and Vignola; Palladio

65

V BAROQUE, ROCOCO, AND PALLADIANISM

Introduction; Bernini, Borromini, ellipses, and western façades; some French examples; Classical Architecture in England; some German buildings; Palladianism

105

VI NEOCLASSICISM AND AFTER
Neoclassicism and Rome; Cordemoy and Laugier; the rediscovery of Greece; the Greek Revival;
the move away from Neoclassicism

145

VII EPILOGUE

169

GLOSSARY

171

SELECT BIBLIOGRAPHY

223

INDEX

226

ILLUSTRATION SOURCES

Sources are given in brackets after each caption, with the abbreviated form of the publication or collection indicated in either the caption or the source in parentheses. Abbreviations indicate the collections from which the illustrations derive, with the reference number or shelf-mark (if appropriate) after the abbreviation. Illustrations in the Glossary are by the author unless indicated otherwise. Sketch-plans and sections are at differing scales. The key to abbreviations is as follows:

A	The author, or from the author's collection.
AFK	Anthony F. Kersting.
Batsford	Archives of B.T. Batsford Ltd, London.
Langley	Langley, Batty. *The CITY and COUNTRY BUILDER'S and WORKMAN'S TREASURY of DESIGNS: Or the ART of DRAWING and WORKING The Ornamental PARTS of* ARCHITECTURE. S. Harding, London, 1745.
Normand	Normand, Charles. *NOUVEAU PARALLÈLE des ORDRES D'ARCHITECTURE des GRECS, des ROMAINS et des AUTEURS MODERNES.* Normand Aîné, and Carillian, Goeury and Dalmont, Paris, 1852.
RCHME	Royal Commission on the Historical Monuments of England.
RCAHMS	Royal Commission on the Ancient and Historical Monuments of Scotland.
SJSM	By courtesy of the Trustees of Sir John Soane's Museum.
Spiers	Spiers, R. Phené. *The Orders of Architecture, Greek, Roman, and Italian. Selected from Normand's Parallel and Other Authorities.* B.T. Batsford, London, 1893.

PREFACE TO THE SECOND EDITION

*The word 'classic' . . . is often used . . . to indicate
qualities which are the special praise of Greek
and Roman work – stateliness, elegance, and
the careful coordination of all the parts of
the composition . . . It [implies] standard
excellence.*

RUSSELL STURGIS (1836–1909): *A Dictionary of Architecture and Building.*
The Macmillan Company, London and New York, 1901, pp. 609–610.

*C*lassical Architecture was very well received when it first appeared in 1992, so it is therefore a source of some satisfaction that it is being re-launched in paperback.

In several countries today, Classicism in Architecture is alive and well, although it gets a bashing in the Public Prints from time to time, usually by those for whom it never had relevance on any level. Yet visitors to old cities in Italy are surrounded by Classical Architecture (which is almost the vernacular style there), and much twentieth-century modern Italian Architecture (not just of the Fascist era) is deeply rooted in Classicism. Rome, for example, is a Classical city *par excellence*. Classicism is dominant in Paris and other French cities, and, in its many transformations, can enchant those who trouble to explore (for example) the exquisite eighteenth-century Rococo churches in Southern Germany. Many great public buildings of the nineteenth and twentieth centuries, familiar to multitudes on both sides of the Atlantic, are fine Classical compositions, and it is probably reasonable to claim that Classical Architecture contributes not a little to the pleasures of travel. It therefore seems sensible to provide a volume that explains what the essence of Classical Architecture actually is, for, although many buildings in different places will be familiar *partly*

because of the Classical language of Architecture employed, the traveller misses much if he or she cannot identify the sources of designs, the stylistic aspects, and even the Classical shadow lurking behind even the most stripped and bare essay in unornamented design.

I have replaced line-drawings with which I was dissatisfied, and have (I hope) excised some infelicities. I still think the designers created something rather beautiful, and the text and illustrations are informative, so I offer *Classical Architecture* once again in the belief that the book has some merits, and will be useful to the student of a great architectural phenomenon.

My gratitude, as always, must be expressed to my wife, Dorota, who has tolerated the piles of paper and drawings that eventually became this volume, and to those of my friends, especially the late Stephen Dykes Bower (1903–1994), who wrote to me about the first edition in most gracious and appreciative terms, and encouraged me to labour on this new edition. Mrs Karen Latimer kindly helped with the revised bibliography.

James Stevens Curl
Holywood, Down, and Broadfans, Essex
2000–2001

Architecture cannot lie, and buildings, although inanimate, are to that extent morally superior to men . . .

Since the early nineteenth century we have depended almost exclusively on what used to be called book learning, so much so that we have become visually illiterate.

JOHN EDWARDS GLOAG (1896–1981): *The Significance of Historical Research in Architectural and Industrial Design.* A Paper read to the Royal Society for the encouragement of Arts, Manufactures, and Commerce. 20 March 1963.

PREFACE TO THE FIRST EDITION

It is not till we come to the rise of Greek architecture that we enter on the great course of European architectural development, in which one style arises in historic succession from another – Roman from Greek, Romanesque from Roman, Gothic from Romanesque, in a steady stream of which the glorious and perfect Art of Greece is the fountainhead.

HENRY HEATHCOTE STATHAM (1839–1924): *A History of Architecture*. London, 1950, p. 43.

When I was a student of Architecture, one had to survey a building of quality and prepare measured drawings based on the survey: the buildings selected for us were usually Classical (either eighteenth- or early nineteenth-century), and our drawings and notes were subjected to close scrutiny, criticized, and then marked. There was a cash prize for the best set of measured drawings, given in memory of the distinguished Architect, Sir Charles Lanyon (1813–1889), who designed the Antrim Coast Road and many of the noblest buildings in Ulster.

This discipline proved invaluable and instilled in me, from my first year of study, a healthy respect for the complexities, subtleties, and qualities of the Classical Language of Architecture. Surveys and measured drawings oblige students to look at buildings and understand them: it is only by surveying and drawing up those surveys that a detailed knowledge of proportional systems, relationships of parts, axial planning, mouldings, and, above all, how junctions are formed in a satisfactory manner, can be acquired. I learned very early in my career (to give some examples) how a moulded skirting stops at a block above which an architrave rises; how a band of mouldings joins another band at right angles; how the features of a room (such as fireplaces, windows, niches, doors, and bays) relate to each other by means of main axes and subsidiary axes; how subtle, recessed bands or planted beads can not only disguise joints, but can help objects to look pleasing by their logical positioning and the resulting subdivision of planes; how plinths, pedestals, rails, and cornices divide and finish the designs of walls; how pilasters can break up a long wall into a series of parts and relate to the design of entablatures and ceiling compartments; how to design a corner (inside and out); and a great deal more. I discovered a rich alphabet to start with, then a vocabulary, and then a whole language capable of infinitely adaptable use. I have always been grateful for that invaluable training, for it enabled me to look at buildings with an informed eye, and has made visiting fine cities, towns, and buildings one of my greatest of pleasures in life, and one that has never palled.

From the 1950s, however, architectural students were required to design in the manner that had become *de rigueur* after 1945: this eschewed all 'historical' references, although it was perfectly all right to crib bits from the works of Le Corbusier, Mies van der Rohe, Marcel Breuer, Walter Gropius, and others currently fashionable. I, like many others of my generation, had to 'design' to comply with the prejudices of those who talked about 'building for our own time', the 'poetry of concrete', the 'honest expression of structure', and other doleful matters.

I realized very quickly that not only was the favoured 'Architecture' promoted in Schools of Architecture arguably not Architecture at all, because it had no vocabulary, grammar, syntax, serenity, repose, quality, or beauty, but also that it was extraordinarily easy to produce, and required the minimum of effort in terms of thought or draughtsmanship. Classicism required study, practice, understanding, scholarship, and thought: it was far too difficult for people who wanted the easy way out, who did not care about the environment or about the past (several individuals expressed a desire to destroy all old buildings, especially cathedrals, churches, museums, country houses, and palaces), and who preferred mouthing cant and cribbing the latest cliché from pictures in one of the 'architectural' magazines to expending any effort on learning about real Architecture. A great language, a mighty and expansive vocabulary, was superseded by a series of monosyllabic grunts, uttered as offensively as possible, and foisted on the populace with a totalitarian disregard for the opinion of those who had not been drilled to conform. Vitruvius, Alberti, Palladio, and all the other great architectural writers were jettisoned in favour of sociological twaddle and mindless sub-Marxist drivel, larded with a few 'calculations' related to reinforced concrete structures.

The quality of the buildings created as a result of the fashions of the 1940s through to the 1980s is on view virtually everywhere: it has been weighed, and, for the most part, has been found wanting. Some very large structures, 'designed' without the slightest regard for quality, and hated by their inhabitants and by those who had to look at them, have already been demolished, long before their construction costs had been paid off, while others are being dressed up with a primitive attempt at architectural language to make them more visually acceptable.

Classical Orders, or sometimes just columns, have reappeared, not always with success, and there have been a number of schemes in recent years that adhere to a system of geometry owing something to Classicism. There have even been some direct Classical quotations in otherwise un-Classical buildings, sometimes referred to by critics as 'witty', depending on the identity of the Architect and his current standing in the favouritism

stakes. Yet there are so many errors being perpetrated it is quite clear that knowledge of the principles of Classicism (and even of basic masonry) is less than rudimentary among Architects of today. One sees stones joined at the mitre, keystones that would never work, lintels that are far too small in height or too great in length, columns carrying pediments with no supporting entablatures, and supports that are far too widely spaced. One has the feeling that games are being played, and that superficiality still dominates the once noble world of Architecture.

This book is an attempt to explain what Classical Architecture is, and to show various permutations, combinations, and types of Classicism in Architecture. It is restricted to being an introduction to the subject because to cover it as fully as possible would make a far bigger volume than my publishers are prepared to allow me. It is hoped that it will help students of Architecture to begin to have a feeling for a great language that can still be studied, not only in some of the best buildings in the world, but in thousands of decent works of Architecture that serve to enhance our towns, cities, and countryside with their well-mannered reticence.

A word is necessary concerning my use of Langley as a source for some of the illustrations. I chose Langley for his practicality and simplicity, and because his plates demonstrate the modules and relationships of parts very clearly. He was, after all, catering for draughtsmen and for people who had to build or make artefacts in the Classical styles.

I am grateful to two of my tutors (the late Mr William Murray and the late Mr Ferguson Sprott) who first gave me a taste for Classicism: the first edition was dedicated to their memories. Mr Timothy Auger, then Editorial Director of B.T. Batsford Ltd, quickly saw the point of such a book as this: I thank him and all his staff for support. Mr Robert Blow and Mr Ian Leith of the National Monuments Record, and the late Mr A. Stuart Gray rendered great assistance in helping to provide some of the illustrations. Mr Anthony F. Kersting, Miss Iona Cruickshank, and Mr Rodney C. Roach helped with the photography and processing. The late Sir John Summerson kindly gave permission to quote from his work. Mr John Gamble, Mr Barry Ketchum, Mrs Vicky Johnson, Mr Jeremy Ridge, and the late Mr Meaburn Staniland all helped to locate books. Many others have influenced the contents of this work in one way or another; shortage of space precludes mentioning them all by name, but my friends are warmly thanked for everything they have contributed over many years.

James Stevens Curl
Burley-on-the-Hill, Rutland
1989–91

I

INTRODUCTION

What is Classical Architecture?
A few definitions

Eighteen centuries ago one magnificent architectural tradition ruled Europe, Africa, and Asia, from the Rhine to the Sahara, from the Atlantic to the Euphrates.

DONALD STRUAN ROBERTSON (1885–1961): *A Handbook of Greek and Roman Architecture.* Cambridge, 1945, p. 1.

WHAT IS CLASSICAL ARCHITECTURE?
A FEW DEFINITIONS

It is perhaps as well, at the very beginning, to be reminded of what is meant by Classical Architecture. The definition[1] that Architecture is the art or science of building or constructing edifices of any kind for human use is surely far too wide, for it includes any building, whatever its quality. John Ruskin (1819–1900), in the *Seven Lamps*,[2] proposed that Architecture was the 'art which so disposes and adorns the edifices raised by man . . . that the sight of them contributes to his mental health, power, and pleasure', a definition that suggests something more than utilitarianism, and indicates a spiritual, aesthetic, and beneficial content. Sir George Gilbert Scott[3] (1811–1878) stated that 'Architecture, as distinguished from mere building, is the decoration of construction', but few would subscribe to that view today. Architecture implies a sense of order, an organization, a geometry, and an aesthetic experience of a far higher degree than that in a mere 'building'.

Sir Henry Wotton's (1568–1639) declaration that 'Well building hath three conditions: Commodity, Firmness, and Delight', is derived from Vitruvius (Marcus Vitruvius Pollio), whose *De Architectura*, written in the reign of the Emperor Augustus, is one of the most important texts dealing with Classical Architecture; it is the only complete work on Architecture that has come down to us from Antiquity. Vitruvius was an Architect, and his treatise is in ten books: they include observations on the education of the Architect; on fundamental principles of Architecture; on building types; and on four of the Orders (not, however, discussed in their logical sequence of Tuscan, Doric, Ionic, and Corinthian). There is a vast amount of information about Architecture and building in Antiquity included in *De Architectura*, but, although Vitruvius suggested appropriate associations for each Order, he did not give them the degree of rule-book significance accorded them later by Renaissance writers.

Vitruvius stated[4] that Architecture depends on Order, Arrangement, Eurythmy, Symmetry, Propriety, and Economy. By Eurythmy he seems to have meant harmony of proportion, or some kind of rhythmical order of elements: central to that concept is beauty and fitness of the elements of a building, involving relationships of height to breadth, breadth to length, and symmetrical balance. These six points appear to come from an Alexandrine text, now lost. Vitruvius also states[5] that works of Architecture should be realized with due reference to durability, convenience, and beauty ('*Ut habeatur ratio Firmitatis, Utilitatis, Venustatis*'): durability depended on foundations and a wise choice of materials; convenience on the arrangement and usability of apartments and on orientation and exposure to the sun and air; and beauty on the appearance of the finished work and on the proportion of the various parts in relation to each other and to the whole. Usefulness, spaciousness, sound construction, and strength are indeed qualities to be expected in good buildings, but the addition of delight, uplifting of the spirits, and aesthetic aspects suggests that Architecture is something more than building. Sir Christopher Wren stated[6] that the principles of Architecture were, in his time, 'rather the Study of Antiquity than Fancy', and that the main principles were 'Beauty, Firmness, and Convenience', the first two depending on the geometrical factors of 'Opticks and Staticks', while the third provided variety in works of Architecture.

Today, the term 'Classical' implies the first rank or

authority, a standard, or a model. It is therefore exemplary, but it specifically suggests derivation from Greek or Roman Antiquity: the term 'Classical' means conforming in style or composition (or both) to the rules or models of Greek and Roman Antiquity. The Classical ideal is characterized by clarity, completeness, symmetry, deceptive simplicity, repose, and harmonious proportions; it is associated with civilized life, perfection, taste, restraint, and serenity. The Classical language of Architecture is not a free-for-all in which elements are arbitrarily thrown together; it is a sophisticated system that was in use throughout the Roman Empire, and its traces survived throughout the centuries, especially in Italy, Greece, parts of France, and the Middle East. Classical Architecture has elements that can be related directly to the architectural vocabulary and language of Graeco-Roman Antiquity (especially Greek temples and the ceremonial, monumental, and public Architecture of Ancient Rome), or are derived as variants from that vocabulary and language: those elements include the Orders themselves (the columns or pilasters *with entablatures*), the frames and heads of window or door openings, pedimented gables, plinths, crowning cornices, string-courses, a range of mouldings, with or without enrichment, and much else.

Classical Architecture, however, does not mean only the application of Orders or other details; those are only the outward and visible distinguishing marks. It suggests that the various parts of Architecture are disposed in some form of harmonious relationship, both to each other and to the whole. Of course, the proportions and relationships of the various parts, including those of solids and voids, are to a very large extent determined by the Orders and by the spaces between columns or pilasters (intercolumniation), and by whether the Orders are physically present or the façades are astylar (without columns or pilasters). There is also, in Classical Architecture, a system by which the geometry of each part is related to the geometry of the whole, giving an harmonious balance and repose to the entire façade, or total building, or both. Thus units, and multiples or subdivisions of such units, have an essential rôle to play in the system of Classical proportion, and the purpose of proportional systems is to help to set up harmony, balance, repose, and an agreeable aesthetic throughout the whole of the building.

A building without overt Classical detail can still be a work of Classical Architecture: designs by Architects such as Claude-Nicolas Ledoux (1735–1806) and Friedrich Gilly (1772–1800), for example, often eschew references to the Orders, architraves, or any other Classical motif, with the result that their buildings have a bare, primitive, stripped appearance, yet the proportions are undeniably Classical; while occasional techniques, such as the use of unfluted, primitive Doric columns, or a cornice based on that of the exterior of the Pantheon drum, suggest Antiquity by the most understated means. Certain Romanesque and Gothic buildings, or parts of buildings, such as porches or western doors, have proportional systems that unquestionably derive from Classical Antiquity, but the Romanesque or Gothic details of colonnettes, capitals, tympana, and mouldings are anything but Classical, and so cannot be considered as Classical Architecture. Sir John Summerson, in his *The Classical Language of Architecture*,[7] has held that Classical Architecture is only recognizable 'as such when it contains some allusion, however slight, however vestigial', to the Antique Orders: such an 'allusion may be no more than' a hint of a cornice, or it could be 'a disposition of windows which suggests' the proportional relationships of pedestals, columns, and entablature. 'Some twentieth-century buildings – notably those of Auguste Perret and his imitators' – are Classical 'in this way: that is to say, they are thought out in modern materials' but in a Classical spirit 'and sealed' as Classical 'only by the tiniest allusive gestures'. I would go even further, and suggest that a building can be Classical in its proportions, its relationships of solids to voids, and the clarity of its expression, but need not have any allusion to an Order *per se*, although, in most true, stripped Classical buildings one can superimpose an imaginary Order that will fit easily on to the basic façade. In some cases, too, an Order or parts of an Order may even be paraphrased: that is, the Order or parts of it may be expressed or suggested by other means; so the language of Classical Architecture can give an Architect who is fluent in all its aspects great latitude. The *sense* of Classicism can be suggested by economical means, and may be *commented* upon by a variety of methods in design. Like all great languages with a huge vocabulary and a vast range of expressive subtleties, Classical Architecture is not a matter of mere imitation (although that is necessary at an early stage of study in order to learn its basic alphabet, vocabulary, syntax, and grammar): it offers enormous possibilities for expression, creative design, and composition.

It should be emphasized that there is far, far more to Classical Architecture than the treatment of surfaces or the design of elevations. It is about three-dimensional Architecture: spaces, volumes, plan shapes; the relationships of one room to another; the setting up of axes about which balance and symmetry can be achieved; proportions of solids to voids; the position of columns in relation to beams, pilasters, corners (inside and out), and design of soffites and ceilings; how one volume can rise up through others or can penetrate surrounding volumes; how axes and entrances can be signalled or emphasized; the framing and finishing of windows, doorways, fireplaces, and niches; the establishment of different planes; the emphasis given to a main floor; and a great deal else besides. It involves using a huge range of motifs, almost 'kits-of-parts', each of which is beautifully designed in itself, and each of which relates to other motifs in a literate, grammatical way: it also can involve being able to experiment with a rich language in order to create new and interesting compositions. An integral part of Classical Architecture is the rhythm set up by the dimensions between elements, which are based upon modules, multiplied or divided: so measurement, mathematical relationships, and geometrical principles are essential. Those modules, rhythms, and proportional systems have important anchors in the Orders themselves. So, even though an Order may not be physically present in a design, its presence may still be overwhelmingly there through the proportional systems and juxtaposition of parts.

1. *The Oxford English Dictionary.*
2. i. § I.7 (1849).
3. *Lect. Archit.* II. 292 (1879).
4. *The Ten Books on Architecture*, Book I, Ch. I, 1.
5. Ibid., Book I, Ch. III, 2.
6. *Tracts on Architecture I, On Architecture; and Observations on Antique Temples, etc.* in the *Appendix* to *Parentalia. The Wren Society*, vol. 19, Oxford, 1942, p.126.
7. London, 1963 and 1980. P.9 in the 1980 edition.

II

THE ORDERS OF ARCHITECTURE AND THEIR APPLICATION

Introduction; the Greek Orders; the
Greek Doric Order; the Greek Ionic
Order; the Greek Corinthian Order; the
Roman Orders; the Tuscan Order; the
Roman Doric Order; the Roman Ionic
Order; the Roman Corinthian Order;
the Roman Composite Order;
application of the Orders

Architecture aims at Eternity; and therefore is the
only Thing uncapable of Modes and Fashions in
its Principals, the Orders.

CHRISTOPHER WREN (1632–1723): *Tracts on Architecture I*, quoted in Stephen
Wren's *Parentalia, or Memoirs of the Family of Wrens* (1750). Reprinted in
The Wren Society, Vol. 19, Oxford, 1942, p. 126.

INTRODUCTION

An Order of Architecture is essentially a vertical post carrying a beam or a lintel, but there is far more to it than that. It is an assembly of parts consisting of a column, with base (usually) and capital, carrying an entablature, proportioned and embellished in consistency with one of the Orders: it is essentially the column and the horizontal element above of a temple colonnade, and it may or may not have a pedestal. The entablature is divided into the architrave, which is the lowest part, resting directly on the abaci of the columns, so the architrave is properly the lintel. Above this lintel-architrave is usually a frieze (omitted in some of the Antique examples of the Orders), and above this is the cornice, which represents the eaves of the building, protects the frieze, and sheds water from the roof.

Vitruvius provided the earliest descriptions we have of the Orders of Architecture in his *De Architectura*, drawn from Greek sources and from his own experiences. The work was composed between 16 and 14 BC, and was dedicated to Augustus. The first seven books of *De Architectura* deal with: Architecture in general (I), building materials (II), the construction of temples (III), the Orders of Architecture (IV), public buildings (V), private buildings in town and country (VI), and ornamentation of buildings (VII); the remaining books cover water and waterways, sundials and water-clocks, and the building of various machines. The Orders, therefore, are described in his third and fourth books. Unfortunately, what was clear to Vitruvius and his contemporaries is no longer familiar, and architectural descriptions are notoriously difficult to interpret in any case, so the text poses some problems. Nevertheless Vitruvius provided descriptions of the Doric, Ionic, and Corinthian Orders,

and brief notes on the Tuscan Order. He suggested the geographical areas where each Order was evolved, and associated the Orders with various deities, indicating an appropriate Order for a particular god or goddess.

Much later, in fifteenth-century Florence, Leon Battista Alberti (1404–1472) prepared the first treatise on the theory and practice of Architecture since Antiquity, in his *De re aedificatoria* (1485), drawing on Vitruvius and on his own acute observations of Antique remnants. Like Vitruvius's *De Architectura*, Alberti's *De re aedificatoria* was divided into ten books, but, unlike the earlier work, Alberti's was written in stylish Latin, and gave a coherent account of the decidedly fragmented knowledge of the Architecture of Antiquity that had survived through the centuries. Alberti established Architecture as an intellectual and professional discipline, and gave it a respectable theoretical substance: in fact he laid the foundations for the development of the theory and practice of Architecture in the Renaissance period. To the four Orders identified by Vitruvius, Alberti added the Composite, which he had observed in extant Roman buildings, as a distinct Order, the capital of which combined Ionic volutes with Corinthian acanthus leaves.

However, the great Renaissance writers on Architecture were to be concerned with five Orders based on Roman exemplars, for the Greek Orders were not to be published in any detail until the second half of the eighteenth century, and a taste for the severe Greek Doric order was not to develop until after such details were available. Among the most influential of Renaissance writers was Sebastiano Serlio (1475–1554), whose *L'Architettura* appeared from 1537 to 1575, and was further embellished with his drawings in 1584. Serlio's great work was essentially practical in that it provided an illustrated textbook describing the five Orders and much else in the way of Classical detail. *L'Architettura* made not only the Orders, but the architectural language of Donato Bramante (1440–1514) and Raffaello Sanzio (Raphael, 1483–1520) familiar throughout Europe. Serlio had inherited many drawings by Baldassare Peruzzi (1481–1536), which were used in the book. *L'Architettura* quickly became the pattern-book of Europe, used extensively (and often indiscriminately) in many countries. In it the five Roman Orders are shown together for the first time, arranged in the Tuscan–Doric–Ionic–Corinthian–Composite sequence, and described by the author as the *Dramatis Personae* of his treatise. Serlio laid these down in a canonical way, giving his successors and his readers the impression that variations on these Orders were not allowed. In the Italian Renaissance, therefore, the Orders acquired great significance as the true foundations of Architecture, and even seemed to be regarded as something approaching the divinely inspired. This is not surprising, given the intellectual atmosphere of the time in which Hermeticism, Alchemy, and the beginnings of speculative Freemasonry were in evidence. Columns had associations with the Divine through the Temple of Solomon, with Ancient Egyptian mysteries, and with ideas of Strength (Doric), Wisdom (Ionic), and Beauty (Corinthian), apart from Vitruvian connections with deities.

Serlio set down proportions, dimensions, sections, and the like as though they were Holy Writ; he used Vitruvius and observed extant Classical Orders, but Vitruvius can be vague or incomplete, and surviving Roman Orders displayed wide variations, so Serlio was obliged to compose his idealized Orders from a variety of sources. His Orders, therefore, were based partly on the Antique and partly on his own invention.

The Five Orders, and illustrations of them, dominate most architectural introductory texts from Serlio's time for the next three centuries. Giacomo Barozzi da Vignola's (1507–1573) *La Regola delli Cinque Ordini d'Architettura* of 1562 set out a simple modular interpretation of the Orders, which provided a straightforward architectural vocabulary, and was immensely influential as well as more accurate and scholarly than Serlio's work. Andrea Palladio's (1508–1580) *I Quattro libri dell' Architettura* of 1570 did not show the Orders together, although his book (and his use of the Orders) was very important as a source. Vincenzo Scamozzi (1552–1616), a gifted follower of Palladio, produced *L' Idea dell' Architettura Universale* of 1615, which set out the Orders with dimensions, and so provided the final codifying of the five Roman Orders: his book had a profound influence on Northern European Architects. Claude Perrault (1613–1688) published his *Ordonnance des Cinq Espèces de Colonnes* in 1683, which was based on all the great Italian works previously published, and included a modular scale system which enabled proportions to be determined very easily. Many other texts with fine illustrations followed, including James Gibbs's *Rules for Drawing the Several Parts of Architecture* of 1732, and Sir William Chambers's *A Treatise on Civil Architecture*, originally published in 1759, republished as *A Treatise on the Decorative Part of Civil Architecture* in 1791, and brought out again in 1825 with an Examination of 'Grecian Architecture' added by Joseph Gwilt. The Greek Orders are described in the Glossary of Terms (p. 171), but a few salient points need to be made here.

THE GREEK ORDERS

There are three Greek Orders: the Doric, Ionic, and Corinthian, and these are distinct from the Roman Orders of the same name. While the Doric column resembles in some respects a rare Egyptian type found, for example, in the rock-cut tombs at Beni-Hasan, it is also like Mycenaean and Minoan types: the capitals of some very early temples of Doric type closely resemble those of the so-called 'Treasury of Atreus' at Mycenae.

There has been a great deal of argument as to whether or not the Greek Doric Order had a stone or a timber origin. The supporters of stone, including H. Heathcote Statham (1839–1924), have argued that the Doric column and capital are stone forms because the oldest examples of column are thick, fat, and squat, while the reverse would have been true had the original columns been of timber, and because the echinus of the capital, under the abacus, is essentially a stone form, and would be difficult to carve in wood. Unfortunately for this view, while it is true that many early Doric columns are thick and heavy, some of the oldest of all are extremely slender, with very widely spreading capitals, and this type closely resembles Doric columns shown in Athenian vase-paintings depicting wooden structures. The remains of 12 columns from the sanctuary of Athena Pronaia at

Delphi are probably the oldest that can be called Doric (seventh century BC), with a height about six and a half times their lowest diameter and a very pronounced taper. We know that Pausanias, the Lydian traveller and geographer who flourished in the second century AD, saw a wooden column, much decayed, and held together only by means of bands of metal, near the temple of Zeus at Olympia; he also saw a low building with columns of carved oak in the market-place at Elis, and there was an ancient temple of Poseidon Hippios, near Mantinea in Arcadia, that was built of oak, carefully fitted together.[1] The pro-stone commentators also suggest that the triglyphs of the Doric Order could not have had a timber origin because they occur on all elevations of a temple, and because it would be difficult to cut the channels across the grain of the wood. However, the form of the triglyph frieze is suggestive of a wooden origin, a suggestion reinforced by the presence of the dowel- or peg-like guttae of the regulae and the mutules. The triglyphs represent the end of beams, and the metopes the spaces between the beams: it may also be that they are not beams, but some kind of early truss-ends, and that the channels represent the joints between the horizontal beams and the sloping members following the rake of the roof. If the triglyphs were stylized and conventionalized very early, even before their translation into stone, it is a short step to continue the pattern of triglyph-metope-triglyph all round the frieze, even though logically there would be no need for the beam-ends or truss-ends on the gabled façades. The fact that the soffite or underside of the cornice is inclined at the angle of the slope of the roof, and has flat blocks called mutules decorated with 18 guttae, suggests that the mutules may be petrified rafters. These mutules are set over each triglyph and each metope, which suggests some kind of structural origin. Occasionally, the part of the soffite between the mutules was ornamented: in the case of the Parthenon, the corner soffites had an anthemion motif [2.1, 2.2].

THE GREEK DORIC ORDER

The Doric Order, then, must be a stylized and conventionalized petrified version of a timber prototype. The column itself could have originated as a tree-trunk, with the outside 'shaved' by means of a series of flat faces to produce a polygonal plan. The hollowing out of each flat face is a further variation. Greek Doric columns sit directly on the stylobate with no base and have a height, including the capital, of between four and six-and-a-half times the diameter at the base of the column. The circular form of the shaft generally has 20 shallow, concave flutes

2.1 *Reconstruction of the Greek Doric Order from the Parthenon (447–438 BC), an octastyle temple with 17 columns on each side. The triglyphs are over the centre-lines of columns or the spaces between columns (intercolumniations), except at the corners, where the columns are moved in from the centre-lines so that the intercolumniations at the corners are smaller. In the Greek Doric Order the triglyph block has to terminate the frieze, and this creates the problem of spacing of columns at the corners. The drawing shows the relationship of triglyphs to the columns and intercolumniations, with a detail of the corner treatment where the three corner-columns are closer together than elsewhere. Between the triglyphs are the sculptured metopes, and in the tympanum of the pediment is another sculptured group. The shafts of the columns are fluted with sharp arrises between flutes, and rest (without bases) directly on the stylobate of the three-stepped crepidoma. Above the shaft is the capital with hypotrachelion (–um), trachelion (–um), annulets, echinus (cushion-like pad) and square abacus-block. The entablature is divided into its three parts: the low, plain architrave (on which circular medallions of bronze have been fixed); the frieze (of triglyphs and metopes separated from the architrave by the taenia, with regulae under the taenia with guttae); and the cornice, which overhangs, and has sloping mutules on the soffite ornamented with guttae, or peg-like drops (there are no mutules on the soffite of the raking cornice of the pediment). At the corners of the building, and at the apex of the pediment, over the cornice, are blocks known as acroteria, on which ornaments were set. Note the antefixa set at intervals over the cornice to cover the ends of the roofing tiles: they are ornamented with the palmette, while a variation on the palmette, the honeysuckle, ornaments the acroterion at the apex. The honeysuckle also occurs on the soffite of the cornice, at the corner, between the mutules (Batsford)*

2.2 *The Greek Doric Order, showing the corner detail, with triglyphs joining at a bevel. The relationships of column, capital, abacus, architrave, frieze, and cornice should be noted. The sloping mutules with guttae on the underside of the cornice relate to the centre-lines of triglyphs and metopes. Note the antefixa (with palmette ornament), lion's mask as waterspout, and guttae under each regula (the short band under the taenia separating the architrave from the frieze)* (Batsford)

2.3 *Reconstruction of the Lion Tomb at Cnidos (fourth century BC), with its engaged unfluted (except for vestigial fluting top and bottom) Greek Doric Order, and stepped pyramidal roof. This is an example of the so-called Hellenistic taste, dating from the middle of the fourth century BC, in which the spacing (intercolumniation) of the columns became much wider; there are two and three triglyphs per intercolumniation instead of the one triglyph usual in Hellenic examples* (Trustees of the British Museum GoR LXIII 806606)

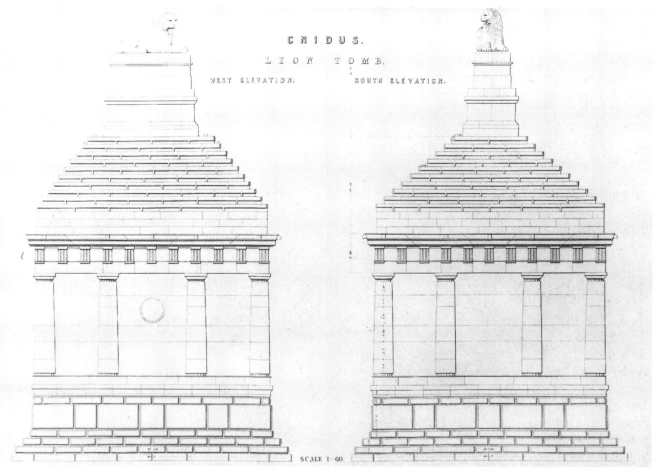

CNIDUS.

LION TOMB.

WEST ELEVATION.　　SOUTH ELEVATION.

SCALE 1 – 60.

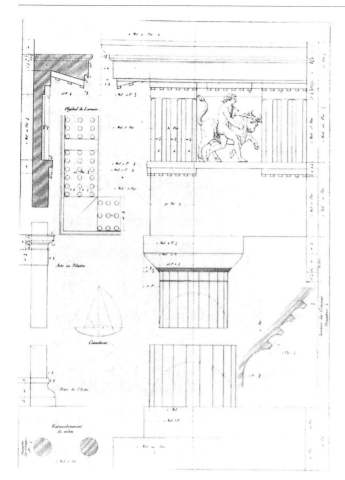

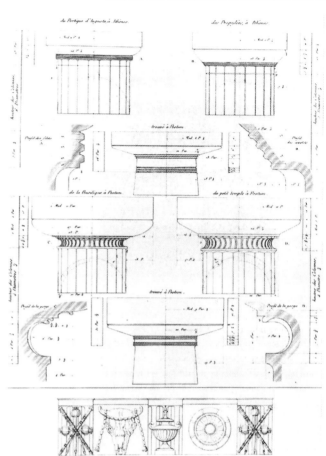

2.4 *Greek Doric Order from the 'Theseum', or Temple of Hephaestus, Athens, of c.450–440 BC, which has an arrangement of 6 × 13 columns around the naos, making it peripteral hexastyle. On the left are details of an anta, the capital and base of which differ from the Order of the columns. Note the two-step crepidoma, the shaft with entasis and flutes with sharp arrises, the hypotrachelion, trachelion or neck, annulets, echinus, square abacus-block, plain architrave, frieze of triglyphs and metopes separated from the architrave by the taenia, the regula-strips with guttae under the taenia, the sloping mutules with guttae under the soffites of the cornice, and the cornice itself. From Normand (A)*

2.5 *Greek Doric capitals. At the top are two Athenian examples. Below is a capital from Paestum showing the exaggerated entasis and the extraordinarily wide abacus and echinus associated with examples there. The remaining three capitals are variations on the Paestum type: note the concave necking which is quite unlike the usual type of Doric trachelion. Below is a frieze of the Roman Doric type with bucranium and patera in the metopes. From Normand (A)*

2.8 *Walhalla, near Regensburg, in Bavaria, by Leo von Klenze (1784–1864) of 1830–42, modelled on the Athenian Parthenon, and set on a stepped podium derived from designs by Karl Freiherr Haller von Hallerstein (1774–1817). Sculpture by Ludwig Schwanthaler (1802–48). Nineteenth-century photograph by G. Böttger of Munich (A)*

2.6 *The Choragic Monument of Thrasyllus, an unusual Greek Doric building of 319 BC, erected as a façade to a cave in Athens. It has two antae, between which is a single square column. The taenia between the plain architrave and frieze has a continuous row of guttae beneath, and the frieze has no triglyphs, but is adorned with wreaths. The attic was added in 279 BC. This monument was derived from the south-west wing of the Athenian Propylaea, which also had three square uprights and a continuous row of guttae. The Thrasyllus Monument was the inspiration for Schinkel's use of square mullions at the Berlin Schauspielhaus (1818–26), and for his continuous guttae at the Neue Wache, Unter den Linden (1816–18). From J. Stuart and N. Revett,* The Antiquities of Athens, *Vol. II, Ch. IV, Pl. 3, London, 1787 (SJSM)*

2.7 *The Greek Doric Order revived. The Anglican chapel at the General Cemetery of All Souls, Kensal Green, London, by John Griffith of Finsbury (1796–1888), of 1837, showing two sizes of Order. Note the prostyle tetrastyle portico and the antae with capitals that are quite different from those of the columns* (A)

2.10 *The Neue Wache, or Royal Guard House, Unter den Linden, Berlin, by Karl Friedrich Schinkel (1781–1841), of 1816–18. A free interpretation of Greek Doric. As in the case of von Klenze's Propyläen in Munich, the prostyle hexastyle portico is set between massive plain pylons. The Order, however, has been adapted: gone are the triglyphs and metopes, and a continuous row of guttae is set beneath the taenia (a motif derived from the Choragic Monument of Thrasyllus [2.6]) and the mutules have been dispensed with. This is an example of an Architect of genius freely altering an Order (A)*

2.9 *Detail of the inner return of the Greek Doric entablature at the Ruhmeshalle (Hall of Fame), Munich (1843–54), by Leo von Klenze. Note the anthemion motif on the soffite at the corner between the mutules with their guttae (A)*

separated by arrises, but there are examples with 12, 16, 18, or 24 flutes. A choice of 20 flutes was more usual because with 20 an arris would occur under the corners of the square abacus, that is, under the diagonals of the abacus, and would permit a flute to occur in the centre of each column as viewed from the centre of each front, back, or sides.

This use of a void (as a flute appears between its arrises) in the centre of a symmetrical composition is essential to much Classical composition. Façades should have a void or a door in the centre, or a space between columns, which means that, in the most satisfactory compositions involving columns or pilasters, there must be an even number of columns (although there are examples in Greek Antiquity where odd numbers of columns create a central column, and therefore confound the normal rule).

Doric shafts are usually composed of drums jointed by means of dowels, and become more slender at the top: in fact, the diameter at the tops of such shafts will be between three-quarters and two-thirds of the base diameter. Furthermore, the shaft has a convex profile, called entasis, which corrects the optical illusion of concavity and apparent weakness in straight-sided tapering columns: the entasis was very obvious at the Paestum temples [2.5]. Occasionally the shaft was unfluted, giving it a primitive look and making it look more sturdy and dumpy, as at the temple of Apollo at Delos: there, and at Cnidos, for example, the flutes appear in a band at the base and top of the shaft [2.3, 2.12]. Flutes serve to accentuate verticality and give the illusion of greater refinement and thinness, especially when strong shadows are cast in the flutes by the sharp arrises.

The shaft terminates at the band known as the hypotrachelion (or hypotrachelium), usually of three grooves in early examples and one in later, above which the flutes and arrises continue (the trachelion or necking) to the capital. This last-mentioned consists of horizontal rings called annulets, above which is the circular, bulbous, cushion-like echinus (so called by Vitruvius because it is like the shell of a sea-urchin), and the plain

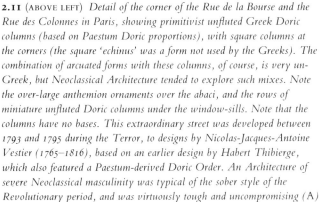

2.11 (ABOVE LEFT) *Detail of the corner of the Rue de la Bourse and the Rue des Colonnes in Paris, showing primitivist unfluted Greek Doric columns (based on Paestum Doric proportions), with square columns at the corners (the square 'echinus' was a form not used by the Greeks). The combination of arcuated forms with these columns, of course, is very un-Greek, but Neoclassical Architecture tended to explore such mixes. Note the over-large anthemion ornaments over the abaci, and the rows of miniature unfluted Doric columns under the window-sills. Note that the columns have no bases. This extraordinary street was developed between 1793 and 1795 during the Terror, to designs by Nicolas-Jacques-Antoine Vestier (1765–1816), based on an earlier design by Habert Thibierge, which also featured a Paestum-derived Doric Order. An Architecture of severe Neoclassical masculinity was typical of the sober style of the Revolutionary period, and was virtuously tough and uncompromising* (A)

2.12 (ABOVE, RIGHT) *The Eben Mausoleum in the Kirchhof I der Jerusalems- und Neuen Kirchengemeinde, Kreuzberg, Berlin, of 1798. This remarkable design, with its primitivist interpretation of an unfluted Doric column (with vestigial flutes between the shaft and the abacus [there is no capital]), is the essence of a late eighteenth-century search for an Architecture that was primitive, blocky, elemental, and reduced to the bare minimum. Probably by Friedrich Gilly* (A)

2.13 (RIGHT) *Portico of the Domkirke (Vor Frue Kirke), Copenhagen, designed from 1808 to 1810 by C. F. Hansen and built between 1811 and 1829. The tympanum is by Thorvaldsen. This portico is very free in its interpretation of Greek Doric: the columns have no entasis, the capital is based on the pattern from Paestum, but, even odder, the triglyphs do not meet at the corner, but leave a portion of metope between them, so they are set on the centre-line of the corner columns. Guttae are not pegs either, but truncated pyramids. This is a Roman-Renaissance arrangement with Greek detailing. Note the anthemion at the corner of the soffite* (A)

square block called the abacus. In early Doric temples the echinus is very bulbous, like a parabolic section, and has a considerable projection, but in late examples, such as the Parthenon, it is only slightly curved from the annulets to just under the abacus, when it curves to the underside of the abacus block. The Greek Doric entablature (about a quarter the height of the total Order, which includes column *and* entablature) is carried on the abaci, and has three parts: the architrave, or beam, with a flat face in one plane, above which is a flat moulding known as the taenia, or tenia, under which, at intervals immediately under the triglyphs, are narrow bands known as regulae, under which are six cones called guttae; the frieze, consisting of vertical slabs known as triglyphs cut with vertical channels (usually two full ones and two halves at the edges), set equidistant from each other over the centre-lines of each column and over the centre-line of each space between each column, and metopes (the panels between each triglyph, set back from the front face of the triglyphs and often ornamented with sculpture in relief); and the cornice, which overhangs the frieze, and consists of a cymatium over a corona or vertical face to a projection, the soffite of which inclines, and has flat blocks, or mutules, like the ends of rafters, over each triglyph and metope, usually embellished with 18 guttae in three rows of six for each mutule.

At the corner of a Greek Doric frieze the triglyphs touch, meeting at the bevel coinciding with the half-channels, with the result that the corner column centre-line is not under the centre of the triglyph. This makes the spaces between the corner column and the columns adjacent to it on each face less than the intercolumniation elsewhere, thus giving the corner the appearance of greater stability. In the case of the Parthenon, too, the corner columns have slightly greater diameters, so the corners are further strengthened in appearance [2.1, 2.2].

Greek Doric channels in triglyphs are rounded at the top, and the mutules slope with the soffite, and project beneath it [2.2, 2.4].

THE GREEK IONIC ORDER

The distinctive feature of the Ionic Order is the volute, or scroll capital, perhaps derived from shells, rams' horns, or stylized scroll forms evolved in Egyptian art, and certainly used decoratively in ancient times. Very archaic Ionic capitals have volutes that seem to derive from plant forms, with palmettes between them [2.14]. Unlike the Doric capital, the Ionic, in its simplest form, is not based on a circle within a square (and therefore is not the same from all sides), but is rectangular, with two volutes visible on both front and back, connected at the sides by cushions (sometimes plain and sometimes ornamented). This elongated form suggests a type of bracket to support the entablature, later ornamented using a design derived from the nautilus shell. The archaic temple of Artemis at Ephesus had capitals about three metres long and one metre wide.

Unlike Greek Doric, the Ionic Order has a base. It consists of an upper and lower torus (convex) separated by a scotia (concave) and fillets, with no square plinth block: this design became known as the Attic base [2.19]. A variant was the Asiatic base, consisting of a reeded drum over which were two scotiae and a reeded torus. The bases of the columns of the archaic Temple of Artemis at Ephesus were very elaborate, with many small rings of convex and concave form.

Ionic columns, therefore, had bases of varying degrees of complexity, and their heights (including bases and capitals) were approximately nine times the diameter at the bottom of the shaft. The usual treatment of the shaft was to have 24 flutes separated from each other by fillets (not sharp arrises), but in archaic examples there were as many as 40 flutes separated by arrises. Fully developed Ionic eschewed the arris and adopted the fillet, and the flutes do not terminate at the bottom of the shaft or at the annulets, but in rounded forms at the top and bottom, leaving a plain circular shaft between the terminations of the flutes and the top of the base and the bottom of the capital.

The Ionic capital, as has been stated, has two pairs of volutes, approximately two-thirds the diameter of the shaft in height, on the front and rear, connected by cushions (plain or enriched) at the sides, and by an echinus enriched with egg-and-dart on the front and back, under which is usually a bead-and-reel moulding [2.15]. At the acute angle between the top of the spiral form and the horizontal line above the echinus is a fragment of honeysuckle or palmette motif [2.16]. Above the subtle mouldings of the volutes and their cushions is an abacus, much smaller than the Doric, and usually moulded and enriched [2.16].

One of the problems with the use of the Ionic capital occurred at the corners of buildings. In some instances, if there were a peristyle (rather than a prostyle portico in front of an anta arrangement), the cushions at the sides did not look well beside a colonnade with volutes, so the two faces were treated with volutes, and the corner acquired two volutes, back to back, and pulled out at an angle from the corner [2.16, 2.17]. A further variation occurred at the temple of Apollo Epicurius at Bassae (where all three Orders are found): at this celebrated

Persischer Säulenknauf (Viçadahyu).

A
Jonisches Kapitell von Neandria.

Grundplan des Tempels (VI Jahrhdt vor Chr.)

C.

D 92.

Arbae.

Suma. D. Firstziegel.

Jonisch-äolische Kapitelle.

B.
Äolisch-jonische Ordnung (Neandria).

Thonziegel.

E.

2.14 *Archaic forms of the Ionic capital from Neandria, called 'Aeolic'. Note that the volutes seem to grow from the shaft, whereas in true Ionic the volutes are part of a cushion-like member laid on the shaft* (Batsford)

2.15 *Capital from the Mausoleum at Halicarnassus (c.353 BC), showing the three-dimensional form with volutes and pulvinated end. The flutes are separated by fillets rather than arrises* (A)

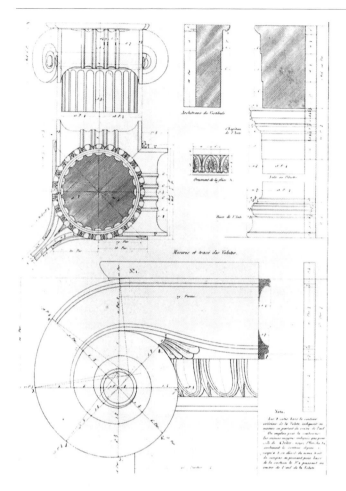

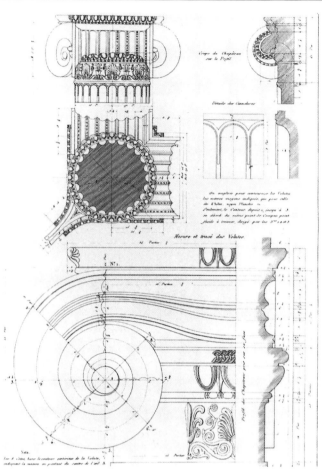

2.16 *Angle capital and anta of the Greek Ionic Order from the Temple on the Ilissus, Athens (c.450 BC). Note how the volute is set out and how the volutes are placed at the corner so that volutes 'read' on the outside faces. Note also how the anta differs from the columnar Order. From Normand (A)*

2.17 *Detail of the Greek Ionic angle-capital from the 'Temple of Minerva Polias' (the eastern part of the Erechtheion in Athens) of c.421–407 BC. Note the extreme refinement of the enrichment. The neck is embellished with palmette and anthemion ornament. Note that the pulvinus has reeding with enrichment. From Normand (A)*

2.18 *Plans, elevations, and sections of columns from the Erechtheion in Athens. Note the elaborate enrichment of the pulvinus and base of each, and the delicate ornamentation of the neck of the column. From Normand (A)*

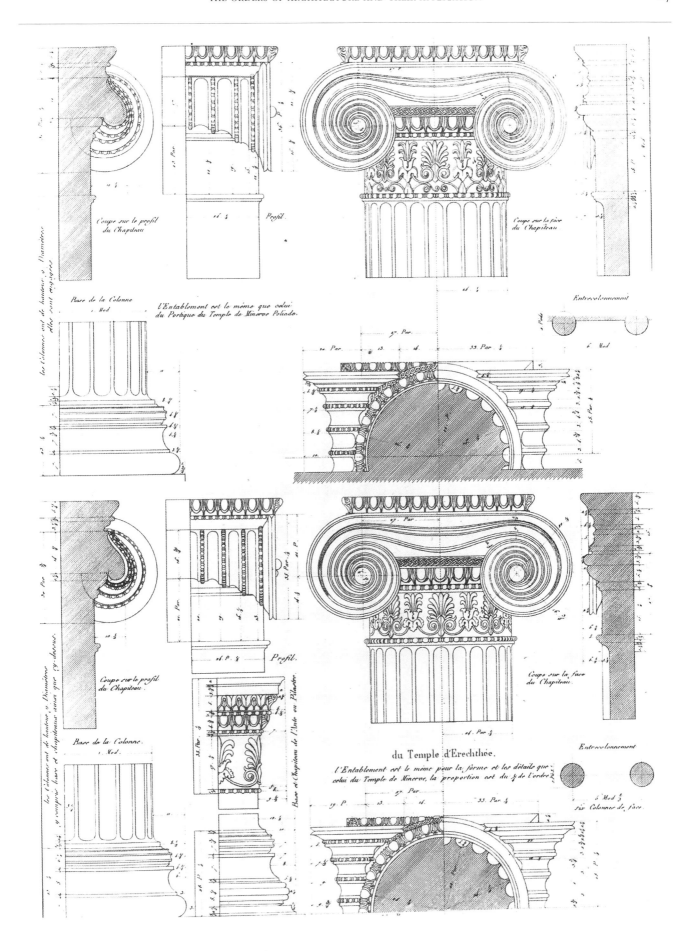

Coupe sur le profil
du Chapiteau

Profil.

Coupe sur la face
du Chapiteau

Base de la Colonne
. Mod .

l'Entablement est le même que celui
du Portique du Temple de Minerve Poliade.

Entrecolonnement

Coupe sur le profil
du Chapiteau.

Profil.

Coupe sur la face
du Chapiteau.

Base de la Colonne.
. Mod .

Base et Chapiteau de l'Ante ou Pilastre.

du Temple d'Erechthée.

l'Entablement est le même pour la forme et les détails que
celui du Temple de Minerve, la proportion est du ⅘ de l'ordre.

Entrecolonnement

six Colonnes de face.

2.19 *Elements of the Erechtheion, Athens. Note the Caryatide porch, with Caryatide Order and plinth. The Caryatide entablature has an architrave divided into three fasciae, but there is no frieze, and there are dentils under the cornice. Flutes on the columns are separated by fillets, and the neck is embellished with palmette and anthemion ornament. The main entablature has three distinct parts, and the architrave is divided into three planes or fasciae: the frieze is plain, and mutules with guttae are no longer present. The base of the column has two torus and one scotia moulding, the so-called Attic base. Note the console at the side of the doorcase, and the paterae, or rosettes, on the doorcase architrave (Batsford)*

2.20 *Greek ornament*
1 & 2 Tops of Greek stelai showing variations on the anthemion and palmette ornaments
3 Pilaster capital from Eleusis showing acanthus and other ornament
4 Rosette from the architrave of the north door of the Erechtheion
5 Anthemion and palmette ornament on the cyma recta of the cornice of the north door of the Erechtheion
6 Detail of the egg-and-dart (top), leaf-and-tongue, and bead-and-reel from the cyma reversa moulding of the anta capital of the Erechtheion
7 Anta capital from the Erechtheion showing the leaf-and-tongue on the lesbian cymatium at the top, with bead-and-reel under, then another lesbian cymatium (or cyma reversa) enriched with egg-and-dart, under which is another astragal enriched with bead-and-reel, under which is the frieze with anthemion and palmette with more bead-and-reel under
8 & 9 Capital of anta from the Temple of Apollo Didymaeus at Miletus, showing the scroll with cushion on the side elevation, and acanthus scroll decoration with anthemion on the cavetto moulding in the centre of the capital
10 Centre panel from the same, showing acanthus scroll and anthemion in the centre
11 Detail of the acanthus-scroll ornament from the roof of the Choragic Monument of Lysicrates in Athens. From Spiers (A)

temple the internal walls of the naos had engaged Ionic columns attached to short cross-walls, and the capitals had corner volutes, so there were four volutes altogether (although C. R. Cockerell (1788–1863) thought there were six [2.21]). These capitals did not have the usual echinus, and the eyes of the volutes were close together. The upper lines of the channel joining the spirals were thrown upwards in a startling curve, and the presence of abaci is still disputed [2.22]. The projection of the volutes at 45 degrees anticipates the four-sided or diagonal Ionic capital developed in Hellenistic and Roman times which had four angle volutes, so that there were eight volutes in all; here the abacus acquired concave sides, thus the problem of a 'special' at the corner no longer arose. These diagonal capitals were models for the Roman Composite Order invented in the first century AD. The bases of the Bassae temple were also unorthodox, for the shafts had a very wide apophyge, and a spread version of the normal

2.21 *Corner of portico of the Ashmolean Museum, Oxford, by C. R. Cockerell (1788–1863) of 1841–5, using a free interpretation of the Greek Ionic Order of the Temple of Apollo Epicurius at Bassae (c.420 BC). Note that the Ionic capital is of the eight-volute type, thus getting over the problem of corners caused when the pulvinated ends of capitals are used. Cockerell's interpretation is free and imaginative (note the drop at the corner between dentils), while the treatment of the frieze is extraordinarily rich (A)*

2.22 *Ionic Order from the Temple of Apollo Epicurius at Bassae (A)*

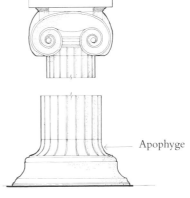

Apophyge

2.23 *Detail of the Greek Ionic Order used by Leo von Klenze at the Glyptothek, Munich, of 1816–30, based on the Erechtheion capitals, but with unfluted shafts. Note the anta capital (A)*

2.24 (ABOVE) *The Glyptothek facing the Königsplatz in Munich by Leo von Klenze, showing the prostyle octastyle Ionic portico. While the portico is based on the Erechtheion, the lower block with its Renaissance aediculated niches and Hellenistic pilasters introduces a syncretic note into this remarkable building, the interiors of which have been disastrously treated after war damage (A)*

2.25 (BELOW) *The Altes Museum, Lustgarten, Berlin, of 1823–8, by K. F. Schinkel, with its great* in antis *arrangement of Greek Ionic columns, like a Hellenistic stoa. Here is the apparently effortless simplicity of Antiquity (it is, of course, extremely subtle and difficult to achieve such effects by means of clarity of forms and archaeological correctness of detail) (A)*

2.26 *A late and less powerful derivative of the Altes Museum. The Haus der Deutschen Kunst in Munich by Paul Ludwig Troost (1878–1934), designed 1933 and completed in 1937. Instead of antae, Troost terminated his simplified Doric colonnade by means of square columns, a device used at the Rue des Colonnes in Paris* (A)

torus, below which was a tall, concave moulding sweeping outwards to a shorter concave moulding under it [2.22].

In the case of the Erechtheion in Athens, the very beautiful Ionic capitals had additional neckings, or a band under the capital proper at the top of the shaft, enriched with the anthemion, palmette, or honeysuckle ornament; this necking also occurs on the antae, and is continued as a variety of decorative frieze under the architrave all round the building [2.17, 2.18, 2.19].

Ionic entablatures are usually about a fifth of the height of the whole Order, and do not have triglyphs or metopes. Architraves are subdivided into three fasciae or planes, like superimposed slabs; friezes are often unadorned, or may have a continuous band of sculpture, but in either case will have no vertical interruption; and the cornice has no mutules, but is often enriched with dentils and crowned by the corona and cyma recta moulding (frequently decorated). In many Asiatic examples of the Ionic Order the frieze is omitted altogether, giving the entablature a curiously flattened appearance.

2.27 *The church of S. Vincent de Paul, Paris, of 1824–44, by Lepère and Hittorff, a Neoclassical composition incorporating a prostyle hexastyle Ionic portico (with sculpture by Lemaire in the tympanum)* (A)

2.28 (ABOVE) *The Schauspielhaus, Berlin, by K. F. Schinkel, of 1818–26, with its prostyle hexastyle Greek Ionic portico based on the Erechtheion, and the square mullions derived from the Choragic Monument of Thrasyllus, Athens [2.6], and from some Egyptian temples which used the square unmoulded column (A)*

2.29 (BELOW) *1–10 Moray Place, Glasgow, by Alexander 'Greek' Thomson (1817–1875), of 1858–9. Photograph by Thomas Annan. Here, Thomson uses the continuous row of mullions which Schinkel had employed in the Schauspielhaus, derived from the Choragic Monument of Thrasyllus (A)*

THE GREEK CORINTHIAN ORDER

The base and shaft of this Order resemble those of the Ionic Order, and the column (including base and capital) is about ten times the diameter at the base of the shaft in height. Corinthian shafts have flutes separated by fillets, like the Ionic Order, but the height of the capital is about one and a half times the diameter of the shaft.

The first Corinthian capital was probably the single example on the central axis of the temple of Apollo Epicurius at Bassae, although the columns on either side of it seem also to have been Corinthian. Pausanias says the temple was built by Ictinus (the Architect of the Parthenon), and it appears to date from the second half of the fifth century, probably around 430 BC.

Although there are wide variations in the details of Greek Corinthian, the capitals consisted of an inverted

2.30 (BELOW) *Greek Corinthian Order from the Choragic Monument of Lysicrates (c.334 BC), Athens. The capital has quite distinct differences from the Roman Corinthian Order, and is taller and more elegant. Note the helices in the centre and the honeysuckle ornament that rises up on the centre of the abacus. From Spiers (A)*

2.31 (ABOVE) *A variation on the Lysicrates Corinthian Order, used in an hotel in Stamford, Lincolnshire, of 1810–29, by J. L. Bond (1764–1837), a sumptuous essay in Greek Revival (A)*

bell-shaped cone, on top of the shaft and separated from it by a horizontal band, sometimes a recess, but more often a convex or torus moulding. The usual and developed type favoured by the Romans consisted of two tiers, each of which is formed of eight acanthus leaves; from between the leaves of the upper row rise eight stalks known as caulicoli, from each of which emerge helices, or volutes, that support the diagonal angles of the abacus and the central foliated ornament: there are four of these ornaments, one on each face; in Greek examples usually of the anthemion or palmette, but sometimes a floral form.

The abacus has four concave sides curving out to a point or chamfered at the angles. An exception is the Tower of the Winds in Athens, which has one row of acanthus leaves with one row of palm leaves above, no caulicoli or volutes, and a moulded abacus square on plan

[2.32]. Extraordinarily elegant are the capitals of the Choragic Monument of Lysicrates in Athens which are taller than is usual, and have several remarkable features: the flutes of the shafts terminate in projecting lotus leaves, and the lower row of capital leaves consists of 16 lotus leaves, leaving a plain channel between the base of the capital and the top of the shaft, which probably contained a ring of bronze; the upper row of capital leaves are those of the acanthus, and between each leaf is an eight-petalled flower resembling a lotus; and, above, the helices are especially elegant, supporting tall palmettes on each face and an abacus with a deep concave moulding all round [2.30, 2.31].

The Corinthian Order has an entablature that is not unlike that of the Ionic Order. A more festive character, the elegance and beauty of the capitals (and their adaptability to any situation including colonnades, corners, and circular buildings), made this the Order favoured by the Romans.

2.32 *The curious palm-leaf and acanthus capital from the Tower of the Winds in Athens (the Horologium of Andronicus of Cyrrhus) of c.50 BC, used in the 'Tower of the Winds', a belvedere at Mount Stewart, Co. Down, of c.1780, by James Athenian Stuart (1713–1788), one of the leading lights of the Greek Revival. Note that this version of the Corinthian Order has no base, and that the abacus is square on plan (A)*

THE ROMAN ORDERS

There are five Roman Orders: the Tuscan, Doric, Ionic, Corinthian, and Composite. All, except the Tuscan, owe much to the Greek Orders.

THE TUSCAN ORDER

This has a plain, unfluted shaft with a base consisting of a square plinth, a large torus, a fillet, and an apophyge connecting the base to the shaft. At the top, the shaft is joined to a fillet by another apophyge, above which is an astragal: then comes the necking, or flat band, like a plain frieze, joined to a circular fascia or fillet with or without an apophyge. Above is an echinus carrying a square abacus, usually with a fillet over the flat sides. The entablature is divided into the usual three parts of architrave, frieze, and cornice, but the mouldings are never enriched [2.33, 2.34]. An even plainer, more primitive type of Tuscan Order eschews the frieze and cornice, and has only an architrave, over which are wide overhanging eaves carried on long plain cantilevered brackets known as mutules. The Tuscan Order was regarded by Serlio as suitable for fortifications and prisons, as it is tough, primitive, strong and manly [2.37].

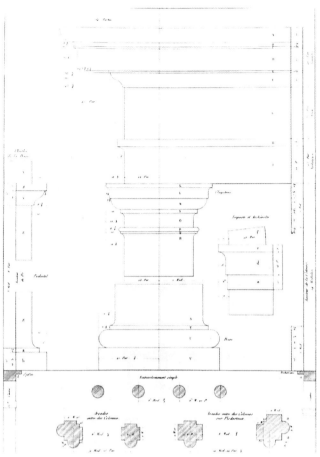

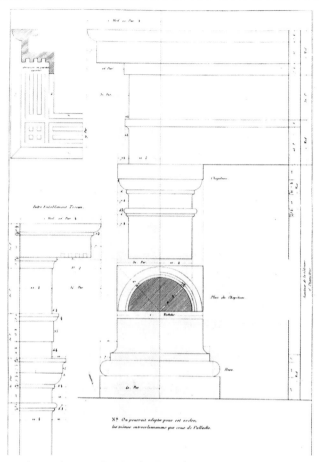

2.33 (ABOVE, LEFT) *The Tuscan Order after Vignola. This Renaissance Order was derived from Roman prototypes, and was the simplest and most severe of all the Classical Orders. From Normand (A)*

2.34 (ABOVE, RIGHT) *Tuscan Order after Serlio. Note the severe treatment of the cornice soffite. From Normand (A)*

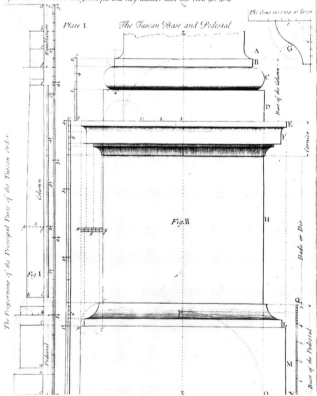

2.35 (RIGHT) *Tuscan base and pedestal. On the left is the Order with a pedestal, the total height divided into five equal parts. One part is the height of the pedestal to the top of its cornice. If the remaining four parts are divided into five parts, the upper part is the height of the entablature, and the remaining four the height of the column.*

If the height of the pedestal is divided into four parts, the lowest part is the height of the plinth, one third of the next part is the height of the moulding at the base of the die, and half of the upper part is the height of the pedestal cornice. Individual mouldings are plain, but can be varied. From Langley (A)

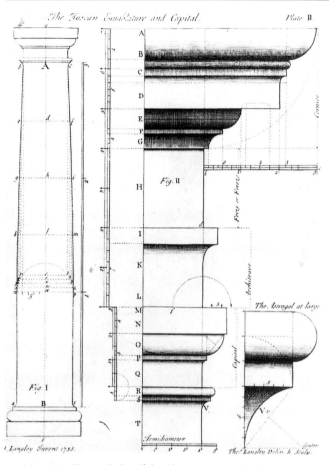

2.36 (ABOVE) *Tuscan Order. If the column is measured at the base of its shaft, then the height of the column (including base and capital) is seven diameters. The heights of base and capital are each half a diameter. The capital consists of three equal parts: the abacus, the ovolo and fillet (the last one sixth of a part), and the neck. The astragal and its fillet are half the height of the neck. The fillet is half the height of the astragal. Note that entasis begins one third of the way up the shaft from its cincture. At the top of the shaft, below the astragal, the diameter is four-fifths of that at the base. The semicircle described one third of the way up the shaft is crossed by two parallel lines dropped from the top of the shaft, and the arcs of the circle between these positions divided into four equal parts. The upper two thirds of the shaft should be divided into four parts, and the lines projected upwards from the circle and its crossing divisions to give the points for the thickness of the shaft rising in a gentle curve. The entablature is divided into seven equal parts: two are given to the architrave, two to the frieze, and three to the cornice. Further subdivision and proportions are given. From Langley (A)*

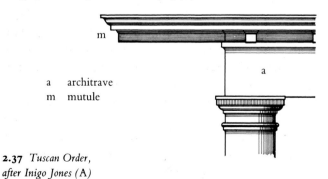

a   architrave
m   mutule

2.37 *Tuscan Order,
after Inigo Jones (A)*

THE ROMAN DORIC ORDER

The Doric temple at Cori has a Doric Order similar to Greek Doric, but more slender, and with other differences, including the flutes and polygonal drums referred to below [2.38]. The column shafts sweep by means of an apophyge to simple circular, pad-like torus bases, and the capitals are very small. A very low entablature and tall narrow triglyphs ensure that three triglyphs are placed over the intercolumniations, so the whole effect of this Order is very un-Hellenic, although the triglyphs touch at the angles of the frieze in the Greek Doric manner. Three triglyphs are also found over the intercolumniations of the lowest storey of the Theatre of Marcellus in Rome, where the engaged columns have no bases, but the columns are unfluted, and the capitals resemble those of the Tuscan

2.38 (BELOW) *The Roman Doric temple at Cori of the first century BC. It stands on a podium and has a deep prostyle tetrastyle portico, with two columns between the angle columns and the antae of the cella. The columns are much more slender than Greek versions, and bases with one convex moulding below a large apophyge, so they differ from Greek examples. The lower parts of the columns are 18-sided polygons set below 18 Doric flutes. The architrave is very low, and the frieze has three triglyphs over each intercolumniation, so the effect is very light and elegant (Batsford)*

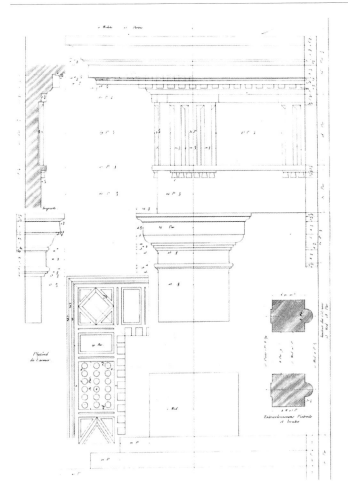

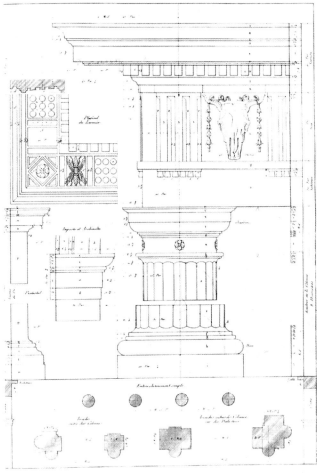

2.39 *Roman Doric Order from the Theatre of Marcellus, Rome (13 BC). Note that the triglyph is now centred on the corner column, leaving a piece of frieze-metope at the return. The soffite of the cornice also differs from Greek Doric, while the capital is quite different. The shaft is unfluted. From Normand (A)*

2.40 *Doric Order of Vignola, based on Roman exemplars. Note that the triglyph block is placed on the centre-line of the corner column, leaving a piece of metope on the corner. The metope has a bucranium, and the neck of the capital has rosettes between the astragal and the capital proper. The tops of the triglyphs are rectangular. Note that the mutules are slightly inclined and do not project below the soffite, and that there are dentils, quite unlike Greek Doric. The ornaments of the soffite have thunderbolts, lozenges, and rosettes, and the columns have bases. From Normand (A)*

Order [2.39]. The bed-mouldings of the cornice contain dentils, however, and the soffite is elaborately enriched with guttae and geometrical mouldings between the mutules.

The more usual type of Roman Doric always has triglyphs on the centre-lines of columns, even at corners, so a portion of metope is exposed at the angles [2.39, 2.40, 2.42]. Columns are usually fluted with arrises, although fillets between flutes, and unfluted examples, are known. Sometimes the shaft has an apophyge terminating in a fillet, as discovered in the Alban countryside near Rome, but it can also be without a base, as in the *Thermae* of Diocletian. Capitals resemble the basic form of Tuscan types, but the necking is often enriched with four or eight rosettes or paterae. Astragals may be enriched with bead-and-reel, and echinus mouldings with egg-and-dart or leaf decorations. Abaci are often not plain, as in Greek Doric, but have a cyma reversa moulding at the top of the plain face, enriched with leaf-and-tongue or other ornament. Architraves are sometimes divided into two fasciae, with mouldings, enriched or plain, between them. Metopes may be embelished with paterae, rosettes, or bucrania. More paterae or rosettes may adorn the coffers between the mutules on the soffites, and intermediate mouldings of the entablature may be ornamented. Bed-mouldings often include dentils and other features.

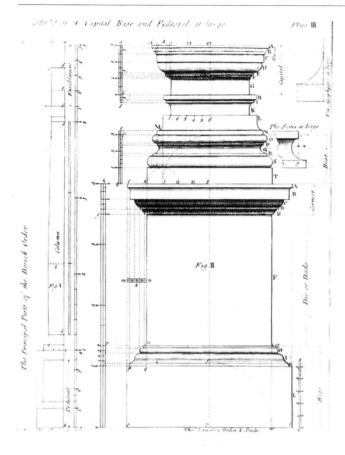

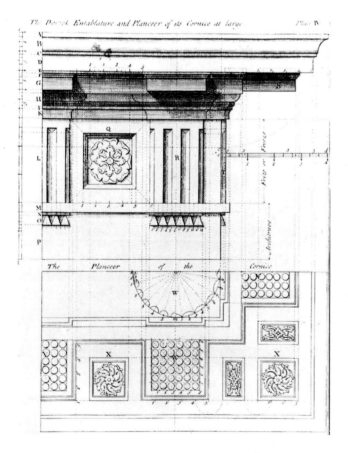

Mutules are usually found, but over the triglyphs only; they are slightly inclined (if at all) and do not project far below the soffites, except in the 'mutule' Order, where the mutules are given prominence. Triglyph channels are rectangular rather than curved at the top.

Doric is associated with Strength and manliness: Serlio suggested it was appropriate in churches dedicated to certain male Saints who were soldiers or who were militant in some other way.

2.41 *Doric capital, Attic base, and pedestal. The height of the Order is divided into five parts, the lowest of which is the height of the pedestal. The remaining four parts are divided into five, the topmost part of which is the height of the entablature. The pedestal is divided into four vertical parts: the plinth is one part high, the base mouldings a third of a part, and the cornice a half part. The column is eight diameters (at the base) high, and the heights of the base and capital are each half a diameter. If the base is divided into three, one part is the height of the plinth, and the system of proportion for the rest is indicated. The capital can also be divided into three parts, the proportions of which are again shown. From Langley (A)*

2.42 *Details of the Roman Doric entablature. The height is divided into eight parts, with two for the architrave, three for the frieze, and three for the cornice. Note the relationship of the mutules to the triglyphs. If the upper part of the two comprising the architrave is divided into three, the upper subdivision is the height of the taenia, and the proportions of the guttae are as shown. The cornice should have its two parts subdivided as shown. Each triglyph is half a diameter wide and each metope is the same width as the height of the frieze. Proportions of glyphs can be arrived at by dividing the triglyph into 12 verticals, which also helps to set out the 6 guttae. Note the overhang of the cornice arrived at by striking a quarter circle as shown. This Order is based on the 'mutule' Order of Vignola, with pronounced mutules, between which are coffers. From Langley (A)*

THE ROMAN IONIC ORDER

Roman Ionic shafts could be fluted or unfluted; Greek examples were always fluted. Bases were usually of the Attic type [2.43, 2.46, 2.47], and capitals often had the pillows between the volutes at the sides enriched with acanthus or other ornament. Roman channels between the volutes are always shallow, and do not dip down in the centres of each face: generally, Roman Ionic capitals look very small and mean compared with the best Greek examples. Although the Romans used the angle-volute (as in the temple of Fortuna Virilis in Rome [2.43, 2.44]), they also favoured the 'diagonal' type with volutes at all four corners (that is, eight volutes in all), thus avoiding awkward 'specials' for the corner details [2.46, 2.47, 2.50].

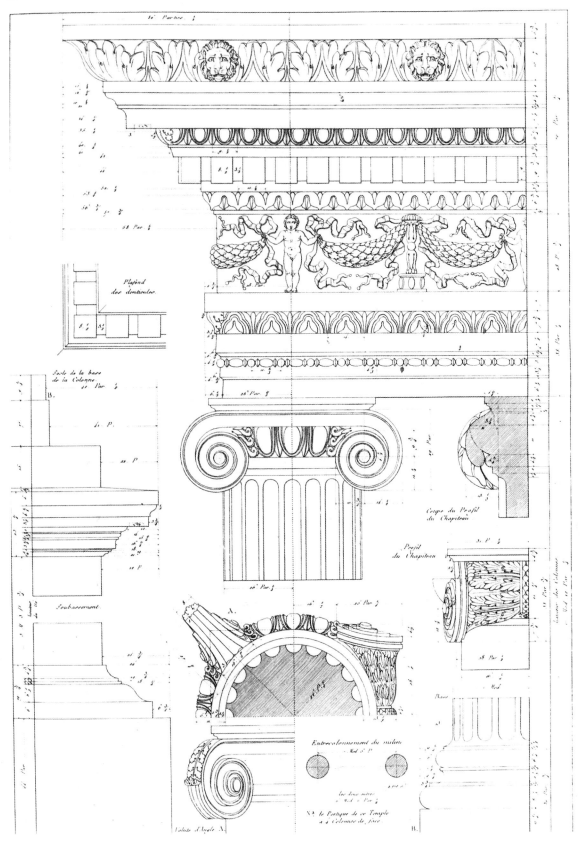

2.43 *Podium and Roman Ionic Order from the Temple of Fortuna Virilis, Rome (c.40 BC), showing how very elaborate and festive the Roman Order could be. Note the angle-volute. From Normand (A)*

2.44 *Temple of Fortuna Virilis, Rome. Note that the Roman temple stands on a podium and that columns are engaged to the wall of the cella rather than carried round as a peristyle as in a Greek temple (Batsford)*

2.45 *Ionic Order after Vignola. An exceptionally rich Order with ornamented pulvinus. From Normand (A)*

2.46 *Ionic Order after Scamozzi. Note the enriched Attic base and the modillions under the soffite of the cornice with rosettes in the coffers between them. The volutes, too, are further ornamented, and there are eight on the capital. From Normand (A)*

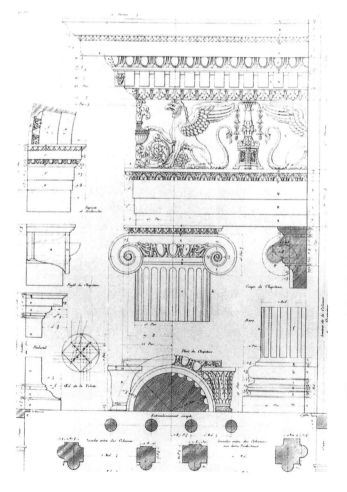

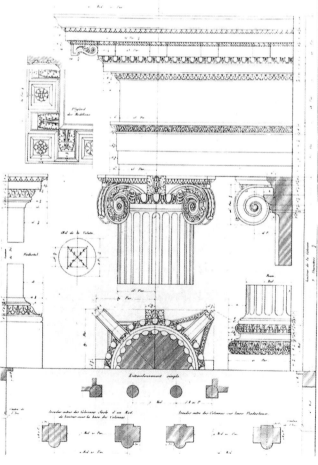

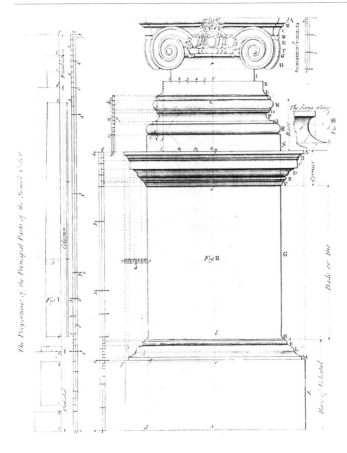

2.47 *The Ionic Order. The whole Order, including the pedestal, is divided into five parts, and the lowest of these is the height of the pedestal. The remaining four parts should be divided into six, the uppermost part of which is the height of the entablature. The height of the pedestal is divided into four, the lowest part of which is the plinth, while the cornice is half a part high. The mouldings above the plinth, including the apophyge, are one third of a part high. The column is nine diameters (at the base) high, with half a diameter as the height of the capital and the height of the base. Proportions of the base mouldings and capitals are as shown. Note that the capital is of the 'diagonal', 'angular', or 'Scamozzi' type, with eight volutes, and is identical on all four elevations, so this Order does not require a 'special' at the angle of a building. From Langley (A)*

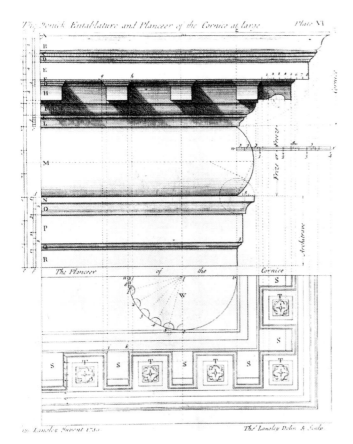

2.48 *The Ionic entablature after Langley. Note the position of the column and the method of subdividing it to set out the flutes, one of which is always in the centre. The frieze is pulvinated. From Langley (A)*

Roman Ionic entablatures often had ornament on every conceivable place, and friezes with garlands, putti, and other features were sumptuous: the whole effect was luxurious, magnificent, and extremely showy. Pulvinated friezes [2.48] were introduced, as at the *Thermae* of Diocletian. On some of the richest examples the channels of the volutes are enriched with leaf and floral decoration [2.46], and in the centres, between volutes, are heads, in deep relief, of Serapis and other deities.

Serlio associated Ionic with female Saints, while to Vitruvius the Order signified feminine slenderness and grace. Ionic has been associated by many writers with scholarship and with Wisdom, and this is especially so of Masonic tradition.

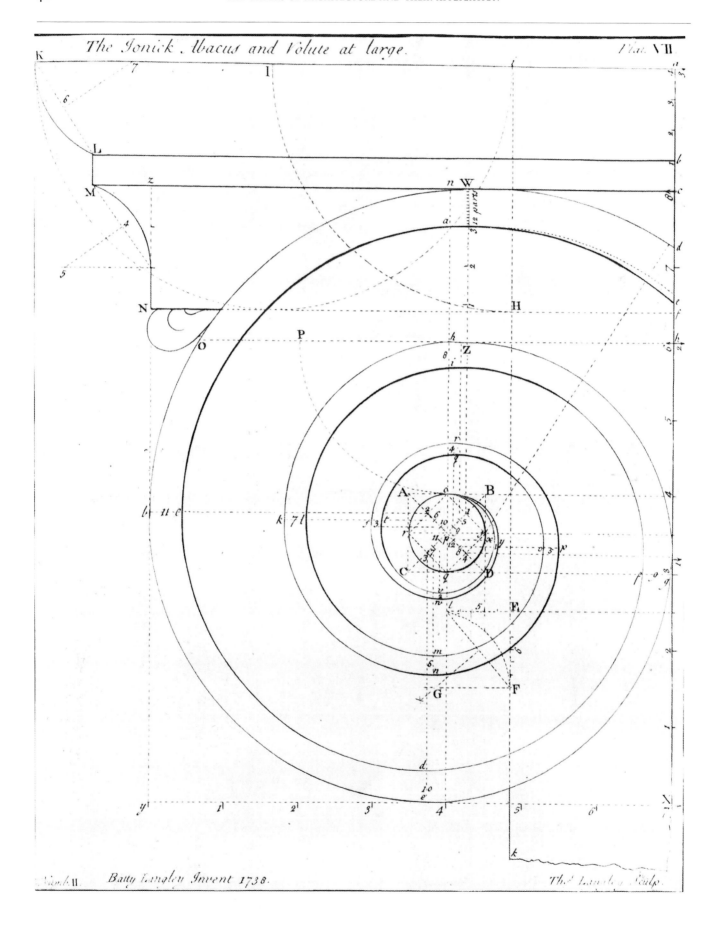

The Ionick Abacus and Volute at large.   Plat. VII.

Batty Langley Invent 1738.   Tho.s Langley Sculp.

2.49 *The Ionic volute. The height of the capital (aX) is divided into three parts, the uppermost of which is divided in two: this half-way line gives the position of the top of the volute (W). A vertical line (n a p q 4) is drawn, divided into 8 parts, and p, the centre of the eye, is 0.225 column diameters from the line Mc, or 4.5 parts below line Mc, where one part is 0.25 of the dimension between Mc and AB. The eye is drawn with p as its centre, using a radius of 0.025 column diameters, or 0.5 of one of the 4 parts between AB and Mc. The horizontal diameter r p s is drawn, and the square r o x q is added within the eye. Diagonal lines are drawn through p to A B C and D, so the eye is held within a square. The arcs nb; ac; be; cd; eg; df; and gh, fi respectively are described as follows: the diagonals 2, 4 and 1, 3 on AD and BC are each divided into six parts labelled 2, 6, 10, p, 12, 8, 4 and 1, 5, 9, p, 11, 7, 3 respectively. Points 1–12 are the 12 centres from which the volute is described. Point 1 is the centre of the arc nb, point 2 of be, point 3 of eg, point 4 of gh, point 5 of hk, point 6 of kn, point 7 of np, point 8 of pr, point 9 of rs, point 10 of sw, point 11 of wy, and point 12 of yo.*

The line WZ (W is obtained by striking a vertical line from arc centre 1) should be divided into four parts, the uppermost of which, na, is the width of the list, which is subdivided into 12 parts. bc = 11 parts, ed = 10 parts, gf = 9 parts, hi = 8 parts, kl = 7 parts, and so on, diminishing by one part with each quarter circle. Subdivide the distances on AD and BC further, between 2 and 6, 6 and 10, etc, setting up 12 new centres for the inner part of the list to give the arcs ac, cd, df, fi, il, lm, mo, oq, qt, tv, vx, and xo. The main problem is the junction between the list and the eye, and if it looks uncomfortable the diameter of the eye can be altered to give a smooth transition from list to eye. From Langley (A)

2.50 *Ionic angle capital, shown so that the volutes are visible on all sides. Circular and square columns are shown. The circumference of the column is divided into 24 equal parts, and each of those parts into 8. Using 3 of each 8 as radii the flutes can be drawn, so each fillet is 2 small parts. In the case of a square column divide each side into 31 parts, giving 6 to each flute and 2 to each fillet. A variation is to have a bead in the angle. From Langley (A)*

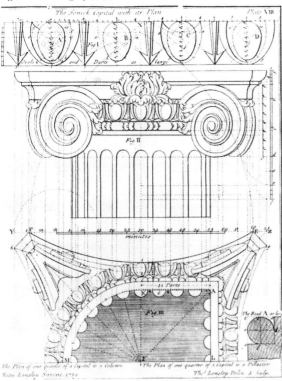

THE ROMAN CORINTHIAN ORDER

This Order was favoured by the Romans, especially during the Empire. Its grandeur, the proportions of the capital, and its elegance made it ideal for important religious [2.60], civic, and Imperial buildings.

Column shafts were fluted or unfluted, and bases were usually of the Attic type [2.51, Fig.51]. The model the Romans favoured for their Order was that of the temple of Zeus Olympios, later the Olympieion, in Athens. Abaci and entablatures were given anything from fairly plain treatments (as at the Pantheon [2.55]) to the most sumptuous (as at the Forum of Nerva [2.54]), where every moulding between fasciae was enriched, friezes were treated with sculptured scenes in relief, and the modillioned cornice was embellished with a wide

2.51 *Corinthian Order from the Temple of Zeus Olympios at Athens, begun in c.170 BC and completed under Hadrian around AD 130. Note the remarkably pointed plan of the elegant abacus and the treatment of the soffite of the cornice. From Normand (A)*

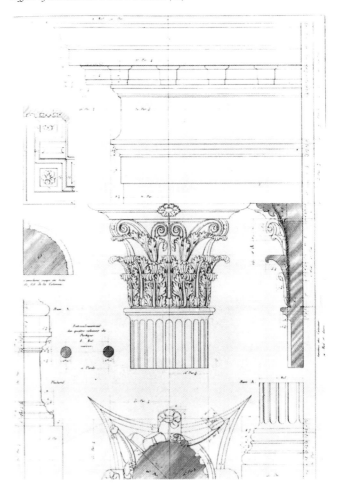

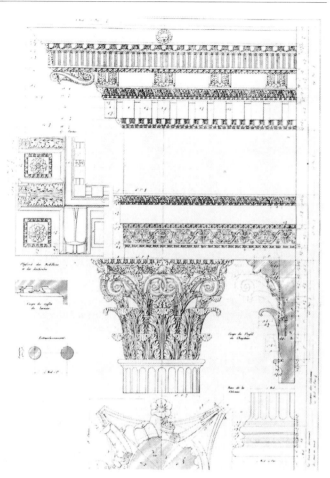

2.52 *Roman Corinthian Order from the round temple by the waterfall at Tibur (known as the Temple of Vesta at Tivoli) of c.80 BC. This very curious Order has a somewhat squat capital and very large volutes, with a big floral device in the centre. It looks like a tentative first attempt at a Composite Order. Note the continuous frieze of bulls' heads and garlands, and the treatment of the soffite. From Spiers (A)*

2.53 *Corinthian Order of the Temple of 'Jupiter Stator' now known as the Temple of Castor and Pollux, in Rome of AD 6. The capitals, with their interlocking inner helices, are exceedingly refined and beautiful, and the Order was used by James Gibbs for his church of S. Martin-in-the-Fields in London. The elaborate entablature with modillions supporting the cornice should be noted. Between the modillions are coffers with rosettes. From Normand (A)*

2.54 *Roman Corinthian Order from the Forum of Nerva in Rome, c.AD 90–7. An elaborate Order with frieze and crowning cornice with dentils, egg-and-dart, modillions, and coffers. From Normand (A)*

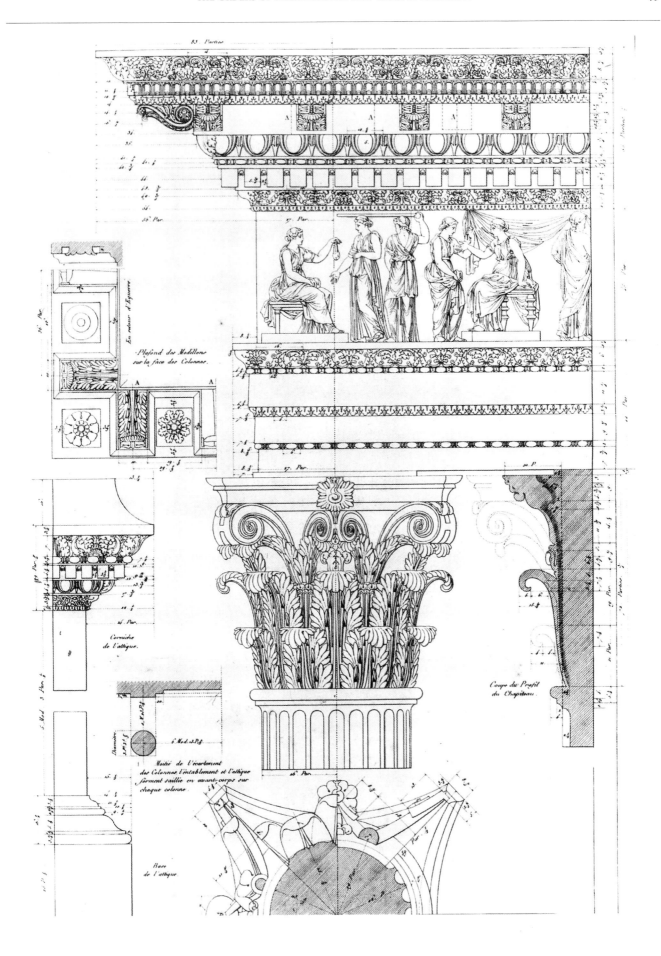

Plafond des Modillons
sur la face des Colonnes.

Corniche
de l'attique.

Moitié de l'écartement
des Colonnes, l'entablement et l'attique
forment saillie en avant-corps sur
chaque colonne

Base
de l'attique.

Corps du Profil
du Chapiteau.

2.55 *The great prostyle octastyle portico of the Pantheon in Rome. The shafts of the columns are unfluted monoliths of marble and granite, with capitals of marble. Photograph by Donald McLeish (Batsford)*

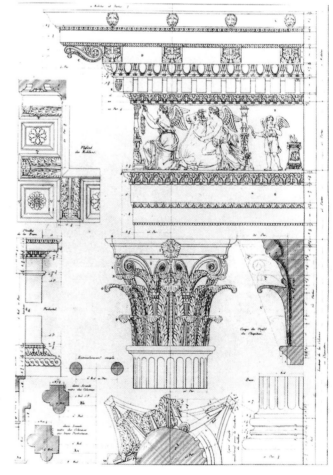

2.56 *Corinthian Order after Vignola, showing the exceptional richness of this development of a Roman Order. The capital is quite distinct from Greek examples. Note the ornament of the horizontal mouldings, the elaborate modillions, and the coffers with rosettes between the modillions in the soffite. From Normand (A)*

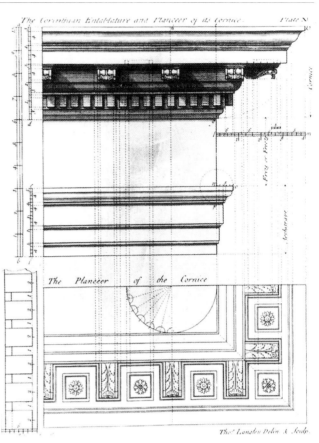

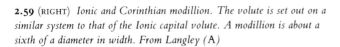

2.57 (ABOVE, LEFT) *The Corinthian Order has a pedestal similar to that of the Composite Order (see* **2.63***). If the total height is divided by 5, the height of the pedestal is equal to 1 part. The remaining parts are divided by 6, the upper of which is the height of the entablature. The Corinthian column is 10 diameters high, the base (including plinth) half a diameter, and the capital one-and-a-sixth diameters high.*

The Corinthian capital can be divided into seven parts vertically, and each part subdivided by 10. The tops of the first range of acanthus leaves are 20 subdivisions high, the second 20, and the third 10. The total height from the astragal to the underside of the abacus is 60 subdivisions, and the abacus itself is 10 high, 5 of which are the cavetto. From Langley (A)

2.58 (ABOVE, RIGHT) *The Corinthian entablature is divided into 10, with 3 for the architrave, 3 to the frieze, and 4 to the cornice. An entablature height of 2.5 diameters is preferable to the 2 advocated by Gibbs. Note the system for subdividing cornice and architrave, and the method of establishing the overhang. From Langley (A)*

2.59 (RIGHT) *Ionic and Corinthian modillion. The volute is set out on a similar system to that of the Ionic capital volute. A modillion is about a sixth of a diameter in width. From Langley (A)*

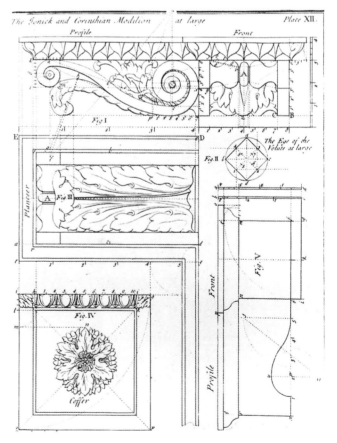

2.60 *The Temple known as the Maison Carrée in Nîmes of 16 BC. This is a small hexastyle pseudoperipteral Corinthian temple on a podium. The plan is typical Graecized Roman-Tuscan, with engaged columns around the cella* (AFK G13845)

repertory of ornament. Coffers between the acanthus-covered modillions were treated with a variety of circular features. However, Roman Corinthian capitals have an important difference when compared with Greek: the acanthus leaves of Greek Orders tend to be taller and more elegant, even spikier, and were probably modelled on *Acanthus spinosus*, or prickly acanthus, while those of Roman Orders are shorter, with blunt ends to the leaves, and were probably based on *Acanthus mollis*. In some cases Roman Corinthian leaves are rather like those of the olive tree, or even resemble parsley. In addition Greek capitals tend to have large scrolls in the centres of each face, half-way between the abacus and the top row of acanthus leaves: these scrolls support palmette orna-ments which usually rise up over the face of the abacus [2.30, 2.31]. Roman volutes in the centres of each side are smaller, sit directly under the abacus, and support a fleuron in the centre of each face of the abacus [2.51, 2.53, 2.54, 2.56, 2.57].

Serlio associated Corinthian with virginity, especially the Blessed Virgin Mary, and Vitruvius thought of the Order as representing the figure of a girl, so it was associated with Beauty.

THE ROMAN COMPOSITE ORDER

This is very similar to the most sumptuous of the Corinthian Orders, but again, shafts can be plain or fluted. Bases were often of the Attic type (sometimes with the torus mouldings enriched), but on occasion extra mouldings were placed between the two torus rings [2.61]. The entablature of the Arch of Titus was exceptionally rich [2.61].

The characteristic feature of the Composite Order is its capital, which combines two rows of acanthus leaves (as on the Corinthian capital) with the diagonal or eight-volute Ionic capital above the top row of acanthus. Although the Romans are credited with the invention of the Composite Order in the first century AD, there were earlier precedents. The temple of Athena Alea, Tegea, had two acanthus rows and corner volutes only, while the 'Corinthian-Doric' temple at Paestum has corner volutes over a row of leaves. Composite presumably signifies the mixing of Wisdom with Beauty.

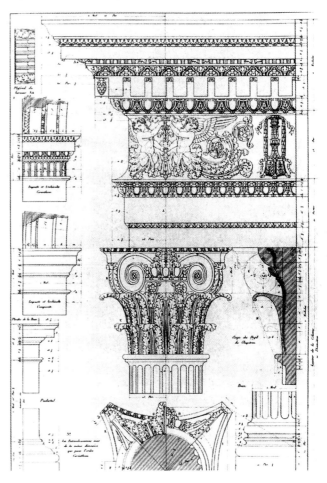

2.61 *Composite Order from the Arch of Titus in Rome of c. AD 82. This highly elaborate Order combines Ionic and Corinthian motifs in the distinctive capital. From Normand (A)*

2.62 *Composite Order after Vignola. There are suggestions of modillions which project only partially below the cornice. From Normand (A)*

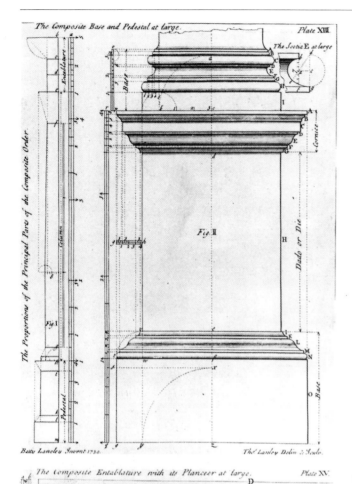

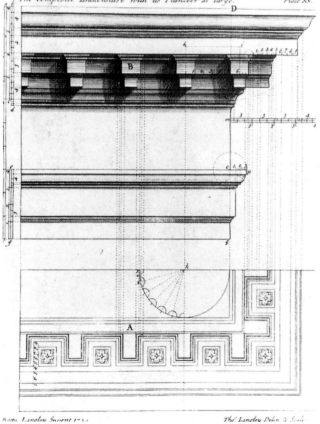

2.63 (ABOVE, LEFT) *The Composite Order. The total Order with pedestal is divided in 5 parts, and the pedestal is 1 part high. The remaining parts are divided into 5 parts, and the upper part is the height of the entablature. If the pedestal is 4 parts high, the plinth is 1 part high and the cornice is half a part high. The mouldings above the plinth are a third of a part high. From Langley* (A)

2.64 (ABOVE, RIGHT) *Composite capital. Like the Corinthian capital the Composite is 7 parts high, each row of leaves being 2 parts high. The volutes are $2\frac{1}{2}$ parts high, subdivided into 8 parts, which set out the main proportions as shown. From Langley* (A)

2.65 (LEFT) *Composite entablature. Divided into 10 parts, the architrave = 3, the frieze = 3, and the cornice = 4. Subdivisions are based on the proportions shown. From Langley* (A)

APPLICATION OF THE ORDERS

Although there are examples of engaged columns in Greek Architecture (temple of Zeus Olympios at Agrigentum (Doric), Lion Tomb at Cnidos (unfluted Doric except at the tops and bottoms of the shafts, with wide intercolumniation [2.3])), temple of Apollo Epicurius at Bassae (four angle-volute Ionic), and Choragic Monument of Lysicrates (Corinthian [2.30, 2.31]), most Greek Architecture is distinguished for its expression of a columnar and trabeated construction. When the Abbé Laugier visualized the Primitive Hut as the precedent for all subsequent Architecture, he argued that the constructional integrity of such a system had been undermined by such 'abuses' as engaged columns, and so real Architecture would express the columnar and trabeated form with clarity. Laugier's *Essai sur l'Architecture* of 1753 heralded a celebration of the column, a seeking for a greater purity of form and construction, and a primitivism in which stereometrical shapes and tough, robust Doric began to be used in reaction to over-refinement and Rococo frippery. Thus the rediscovery of Greek Architecture occurred at a time when philosophically a return to basics was being demanded, and the uncompromising strength and severity of Greek Doric began to

2.66 Merging of arcuated and columnar and trabeated forms at the Colosseum, Rome (AD 75–82). The superimposition of Orders involves widely spaced engaged columns of the Tuscan Order, over which is an Ionic Order, above which is a Corinthian Order. The wide spacing derives from Hellenistic and Roman examples, but the arch, which combines with the trabeated Orders, makes the spacing visually acceptable (Batsford)

2.67 Detail of the superimposed Orders of the Theatre of Marcellus (13 BC) in Rome, showing the Doric entablature with three triglyphs over the intercolumniation with an engaged Ionic Order above (Batsford)

be admired as the direct result of the Primitive Hut. Nevertheless, as scholarship revealed more and more of the refinements of Greek Architecture, it was found that even the Greeks employed antae (a species of pilaster used to terminate the side walls, with bases and capitals differing from those of adjacent columns, and, unlike pilasters, having straight sides rather than entasis), and used canephorae and caryatides, on occasion, instead of columns.

Superimposed columns are found inside Greek temples, but using the same Order. Two or three Orders could be employed in Greek buildings, but not superimposed. That remained true until the Hellenistic period, when rules governing the syntax of the Orders were relaxed. Ionic colonnades over Doric (the entablature over the Ionic columns being Doric) are found at the portico of the sanctuary of Athena at Pergamon (second century BC), and constitute only one example of an overall loosening of practice, and a greater freedom of expression. Generally speaking, Hellenistic spacing of columns became very wide, as the one-metope-per-intercolumniation began to seem too severe and heavy when lighter, more spacious effects were sought by Architects.

This wider Hellenistic spacing was ideal for mixing the Orders with arcuated forms [2.66–2.68]. The Record Office in Rome of 78 BC had concrete vaulting, and piers adorned with Doric engaged columns and entablature with four triglyphs per intercolumniation: it was a similar Order to that used at Cori [2.38]. This type of arcuated façade, to which Orders are engaged, was further developed at the Colosseum, begun by Vespasian, and completed under Titus and Domitian. The outer wall of this elliptical building consisted of eighty piers connected by barrel-vaults, with the arches expressed on the outside. An engaged Order of Tuscan columns carried an entablature, over which was the second storey of unfluted Ionic: above was a third arcaded storey with an engaged Corinthian Order, on the entablature of which was a wall without arcades, but

2.69 *The Khazna at Petra of* c.AD 120 *or earlier, that incorporates a considerable degree of architectural sophistication. Note the circular pavilion in the centre set between a broken pediment. The whole effect is daringly proto-Baroque* (AFK H17408)

2.68 *The columnar and trabeated form merged with the arcuated principle. The Arch of Titus in Rome of* c.AD 82 *showing the engaged Composite Order and the attic storey. The Roman triumphal arch was an important precedent followed by Architects of the Renaissance period. Its three divisions, the unequal spacing of the columns, and the combination of arched form and Order made it a versatile model. The very wide spacing of the central pair of columns would not work if the Order were not engaged, as it would look weak: with the arch and the background of masonry, however, the composition works* (A)

with every other bay pierced by a small rectangular opening. This wall was divided into bays by means of tall pilasters on pedestals of a unique, vaguely Composite Order [2.66].

Widely spaced columns, engaged or standing before the arcuated structure behind, can also be found in Roman triumphal arches [2.68], but here the intercolumniation varies: it is wider in the centre than at the sides in order to accommodate the great central arch. Thus, the Orders were further freed from Antique usage, but new proportional systems and relationships were established.

The mixing of arched forms with the columnar and trabeated language of the Orders produced further variations. The traditional triangular pediment was often broken (as at the Khazna in Petra [2.69]), and sometimes alternated with segmental pediments, a form associated with the Isiac moon and the bow of Diana. Broken-bed pediments with segmental vaults were used in the 'Temple of Bacchus' at Baalbek, where the entrance portico to the temple complex also had a colonnade with

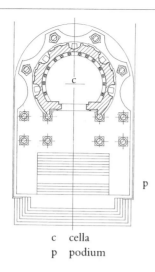

c cella
p podium

2.70 *The third-century 'Temple of Venus' at Baalbek, showing Roman Imperial tendencies towards proto-Baroque forms (A)*

a central arch, the entablature being carried in a semicircle over the arch, and set in a triangular pediment. A similar motif occurred at the second-century temple at Termessus in Pisidia and at the Palace of Diocletian at Spalato, and it is probably the model for the Serliana of Renaissance times.

It was but a small step to forming vaults springing from columns and entablatures, as at the *Thermae*, and to inventing complex proto-Baroque plan-forms, like the round temple at Baalbek, with its entablature containing five concave indentations over a circular drum [Fig.2.70]. Such variations and combinations were to form the basis for an astonishing range of further invention from the early Renaissance period. Hellenistic and Roman exemplars, then, took over from Greece as the main sources for later Classical Architecture, until Greece was once again rediscovered during the eighteenth century.

1. Pausanias, *Itinerary of Greece*, Book V, 20, 6, and Book VIII, 10, 2.

III

THE GRAECO-ROMAN ROOTS OF CLASSICAL ARCHITECTURE

The main sources of Classicism: Greek Architecture; Roman Architecture; concluding comparative remarks

Greek architecture, while the fruit of all the civilisations which preceded the great period of Greek culture, did not live for itself alone; for it has sown the seed of European architecture, and has determined the future form and growth of most subsequent European art.

WILLIAM BELL DINSMOOR (1886–1966): *The Architecture of Ancient Greece.* London, 1950, p. xv.

THE MAIN SOURCES OF CLASSICISM

GREEK ARCHITECTURE

The lands that lie around the Mediterranean Sea produced Architecture long before what we now recognize as Classicism developed into its mature forms. Millennia before Augustus, even before the maturing of the Greek Doric Order in the early seventh century BC, the Egyptians were building great works of Architecture, and evolved sophisticated columnar and trabeated systems with capitals and cornices. There can be no doubt at all that the square, plain columns and simple architrave and cornice (such as those of the remarkable Temple of Queen Hatshepsut at Dêr el-Bahari, and in other buildings employing the square column as a peristyle around a cella, like the temple at Elephantine) influenced European Architects working in Neoclassical styles, notably Schinkel [2.28], Thomson [2.29], von Klenze, Kreis, and Speer. Less clear is the influence of the polygonal columns of parts of the Dêr el-Bahari complex, or of the rock-cut tombs at Beni-Hasan (erected perhaps some two millennia before Christ) on the evolution of the Greek Doric Order. It is improbable that stone columns of circular or polygonal section were used in the Aegean area or in Italy before the seventh century BC, even though they were not unusual in Egypt for many centuries before that. It does seem that timber was the favoured material for columns in Greece and Italy, and that wood was superseded by stone, perhaps through Egyptian influences, from the seventh century in Doric Architecture, but that wood remained in use, often in combination with stone and terracotta, in Italy until much later.

Early Greek Architecture from the seventh century seems to have been a development of well-established local traditions of building in timber and stone, and Egyptian influences helped to encourage an Architecture primarily of masonry. Probably the most important of all the Asiatic imports to affect Ancient Greece was the prototype of the Ionic capital. Early capitals, such as the Aeolic type [2.14] from Neandria, have two volutes springing upwards and curling outwards from the top of the shaft, rather like a sapling being split at the end and the two halves bent outwards into spirals. Between the spirals is a fan-like pattern rising to a flat top that supported the beams. This type of capital is really a variety of the palmette [Fig.7] pattern found in Egyptian and Cretan designs for paintings and reliefs. In true Ionic, however, the volutes do not rise from the shaft; they are quite definitely laid, like a mattress with both ends rolled up underneath to form two whorls, on top of the shaft, but separated from the shaft by the circular echinus (ornamented with egg-and-dart) which carries the central channelled portion joining the volutes [2.15–2.19]. Subsequently, of course, and certainly from the time of Alexander the Great, the process of syncretism accelerated, when Egyptian deities merged with those of the Greek civilizations. It is likely that Egyptian and Asiatic influences had an impact much earlier, even on the prehistoric Architecture of Crete, but this does not mean that Cretan civilization did not have strong native roots. The whole point to remember about the cultures of the lands in and around the Mediterranean is that the sea was the highway, and that artistic and other cross-currents were there from the very earliest of times.

What we now call Classical Architecture seems to have evolved with similarities sufficient to identify it as a language, but it did have several distinct regional variations, which we might term Schools, evolved for different racial, religious, geographical, geological, and other reasons. First of all there was the School of Greece and of its colonies in Southern Italy and Sicily, dating from around the early part of the seventh century to around 150 BC, with the Doric Order much in evidence [2.1–2.13]. Then there is the School of the Greek colonies in Asia Minor, in which the Ionic Order is very much to the fore, from the sixth-century temples and treasuries to those of the second century BC. This does not mean, of course, that the Ionic Order was not found in mainland Greece: both the Temple on the Ilissus [2.16] and the Erechtheion [2.17–2.19] are fifth-century examples of the most refined Ionic, but the archaic temple of Artemis at Ephesus in Asia Minor is sixth century in date. Corinthian seems to have evolved from the fifth century as a more decorated variant of Ionic, and was first used internally at Bassae, Delphi, Tegea, and Epidaurus. The Corinthian Order used externally in temples seems first to have occurred in the third-century Temple of Zeus in Cilicia, which may even be Alexandrian in date, and later at the Temple of Zeus Olympios in Athens around 170 BC. The celebrated Choragic Monument of Lysicrates in Athens has six engaged columns around a hollow but inaccessible cella, and dates from the fourth century [2.30].

We can perhaps use the term 'Hellenic' to indicate the Architecture of Greece proper and its colonies from the seventh to the middle of the second century BC. Hellenic Architecture, therefore, includes celebrated monuments such as the Parthenon (447–38) [2.1–2.2], the temple of Aphaia at Aegina (c.490), the stupendous sturdy Doric temples at Paestum (sixth century), the temple of Apollo Epicurius at Bassae (c.420), the Athenian Ionic masterpieces such as the temple on the Ilissus (c.450) and the Erechtheion (c.421–407), and the Corinthian Choragic Monument of Lysicrates (334).

On the other hand, the term 'Hellenistic' suggests the use of the Greek language, the adoption of Greek modes of thought, and the employment of essentials of Hellenic Architecture modified by the incorporation of new or foreign, non-Hellenic elements: 'Hellenistic' implies the Architecture of the Greek-dominated world from the time of Alexander the Great (born 356, acceded 336, died 323 BC). Hellenistic Architecture is mostly associated with settlements east of the Aegean and Mediterranean Seas, especially in Asia Minor in what were known as Mysia, Lydia, Caria, and Lycia. The most obvious Hellenistic modifications in Doric, for example, include the multiplication of triglyphs, with two or even more, over the intercolumniations (a good example is the Lion Tomb at Cnidos [2.3]): this occurred because Hellenistic

taste favoured entablatures of less depth than Hellenic examples, so the shallower frieze conditioned the width of triglyphs and metopes (since proportions had to remain similar), and because Hellenistic spacing of columns generally tended to be much wider, to give a lighter, airier, less massive effect. In addition, Hellenistic columns tend to be more slender than earlier Hellenic examples, perhaps influenced by the refinement and narrowness of Hellenistic Ionic column shafts. The Nereid monument at Xanthos (c.405), which is earlier than the time of Alexander, had very slender and widely spaced Ionic columns, so the tendency to bigger intercolumniations, reducing the height of the entablature, and making buildings appear less robust, but lighter and more elegant, was already present in Greek Architecture, but became favoured after the conquests of Alexander, especially in Asia Minor.

Hellenistic Corinthian Orders were treated very freely, and show varied local designs, often of great refinement. The temple of Apollo Didymaeus near Miletus (c.330) is one such example, where large acanthus leaves sweep up under the corner volutes. It was the great temple south-east of the Athenian Acropolis, however, which appears to have been among the first Corinthian temples on a grand scale. The temple of Zeus Olbios in Cilicia, of the third century, was probably the earliest, but that of Zeus Olympios at Athens, resumed in the first half of the second century BC by King Antiochus Epiphanes of (significantly) Syria, was undoubtedly bigger and more splendid. Its fully developed Corinthian (completed under Hadrian) was the model for much Roman work of this Order, and therefore for standard Renaissance Corinthian, because Sulla adorned the temple of Jupiter in Rome with columns removed from the Athenian Olympieion.

ROMAN ARCHITECTURE

The important feature of Greek Architecture (be it Hellenic or Hellenistic) was that the column and entablature were very much in evidence in most of the significant buildings. That is, the Greek Orders were the chief architectural expression in a wide range of structures, especially temples, where porticoes and peristyles were essential elements. All of which leads us to the various Schools associated with Rome. First, there is the School of Etruria and Latium, quite distinct from the Greek Schools, and dating roughly from the sixth to the second century. From this derive the Tuscan Order and the Roman temple type, with its prostyle portico, bare cella, and more steeply raked roof. The Roman Republican School (150 to the end of the first century BC) has examples of Roman Doric, Ionic, and Corinthian Orders, but the appearance of buildings – temples on podia, columns engaged with cellae, as with the temple of Fortuna Virilis in Rome (Ionic) of c.40 BC – differed from that of Greek, or Greek colonial, examples, in spite of superficial similarities [2.43, 2.44].

However, the decoration of early temples in Italy has strong affinities with Greece, although the architecture of Campania, Latium, and Etruria are similar in type, and are distinctly Italian. The temples built were mostly of timber and brick, while entablatures were of wood, often decorated with painted terracotta. The buildings stood on high podia with steps at only one end, a feature that is very rare in Greece, but was adopted universally by the Romans. Vitruvius describes an Etruscan temple [3.1] which consisted of three cells separated by walls, with a door each, opening to a large portico of two rows of four widely spaced columns. The eaves and gabled end had very wide projections.

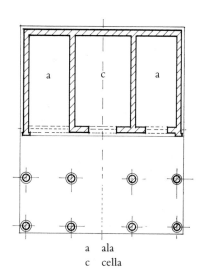

3.1 *Etruscan temple, after Vitruvius* (A)

consisting of one torus below a large apophyge: the shafts had 18 Doric flutes on the upper two-thirds, but the lowest third consisted of an 18-sided polygon. Below the capital, which consisted of a small abacus and echinus, was a smooth band. The low entablature ran all the way round the building, and there were three triglyphs to each intercolumniation: like Greek Doric examples, the triglyphs at the corner met, so the corner columns were not on the centre-lines of the triglyphs. The basic form of the temple of Fortuna Virilis [2.43, 2.44] in Rome was similar, except that it was Ionic and had engaged columns round the cella with the same intercolumniation as that of the porticoes. With the coming of the Empire and the Age of Augustus and Tiberius (31 BC–AD 37) the temple type continued, notably with the *Maison Carrée* in Nîmes (16 BC), a hexastyle pseudo-peripteral Corinthian temple on a podium, so the form is Hellenized Roman-Etruscan [2.60]. Many temples were of great magnificence, and the Corinthian Order was much favoured, with elaborate and deeply carved entablatures, and vigorous capitals. The Augustan temple of Mars Ultor (2 BC) [3.2] had a peripteral colonnade on three sides terminating in a mighty wall, into which the apse, with its concrete hemidome, was set at the end of the cella.

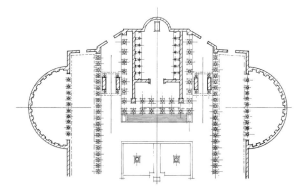

3.2 *Rome: Temple of Mars Ultor* (A)

It seems that strong Hellenistic influences merged with the traditions of native Italian temple Architecture to produce the type favoured during the later Republic. The Doric temple at Cori [2.38], of the first century BC, is one of the best preserved of all Republican temples. The plan is similar to that evolved in Etruria: it stood on a high podium approached by steps at one end, and had a deep prostyle tetrastyle portico, with two columns between each of the angle-columns and the wall of the cella, which had a central door. There were antae at all four corners of the cella. The columns were very slender, with bases

The most interesting innovations during the Empire included the mixing of arcuated forms with the Orders, and the development of vaults and domes, often employing concrete. Under the Flavian Emperors (AD 69–96), the use of superimposed Orders in storeys mixed with arcuated structure occurred in the Colosseum (c.AD 75–82) [2.66], while the Arch of Titus (c.AD 82) has a single arch, the early engaged Composite columns with varied intercolumniation and elaborate entablature, and a mighty attic storey with inscription panel [2.61, 2.68]. Later triumphal arches, notably those of Septimius

Severus (AD 203) and Constantine (*c*.315), are highly sophisticated compositions involving three arches (one central large one and two smaller flanking arches) with superimposed detached columns, entablatures, and elaborate attic storeys, and were potent models for later Architects of the Renaissance period [3.3–3.5].

From 96–138 of our era date the Pantheon [3.6] in Rome (with its great drum, coffered brick, mortar, and concrete dome with oculus, and heroic pedimented prostyle octastyle portico [2.55]); the large complex of the Villa Adriana at Tivoli (involving much concrete vaulting and complex allusions to various parts of the Empire); and the huge circular mausoleum of Hadrian. Massive vaults and concrete domes were being fully

exploited at that time, and complicated arcuated structures, with plans of increasing geometrical intricacy, were not uncommon. At both Heliopolis (Baalbek) and the Villa Adriana there appeared a new freedom in the treatment of the Orders, involving curved entablatures and elements that are astoundingly anticipatory of seventeenth-century Baroque developments [2.70].

Under the Antonine Emperors (138–193) architectural and structural innovations continued, but from Pertinax to Alexander Severus (193–235) the monuments associated with Septimius Severus and the mighty *Thermae* of Caracalla were built, demonstrating a complete assurance in the combinations of vaulted, arcuated, and columnar and trabeated forms. The *Thermae* also demonstrate a mastery of the problems of planning very large and complicated buildings, incorporating big vaulted public rooms, gardens, and various geometries in one symmetrical composition [3.7].

From 235–330, that is from Maximin to the founding of Constantinople, date Diocletian's palace at Spalato (or

3.3 *The triumphal arch theme. The Arc de Triomphe de l'Étoile, Paris, begun in 1806 to designs by J.-F.-T. Chalgrin, and completed by G.-A. Blouet in 1836. The arch is astylar, that is without an engaged Order (Batsford)*

3.4 *The triumphal arch theme. The Arc de Triomphe du Carrousel, erected 1805–9 to designs by Percier and Fontaine, and based on the arch of Septimius Severus in Rome, although the attic storey is based on that of the Arch of Constantine in Rome* (Batsford)

3.5 *The triumphal arch theme. The centrepiece of the Grand Palais in the Avenue d'Antin, designed by Deglane, Louvet, and Thomas* (Batsford)

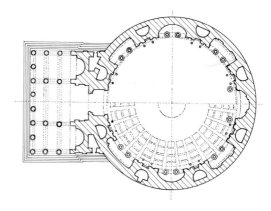

3.6 *Rome: plan of the Pantheon* (A)

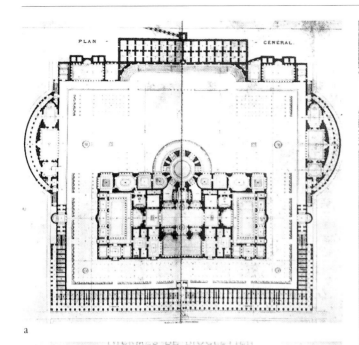

a

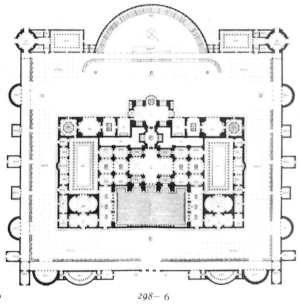

b

3.8 *The Mausoleum of Santa Costanza in Rome of c.AD 325 or later, showing the paired Composite columns, entablature with pulvinated frieze, and arcuated system of annular vault around the central space* (Batsford)

3.7 *The Roman* Thermae: *(a) The Thermae of Caracalla, Rome, AD 211–17, (b) The Thermae of Diocletian, Rome, AD 298–306. Both baths demonstrate the principles of Roman Imperial planning, with vast, formal, symmetrical arrangements of elements, main axes and subsidiary axes, curved exedrae, enormous vaulted spaces, and rooms exploring circles and parts of circles on plan* (Batsford)

Split) and the *Thermae* of Diocletian [3.7], both highly sophisticated essays in planning vast buildings housing various functions and employing many axes, systems of symmetries, and even greater freedom with the Orders. This period also saw the development of circular and polygonal structures, including various mausolea: Santa Costanza in Rome is an example [3.8]. At the same time, complex geometries of plan-form were exploited in many projects.

The Orders were used in basilican churches, often looted from earlier structures [3.9], and incorporating sometimes whole entablatures and occasionally arches; there are many examples, especially in Rome. Certainly

Classical elements were employed in church buildings well into the Christian era, and indeed in parts of Italy the Classical thread never seems to have been completely lost. The Architecture of the Eastern Empire, which we know as Byzantine, tended to accentuate the arcuated and domed Architecture developed by the Romans, and, although columns and other details sometimes suggested Classical prototypes, the pre-eminence of the Orders passed for a while into abeyance.

3.9 *Interior of S. Maria Maggiore, Rome, a huge basilica dedicated to Sancta Maria Mater Dei shortly after the Council of Ephesus sanctioned this unquestionably Isiac appellation of the BVM in AD 431. The marble columns are Antique, and the coffered ceiling dates from 1493–8, and is gilded with some of the first gold brought from America. The baldacchino is carried on four porphyry columns with spiral designs, a reference to the spiral columns above the tomb of S. Peter in the Constantinian basilica and the spiral columns associated with the Temple of Solomon. Note that the clearstorey is carried on a colonnade, and the effect is grave and Antique (AFK H10332)*

CONCLUDING COMPARATIVE REMARKS

Hellenic plans are often very simple, and buildings relatively small. Structure, dictated by the columnar and trabeated form, was limited in scope, and the column was pre-eminent, exploited for the beauty of its form and the expression of its function. Details, such as friezes, metopes, and sculptural elements, were often extremely refined and beautiful, in spite of the limited vocabulary of ornament employed.

Roman structural methods, employing the true arch, the dome, the vault, and concrete enabled buildings of enormous size to be erected, while plans, employing a variety of geometrical forms, were often complex and intricate, as in the *Thermae*, palaces, and fora, and involved main and subsidiary axes. The mixing of arcuated with columnar and trabeated structural elements (the latter adapted from Hellenistic types) created

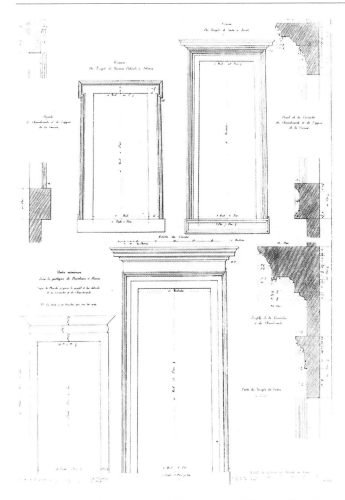

3.10 *Architraves from Antiquity. The example top left comes from the Erechtheion and has ears. The other examples are Roman. Top right and bottom centre are from the Temple of Vesta at Tivoli, and that bottom left is from the Pantheon. From Normand (A)*

an entirely new form of architectural expression, and one that was to be of great importance from Renaissance times. The Romans also superimposed different Orders on storeys, continuing a feature invented in Hellenistic times, but added the Orders to arcuated storeys.

Greek colonnades often rendered the openings in walls of lesser importance in external treatment. In the case of a few buildings such as the Erechtheion, however, the door surrounds were given exquisite treatment, with architraves, a cornice carried on consoles, and a pronounced batter, like the shape of an Egyptian pylon [3.10]. Roman doorcases were also framed, but the variety of treatment was greater [3.10–3.11].

Windows did not, on the whole, merit architectural emphasis in Greek Architecture, but in grander Roman work had segmental heads, or were semicircular with two mullions, the so-called Diocletian Window. High-level windows associated with arcuated and vaulted construction provided lighting even in highly complicated and large buildings. The uses of circular, polygonal, and other forms in plans were often responsible for creating very elaborate effects, and even suggesting swaying convex and concave entablatures over circular

3.11 *Roman ornament:*
a Enrichment of cyma recta moulding showing acanthus and palmette variants
b Left: enrichment of cymatium or cyma recta, with anthemion and acanthus. Right: acanthus enrichment on cavetto moulding
c Left: egg-and-dart over bead-and-reel. Right: variant on egg-and-dart, much enriched with acanthus. Both these examples are, essentially, enriched ovolos, the one on the left having a fillet and bead under
d Typical enrichment of cavetto and ogees or cyma reversa
e Left: enrichment of cyma reversa. The two larger examples show enrichment of cyma recta mouldings with acanthus and anthemion variants
f Left: leaf-and-tongue. Right: leaf-and-tongue variant in the form of leaves and acorns
g Three examples of enriched cyma reversa mouldings
h Astragals ornamented with bead-and-reel
From Normand (A)

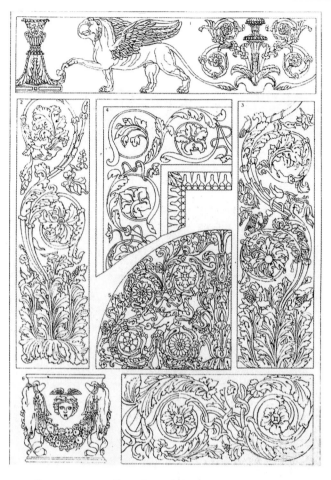

3.12 *Roman ornament. From Spiers (A)*

plans, as at Baalbek; architectural devices that are akin to seventeenth-century Baroque designs.

Classical mouldings were evolved as essential elements of Architecture, and especially of the Orders. An entablature with no mouldings would be only a beam, while the refinements of detail, of cast shadows, and of ornament, so important in great Classical buildings, enhance the qualities of those buildings, so that their excision would be calamitous.

Mouldings help buildings to weather gracefully, and they can protect detail and sculpture from the elements. Greek mouldings had very graceful sections and were enriched with refined carvings that did not disguise the sections or profiles. Many Greek buildings were of marble, which can be cut to precise degrees of accuracy. Roman decoration is often superabundant, and mouldings are usually segments of circles in section.

Familiar ornaments such as dentils are more widely spaced in Greek than in Roman examples, and are as deep as the moulding on which they are set; Roman dentils often have a fillet below and a small fillet between the dentils at the top; Greek consoles, which are often exquisitely shaped and carved, are used vertically as supports for the cornices of openings, whereas Roman consoles also occur set horizontally as modillions on cornices, and on keystones, when they are termed ancones.

Honeysuckle ornament is commonly employed in Greek Architecture, together with the lotus and scroll. In Roman work the acanthus is the commonest form. Egg-and-dart is taller and more elegant in Greek than in Roman work, while the profile is more subtle.

Roman ornaments, such as dolphins or bay-leaf garlands, are specifically Roman, but there are many instances in which Hellenic-Hellenistic-Roman themes mix, coalesce, and become transmogrified in subtle ways. Discussion of these permutations alone would fill a book; the present Glossary and illustrations must suffice to give a flavour of the range of ornament used in Classical Architecture [3.11–3.12].

IV

THE RENAISSANCE PERIOD

Columns, pilasters, antae, and piers; key
buildings of the Early Renaissance; later
Palazzi; Venetian *Palazzi*, Sansovino,
and Alberti; centralized and circular
plans; Michelangelo; Serlio and Vignola;
Palladio

Modern Rome *subsists still, by the Ruins and
Imitation of the old . . .*

CHRISTOPHER WREN (1632–1723): *Tracts on Architecture I*, quoted in Stephen
Wren's *Parentalia, or Memoirs of the Family of Wrens* (1750). Reprinted in
The Wren Society, Vol. 19, Oxford, 1942, p. 126.

COLUMNS, PILASTERS, ANTAE, AND PIERS

The Orders offered Architects a wide range of expression, from the primitive to the luxurious. When the Romans combined columnar and trabeated forms derived from Greek (and especially from Hellenistic [4.1]) exemplars with arcuated and vaulted systems, even piled up in storeys, they invented a new type of Architecture in which the Orders imposed a system of controlled rhythms on façades and gave a sense of decorum and celebration to the underlying structure. It is important to understand that the vertical and horizontal elements of the Roman Orders were fully integrated with the massive structure, and not simply stuck on. Arcuated and vaulted structures require mass to take the loads. In fact, massive piers carry loads and arches which could not be held by a columnar and trabeated system, so the two types of structure are married [2.66–2.68].

This brings us to a consideration of the nature of columns, piers, antae, and pilasters. Much of Greek Architecture had columns holding entablatures, but occasionally columns were engaged. It is important to distinguish between several kinds of vertical support. Associated with the Orders are columns, antae, pilasters, and piers. A column is an upright element, circular on plan, and consists of a base (except in the Doric Order), a shaft, and a capital. It tapers towards the top, is of considerably greater length than diameter, and supports the entablature. Sometimes, as in the cases of Trajan's column in Rome, Nelson's column in Trafalgar Square, or the Downshire column at Hillsborough it stands alone without an entablature, and carries a statue on its abacus. A column can also be engaged, that is attached to a wall or a pier; half or less than half of the diameter of the column can be engaged with, applied to, attached to, or inserted in the mass behind it.

Greek columns were constructed of drums pegged together, and stood on a stepped crepidoma, the top of which was termed the stylobate.. Pedestals were used occasionally, as in the temple of Artemis at Ephesus. Roman columns, on the other hand, were often vast monoliths, and when hard stones like granite were used they were unfluted [2.55]. Greek Architects used super-imposed Orders inside temples, Hellenistic Architects used different Orders superimposed (often with the 'wrong' entablature for the Order of the columns), and the Romans used not only several storeys of different superimposed Orders, but the Orders engaged with arcuated forms [2.66–2.68].

Then there are detached columns, which have a wall behind them (usually quite close) and an entablature connected with the wall. The Romans used this device as well as the fully engaged Order.

A pilaster is shallow, projects from a wall, and is rectangular on plan; it will resemble in all respects the columns of the Order with which it is being used. In other words it will have a base, its shaft usually will taper and have entasis, it may or may not have flutes, and it will have a capital to match that of the column. It might be used on the wall of a gallery that is open on one side and has columns with an entablature conforming to beams that would be related to the pilasters. So, pilasters are like square columns that have had most of their volume buried in the wall.

Antae do not necessarily have bases or capitals conforming to the Order with which they are associated: Ionic antae, for example, do not have volutes at all. Antae are usually on the terminating features of walls in a Greek or Greek Revival pronaos or portico. Columns between the antae are called *in antis*. The Romans used pilasters as features on the ends of walls of temple cellae, but the Greeks used antae to emphasize, terminate, and strengthen the ends of their naos walls. Antae do not taper and have no entasis, so they are unlike pilasters, although they have been described as a species of pilaster.

Piers are structural elements of solid material, or the solid mass between openings in a wall. They are quite distinct from columns, although columns or pilasters may be attached to them. Piers themselves do not necessarily have capitals or bases, but they may do, and if so, usually conform to the main mouldings of the Order used in the columns and pilasters. The Colosseum is a prime example of a building with piers carrying arches with engaged superimposed Orders rising in storeys and framing the arches.

So, the Romans evolved a development of the Classical language of Architecture, and the engaged Order/arcuated structure theme was used further, and with even more variations, by Renaissance Architects. Another important Roman theme, that of the triumphal arch, with its varied intercolumniation, engaged or detached columns, entablature breaking forward over the columns, keystones touching the undersides of string-courses and architrave, coffered vaults, and richly ornamented surfaces, was adopted by Renaissance designers.

There can be no doubt that all through the Middle Ages Antiquity was never entirely submerged: it was always there, obscure perhaps, and even misinterpreted, but present nevertheless. The first conscious attempts to revive Classicism took place during the Carolingian period of the early ninth century, when some semblance of Imperial unity once more occurred.

In Italy, however, Classical elements can be found in some mediaeval Architecture, especially in Pisa and Pistoia Cathedrals, while the eleventh-century church of S. Miniato in Florence displays certain proto-Renaissance features that point to an attempt to revive Classical architectural forms [4.3]. Some west fronts of churches, like those of Notre Dame at Poitiers, Saint-Gilles near Arles, the celebrated porch of Saint-Trophîme, Arles, and the west front of the church at Echillais, display vestiges of the composition of a Roman triumphal arch, which is not surprising considering the many Roman remains in what is now France, and the importance of Rome as a place of pilgrimage. In fact, in spite of the clear stylistic differences, it is hard to imagine the development of Western European Romanesque and Gothic Architecture, especially in the greatest cathedrals and churches, without the precedents of so many Roman buildings; and without the Greek Orders there would not have been those of Rome, or the invention of a new developed language.

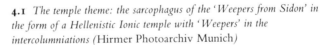

4.1 *The temple theme: the sarcophagus of the 'Weepers from Sidon' in the form of a Hellenistic Ionic temple with 'Weepers' in the intercolumniations (Hirmer Photoarchiv Munich)*

KEY BUILDINGS OF THE EARLY RENAISSANCE

Florentine Renaissance Architecture of the fifteenth century has certain similarities at times to eleventh-century Architecture, but the reappearance of the Orders, complete with entablatures, great *palazzi* capped with the elaborate *cornicione*, and the evolution of astylar façades first occurred there, with much use of arcuated forms. There can be no question that eleventh-century Tuscan proto-Renaissance Architecture had a profound influence on Filippo Brunelleschi (1377–1446), whose Foundlings' Hospital in Florence of 1419–1424 [4.2] has a loggia of arches and sail-vaults carried directly on the abaci of Classical columns; the building aims at an effect of Antiquity, but owes as much to the church of S. Miniato al Monte [4.3]. His S. Lorenzo (from 1421) and S. Spirito (from 1436) both have domes over the crossings, and both employ sail-vaults over the aisles, but the nave arches rest on a slightly clumsy version of complete Orders [4.4], that is the column with entablature, rather than on the abaci. In fact, the entablatures consist of a cornice, an architrave of three exaggerated fasciae and a frieze which is more like a dosseret.

In Brunelleschi's Pazzi chapel of the 1430s a Corinthian Order of pilasters is combined with vaults (both the porch and the chapel have a dome on pendentives in the centre) and arches, giving a remarkable and severe Roman effect enhanced by the cabling in the lower third of the pilasters and the gravely subdued decorative treatment. Yet the handling of the corners in the interior is weak, involving fragmentary and return pilasters. In this interesting building the grammar and discipline of Classical Architecture were being re-established, not by mere imitation, but by using and reviving the language, yet there are uncertainties, clumsy and hesitant corners, and a sense that nuances of language are not fully understood [4.5–4.8].

With Leon Battista Alberti, an Architect of genius, Renaissance Architecture acquired its first important theorist. His first building, the extraordinary church of S. Francesco at Rimini, of *c*.1450, known as the Tempio Malatestiano, incorporates a west front directly inspired by the triumphal arch of Augustus at Rimini [4.9] and robust, arcaded side elevations of a gravely Roman type

4.2 *The Foundlings' Hospital in Florence, arcade by Brunelleschi of 1419–24. Note the long entablature carried on pilasters* (Batsford)

4.3 *S. Miniato, Florence, of c.1090. The west end of a basilican church with high clearstoreyed nave, lean-to aisles and blind arcade with Corinthian capitals. The top of the gable is reminiscent of a pediment. In the thirteenth and fourteenth centuries this Romanesque building was believed to be very much older, and therefore represented Antiquity. It was thought to be a survival from the Roman past, and a model for imitation. Photograph by Donald McLeish (Batsford)*

4.4 *Interior of S. Spirito, Florence, by Brunelleschi, 1434–82. The Corinthian capitals support a full entablature, so a full Order supports the arcade. This is more genuinely 'Antique' than the somewhat hesitant arcade of the same Architect's Foundlings' Hospital [**4.2**] (Batsford)*

4.5 (ABOVE) *The Pazzi Chapel in the cloisters of Sta Croce, Florence, by Brunelleschi, 1429 and later. Almost a variation on the triumphal arch theme, it also suggests the prototype of the Serliana* (A)

4.6 (BELOW) *Interior of Pazzi Chapel. Note the uncomfortably bodged arrangement of pilasters in the corners* (Archivi Alinari)

very like the Colosseum arches *minus the Orders*. In these arches, on the sills, lie the severe Classical sarcophagi of Sigismondo Malatesta's courtiers. In his native city of Florence, Alberti designed the Palazzo Rucellai (from 1446), the first domestic Renaissance building in which each storey is defined by an Order [4.10]. The base is formed of a continuous ledge with a band carved in a diamond pattern emulating Roman *opus reticulatum*: this makes a plinth on which the Tuscan pilasters stand. The *palazzo* combines the superimposed Orders, channelled rustication of the panels bounded by pilasters and entablatures, and arched windows: the whole has a remarkably Antique feeling about it enhanced by a great *cornicione* derived from the Colosseum.

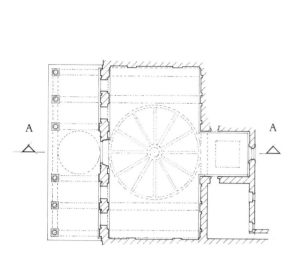

4.7 *Pazzi Chapel: plan (A)*

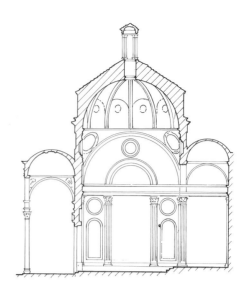

4.8 *Pazzi Chapel: section A–A (A)*

4.9 *The triumphal arch theme. The church of S. Francesco in Rimini, known as the Tempio Malatestiano, by Alberti, from 1450. This was the first Renaissance example of the application of a Classical façade to a traditional church form, that is, with a high central nave and lower lean-to aisles on either side. Although the façade is unfinished, it has an arrangement based on a Roman triumphal arch over which was to be a central arched opening flanked by pilasters, with low segmental screen walls hiding the roofs of the aisles. In the arched openings at the side of the temple are sarcophagi (AFK H11916)*

4.10 *The Palazzo Rucellai in Florence by Alberti, begun 1446. Note the superimposed Orders, the arches, and the rustication. This was the first attempt to apply the Classical Orders to a palace front in Renaissance times (A)*

4.11 *The Palazzo Medici (Palazzo Riccardi) in Florence, by Michelozzo Michelozzi, begun in 1444. The Classical cornicione should be noted. Michelangelo filled in the arches and designed the ground-floor windows early in the sixteenth century (A)*

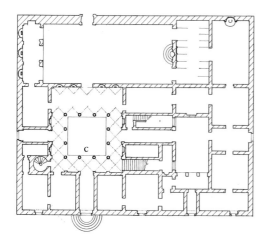

c   cortile

4.12 *Palazzo Medici: plan (A)*

Almost exactly contemporary is the astylar Palazzo Riccardi in Florence [4.11] (originally the Palazzo Medici [4.12]) by Michelozzo Michelozzi (1396–1472), otherwise known as Michelozzo di Bartolommeo. Building began in 1444, and the three storeys are indicated by string-courses which coincide with the sills of the semicircular-headed windows. The ground floor is faced with cyclopean, or rock-faced, rustication and is pierced with round-headed openings, some of which were filled in and acquired windows designed by Michelangelo in the early sixteenth century. Voussoirs are boldly expressed. The windows of the *piano nobile* are symmetrically disposed, but are not related to the openings below, although they are to those of the second floor. The whole composition is capped by a mighty *cornicione* that draws heavily on Roman Antiquity, while the plan, too, with its arcaded *cortile* [4.13] is also derived from Antique prototypes.

Of similar astylar rusticated type with massive *cornicione* is the Palazzo Strozzi, begun in 1489 to designs by

4.13 Cortile *in the Palazzo Medici by Michelozzi, which is basically the arcade of the Foundlings' Hospital wrapped round the court, with a correspondingly weak corner detail (A)*

Simone del Pollaiuolo Cronaca (1457–1508) and Benedetto da Maiano (1442–1497). These *palazzi* allude to Antiquity in several ways, not least by the manner in which Alberti suggested *opus reticulatum* in the base, the superimposed Orders with arches, and the cornice based on that of the Colosseum in the façade of the Palazzo Rucellai. The arrangement of rooms around a central court or *cortile*, the main rooms on the *piano nobile* above the street level, and much else are not unlike Roman apartment blocks designed a millennium and a half earlier, some of which can still be seen in Ostia and elsewhere; the vestibule from the street, and the central court with rooms disposed about it and with columns at the lowest level owe much to Graeco-Roman house plans; and the string-courses and *cornicione* derive directly from Roman buildings. Yet the *cornicione*, with its massive overhang, had no frieze, no architrave and, in Riccardi and Strozzi, no columnar or pilaster system, so it had to be deliberately oversized. This in itself was a new invention of the Renaissance.

LATER *PALAZZI*

The internal *cortile* of *palazzi* became more assured in design with the Palazzo Cancellaria of 1486–96 [4.14] and the Palazzo Venezia of 1467–71, both in Rome. In the Venezia the two storeys of arches in the *cortile* have engaged Tuscan and Corinthian Orders and the angles, being piers, are much more confidently handled than in the Palazzo Riccardi (where Michelozzo crashed two arches, based on Brunelleschi's loggia to the Foundlings' Hospital, down on a single column [4.13]); in the Cancellaria [4.14] L-shaped piers at the corners of the *cortile* successfully terminate the arcades, allowing the arches (which are carried on columns between the piers) to rest on abaci with the archivolts intact. Even more

elegant is the corner treatment of the *cortile* of the Ducal Palace at Urbino (1465–1479) [4.15] by Luciano Laurana (*c*.1420–1479): there, the arcades terminate in L-shaped piers, taking Florentine precedent to heights of sophistication. The ends of the L-shaped pier have engaged half-columns terminating the arcades, and the front of the pier is faced with two pilasters in the angles, which carry the entablature [4.16].

Clearly related to the *insula*, or block of flats, of Classical Antiquity is a type of *palazzo* with shops set in a heavily rusticated, arcaded ground floor. The House of Raphael of *c*.1512 by Donato Bramante (*c*.1444–1514) had a façade of five bays disposed symmetrically about the central axis, with a *piano nobile* separated from the rusticated ground floor by a plain string-course: the *piano nobile* bays were divided by pairs of unfluted Tuscan columns carrying an entablature with three triglyphs over the intercolumniations. Each window had an

4.14 Cortile *of the Palazzo della Cancellaria, Rome, of 1486–96, influenced by Alberti. Note the elegant manner in which the arcades meet at the corner* (Batsford)

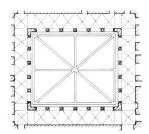

4.15 *Urbino: Palazzo Ducale cortile, showing stronger and aesthetically more satisfactory corners (A)*

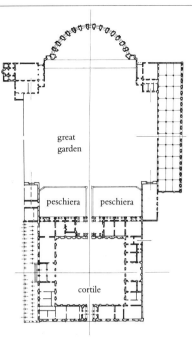

4.17 *Palazzo del Tè, Mantua: plan (A)*

4.16 Cortile *of the Palazzo Ducale at Urbino of 1465–79 by Luciano Laurana, showing the arcades terminating in L-shaped piers (*Archivi Alinari*)*

4.18 *Palazzo del Tè, Mantua, by Giulio Romano of c.1525–34: garden front. Repetition of the so-called Palladian motif, or Serliana* (Archivi Alinari)

4.19 *Palazzo del Tè: part of the elevation of the inner court, containing many Mannerist features. Keystones seem to slip down or up, while the feeling of instability is enhanced by the 'slipping' triglyphs and architraves* (Archivi Alinari)

architrave, over which was a frieze and a triangular pediment. Directly influenced by this design was the Palazzo Vidoni Caffarelli of *c*.1515, attributed to Raphael or to his assistant Lorenzetto, with its *piano nobile* treated in a similar way, but with the pediments over the windows replaced by cornices.

With the Palazzo del Tè in Mantua [4.17] (1526–1534) by Giulio Romano (*c*.1499–1546), the plan of an Antique Roman villa is merged with that of Raphael's (1483–1520) Villa Madama in Rome (itself much influenced by Roman *Thermae*), begun in *c*.1516; but the elevations are extraordinarily original: one has an Order of Tuscan pilasters carrying a Doric entablature, while the rusticated façade has the string-course-cum-window-sills of the plain upper windows flush with the faces of the pilasters, and tied to the huge keystones of the lower windows; another has repeated Serliana motifs [4.18]; and the inner court elevations have keystones that drop down, some triglyphs that are designed to slip below the frieze, bringing the architrave with them in places, and oversized keystones that crash upwards into pediments [4.19]. Thus a sense of instability is created and a kind of deliberate uneasiness that is one of the characteristics of Mannerism (described in the Glossary). Giulio's Cortile della Mostra (or Cavallerizza), in the Palazzo Ducale at Mantua of 1538–39, has tortured, engaged, irregular spiral columns above a rusticated base, but the columns sit on pedestals carried on chunky rusticated consoles:

4.20 *The Cortile della Mostra, or Cortile della Cavallerizza, Palazzo Ducale, Mantua, by Giulio Romano, of 1538–9 – an extraordinary* tour-de-force *of rustication. The Doric columns have become grotesquely twisted and grooved, probably in reference to the 'Solomonic' columns of S. Peter's in Rome. Here is Mannerism carried to extreme lengths (Archivi Alinari)*

4.21 *The Porta Palio, Verona, by Michele Sanmicheli (c.1484–1559), a fortified gate that looks as though it could do its job: this impression is given because of the massive rustication, the choice of the Roman Doric Order, and the massive voussoirs and keystones. The effect is increased by the two distinct layers of rusticated masonry, set behind the engaged Order: the ensemble dates from the 1540s (Batsford)*

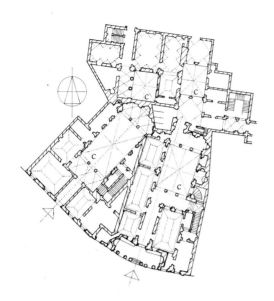

4.22 *Palazzo Massimi alle Colonne, Rome, by Peruzzi, c.1532 and later. A highly ingenious plan on a difficult site, with internal courtyards. Note how the axes are set up on two separate entrances, one for each palace: the Palazzo Angelo Massimi (left), and Pietro Massimi (right) (A)*

4.23 *Palazzo Massimi: A unique curved façade with pilasters and columns of a severe Tuscan Order with a piano nobile and two smaller floors over it. Note the alternating rhythms of the colonnade. The elaborate frames around the upper windows have Mannerist ornament later developed by Serlio as the strapwork which became universal in northern Europe during the late sixteenth and early seventeenth centuries (Batsford)*

c   cortile

4.24 (ABOVE) *The enormous Palazzo Farnese, by Antonio da Sangallo the Younger and Michelangelo, of 1515–46. The gigantic cornicione is Michelangelo's and the façade is astylar, that is, without columns or pilasters. Floors are separated by cornices and by bands of stone coincident with the cornices of the pedestals supporting the aedicules that frame the windows. This important design was very influential (Batsford)*

4.25 (BELOW) *Cortile of the Palazzo Farnese, Rome, begun 1515. This clearly derives from the Theatre of Marcellus and the Colosseum, and consists of superimposed Orders with arches. The ground floor has a Doric Order (unfluted), and above is an Ionic Order, also with arches, and above, an Order of Corinthian pilasters. Antonio da Sangallo the Younger was the Architect, but Michelangelo was responsible for filling in the arcades of the first floor, and rebuilding the top storey (Batsford)*

4.26 *The Northern Bank, formerly the Head Office of the Belfast Bank, Belfast, remodelled in 1845 on the Italian* palazzo *style by Sir Charles Lanyon (1813–89). Note the aediculated windows* (A)

thus the theme of Raphael's House is mixed with that of the Colosseum, but rendered strangely unstable in this Mannerist creation of c.1539 [4.20]. Another important Mannerist monument of the period is the Porta Palio in Verona [4.21].

Baldassare Peruzzi's (1481–1536) Palazzo Massimi in Rome [4.22] has a curved façade to the street with Tuscan columns and pilasters on the ground floor arranged in pairs [4.23]; the whole front is rusticated, and the *piano nobile* is separated from the ground floor by an entablature. Above the *piano nobile* are two rows of small windows, the lower of which has architraves with elaborate frames, the patterns of which were to be developed as strapwork by Serlio and disseminated through his publications all over northern Europe. The *palazzo* has two courts, designed to be similar to a Roman atrium, and arranged on two cunningly contrived axes [4.22].

Contemporary with the Palazzo Massimi is the huge Roman Palazzo Farnese by Antonio da Sangallo the Younger (1484–1546), but finished by Michelangelo after 1546 [4.24]. It is arranged around a central *cortile* that owes much to the theatre of Marcellus and to the Colosseum for its arcuated superimposed storeys, with engaged Orders [4.25]. The main elevation of the Palazzo, however, with its aediculated pedimented windows and huge *cornicione*, was immensely influential on later Architects: Barry's Reform Club and countless stucco-faced houses in Kensington are directly derived from the Farnese Palace [4.26].

VENETIAN *PALAZZI*, SANSOVINO, AND ALBERTI

Venetian *palazzi* are quite different. The typical *palazzo* has an entrance at canal level, off which are a staircase and various store-rooms above the water-level. The *piano nobile* is above, and is given greater architectural expression: the main room is usually in the centre of the front, with smaller rooms on either side expressed by smaller windows, and the *Gran Salone* is usually indicated in the middle by very large windows. Because such *palazzi* are on restricted sites, and are built on piles, there are not always internal courts. So Venetian *palazzi* have façades that are symmetrical, and rise in distinctly expressed parts, usually three. Typical Venetian *palazzi* façades include Corner-Spinelli of *c.*1480, Véndramin-Calergi of *c.*1500–09 [4.27], and the brilliant Palazzo Corner della Ca'Grande [4.28], begun in 1537 to designs by Jacopo Sansovino (1486–1570). The last-mentioned *palazzo* has a rusticated lower floor with a triple-arched entrance and a mezzanine, then the *piano nobile* with arched windows and engaged pairs of Ionic columns, and on top a further floor treated similarly, but with paired, engaged Corinthian columns. The mezzanine windows are flanked by volutes, a Mannerist device reminiscent of Michelangelo's work in Florence.

4.27 *Palazzo Véndramin-Calergi, Venice, begun c.1500–9, by Pietro Lombardo. This has three storeys of Orders, and the internal arrangement is clear, with the* Gran Salone *in the middle. The windows, separated by single columns, are of the Venetian type, that is with two arches and a roundel over held within a semicircular arch (A)*

4.28 *The Palazzo Corner della Ca' Grande in Venice by Sansovino,*
begun 1537 on the right. The rusticated basement has a triple-arched
entrance and there are two superimposed Orders with twin columns rising
over (A)

The Palazzo Corner della Ca'Grande [4.28] is an
example of Orders used above a rusticated ground floor
with a mezzanine that becomes, effectively, a plinth or a
podium. The Palazzo Véndramin-Calergi [4.27] has
three superimposed Orders and no rustication, but the
tripartite form of the façade is emphasized by flanking the
single windows on either side of the façade with pairs of
engaged columns. Corner-Spinelli has superimposed
pilasters at each end of the front only. Sansovino's Corner
della Ca' Grande was the model for later *palazzi*, such as
the Palazzi Pésaro (begun 1652) [4.29] and Rezzonico
(begun 1667) by Baldassarre Longhena (1598–1682) but
these, with their rusticated basements, luxurious carving,
and deeply recessed modelling, add Baroque extremes to
the Sansovinoesque theme.

Sansovino used the superimposed Orders with arches
to even sturdier effect at the great Biblioteca Marciana,
begun in 1537, and completed by Vincenzo Scamozzi in
1588. The references to Antiquity are to the Theatre of
Marcellus and to Vitruvius. Sansovino used heavy piers

at the corners of the library, and a half-metope to turn the frieze [4.30], with pilasters slightly wider than the Roman Doric columns on each face of the pier. The Ionic Order on the first floor means that this floor is taller than the ground floor; the problem of such a difference in height is resolved by carrying the arches of the first floor on a subsidiary pair of small Ionic columns, fluted to make them even more jewel-like compared with the massive, unfluted shafts of the main Orders. The massive entablature has an ornate frieze with swags, and is pierced with small windows; it is crowned by a balustrade with statues on the pedestals. Thus the Colosseum–Marcellus theme acquired even greater richness of expression.

Next to the Library, Sansovino's La Zecca (the Mint, completed in 1545) has a rusticated astylar arcade as the ground floor, over which are two (originally one) storeys of dramatically 'Rustic Orders', that is, with banded columns, which became a common feature throughout Europe from the later sixteenth century, after it was made familiar by Serlio in his textbooks.

4.29 *Palazzo Pésaro, Venice, of the late seventeenth century, by Longhena. Note the rusticated plinth and the two superimposed Orders. It has an arrangement of arched windows carried on a subsidiary Order (A)*

4.31 (OPPOSITE) *The west front of S. Maria Novella in Florence by Alberti, begun 1458. This is a variation on the problem of providing a façade for the traditional basilican shape of clearstoreyed nave and lean-to aisles, and was very influential. In the centre of the façade the Orders framing the door and the blind arcading merge the triumphal arch theme with the S. Miniato treatment. The pediment is carried on an entablature and four pilasters, suggesting the temple front, and the scrolls hide the roofs of the aisles* (Batsford)

4.30 *Corner detail of the Biblioteca Marciana in Venice, by Sansovino, begun 1537, and completed by Scamozzi in 1588. There are two superimposed Orders with reference to the Theatre of Marcellus in Rome. The corner is ingenious, for Sansovino used a Doric Order with heavy piers and got a full half-metope at the angle. The Ionic Order above is taller, of course, and the problems of proportion are solved by carrying the arches on a subsidiary Ionic Order of fluted columns (the main columns are unfluted). Notice the rich entablature with the high carved frieze that does not conform to standard rules of proportion* (Batsford)

4.32 *The triumphal arch theme. The west front of Alberti's church of S. Andrea, Mantua, of 1472, showing the triumphal arch with superimposed pediment instead of an attic storey* (Archivi Alinari)

4.33 *The triumphal arch theme. The interior of S Andrea, Mantua, with its series of alternating large and small spaces opening off the barrel-vaulted nave, giving the effect of a series of triumphal arches* (Archivi Alinari)

Alberti's Classical solution to the west front of the Tempio Malatestiano [4.9] was followed by his completion of the marble polychrome façade of S. Maria Novella in Florence (begun 1458) [4.31]. There, he created a grandly Antique effect, vaguely suggestive of a remembered triumphal arch over which was a tetrastyle temple front with pediment. There are close geometrical relationships between the various parts of the façade and the whole. Alberti's invention of mighty volutes on either side of the upper 'temple' front to hide the tops of the aisles was to prove very influential in the coming three centuries.

Alberti's conscious drawing on Roman exemplars is nowhere more clear than in his great church of S. Andrea in Mantua, designed in 1470 [4.32–4.34]. The plan is cruciform and the nave is roofed with a gigantic barrel vault, the largest and heaviest to be erected since Antiquity, painted to suggest it is coffered. To carry this, Alberti drew on the structural principles of Roman Thermae, and formed massive abutments at right angles to the axis of the nave, between which he created large and small chapels in what would have been the 'aisles'. The elevation of the nave arcades consists of three interlocked triumphal arches, and the west front combines an Antique temple with a triumphal arch that echoes the arches of the interior. So, Alberti used several motifs from Roman Antiquity, and combined them in a logical and consistent manner. Bramante's designs for the Belvedere Court at the Vatican also employed repeated versions of the triumphal arch theme.

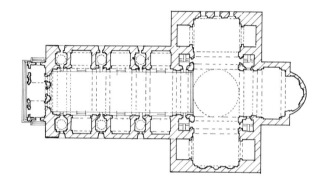

4.34 *S. Andrea, Mantua: note the massive wall-piers, hollowed out (A)*

CENTRALIZED AND CIRCULAR PLANS

Thus, so far, the Orders, the Colosseum, the triumphal arch, *Thermae*, various vaults, domed and arched forms, the pedimented temple front, and the house with its courtyard or atrium, all had played their parts in Renaissance Architecture, together with quotations from great Roman entablatures in the *cornicione* of many a *palazzo*. However, although the rectangular Classical temple was alluded to as a pedimented temple-front in Renaissance and post-Renaissance Architecture until the *whole* temple form was revived in the eighteenth century, the *circular* temple was of considerable importance as a model from quite early in the history of Renaissance Architecture. The Pantheon was, of course, *the* great Roman circular temple, with its vast drum, dome, and Corinthian pedimented portico [2.55, 4.35].

Early in the Italian Renaissance, Architects began to concern themselves with centralized, circular, or polygonal plans. Brunelleschi's octagonal dome for Florence Cathedral (relating to the freestanding octagonal Baptistry which, like S. Miniato, was thought at the time to be a survival from Antiquity), and his plan of *c.*1434 for S. Maria degli Angeli in Florence [4.36], which is related more closely to the Antique temple of 'Minerva Medica' in Rome [4.37], are examples of this. Of course, the crossings of S. Lorenzo and S. Spirito, S. Andrea at Mantua, the Old Sacristy at S. Lorenzo, and the Pazzi Chapel all have domed structures, but the full expression of a circular form was still to come. Important developments of Brunelleschian ideas of centrally planned churches were S. Maria delle Carceri at Prato (begun 1485) by Giuliano da Sangallo (*c.*1443–1516) and S. Maria del Calcinaio, Cortona (late fifteenth century), by Francesco di Giorgio.

Donato Bramante, the first of the High Renaissance Architects, built the *Tempietto* [4.41] (1502) in the cloisters of S. Pietro in Montorio in Rome, and this heralded a revival of interest in some of the circular temples of Antiquity (of which the so-called Temples of

4.35 *The prototype of large centrally planned churches is the Pantheon in Rome (second century AD), in which a great circular space is roofed by a coffered dome of brick and concrete on a massive brick drum. Note the marble columns in antis leading to the exedrae built into the thickness of the wall. Projecting aedicules for altars are, of course, later additions. The attic, or upper part of the circular wall, was originally lined with marble pilasters (A)*

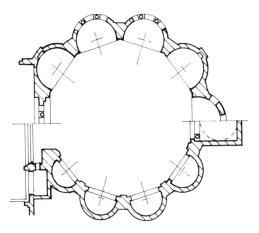

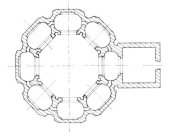

4.36 *Florence: S. Maria degli Angeli, begun 1434. A plan based on Roman Antiquity (the Temple of Minerva Medica, Rome) (A)*

4.37 Above: *Temple of 'Minerva Medica', Rome, c.AD 250. Below: east end of SS. Annunziata, Florence, by Michelozzo di Bartolommeo (1396–1472), begun in 1444. An example of a Renaissance Architect evolving a solution to a problem by reference to Classical Antiquity (A)*

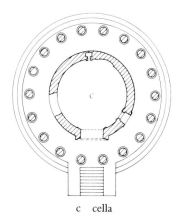

c   cella

4.38 *Temple of Vesta at Tivoli, showing circular peristyle (A)*

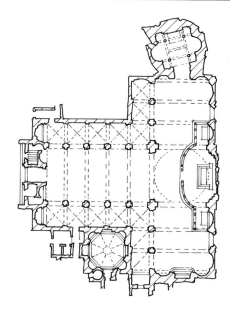

4.39 *Plan of S. Maria presso S. Satiro, Milan, by Bramante. Chapel of S. Satiro above, Baptistry below*

4.40 *The Order and the Arch. The cloister of S. Maria della Pace, Rome, by Bramante, of 1500–04. Note the columns over the centres of each arch. Again, if the arches were not there the very wide spacing of the pilasters would look wrong. It was a legacy of the Roman joining of columnar/trabeated and arcuated forms which produced this expression, so exploited in the Renaissance period (AFK G23926)*

Vesta, in Rome and in Tivoli were examples [2.52, 4.38]). Palladio was to recognize Bramante as the first Architect to bring the gravity of Antiquity into the light of day, although there can be no doubt of Alberti's influence on Bramante. It was Bramante who, at S. Maria presso S. Satiro [4.39] in Milan, built a dome with the first coffered interior since Antiquity, and made the east end appear as a deep chancel by means of theatrical perspective techniques, although it is, in fact, only a shallow recess. The dome sits over a T-shaped plan, and attached to the cross-arm of the T is the chapel of S. Satiro, a Greek cross inside a square within a drum: this is the ancestor of many later churches, and has an octagonal clerestorey supporting a drum. In this chapel Antique, Early Christian, and Brunelleschian prototypes merge. A centralized domed plan also occurs at Bramante's S. Maria delle Grazie in Milan, of the later 1480s.

Bramante went to Rome in 1499. His first works there are of considerable importance: the elegant cloisters of S. Maria della Pace [4.40], begun in 1500, and the tiny *Tempietto*. Circular plans were based on Antique forms it is true, but they do have important precedents in the *martyria* of Early Christian churches. Bramante's *Tempietto* [4.41] has a drum surmounted by a dome, and is surrounded by a peristyle of the Tuscan Doric Order, with two triglyphs over each intercolumniation; the effect is graceful, serene, and Antique. Tuscan Doric was used because of its association with the strong masculine character of S. Peter, whose martyrdom the building commemorates by its circular form. The *Tempietto* was to have had a remodelled circular cloister around it, with a concentric row of columns, and a thick wall embellished with niches and deep, chapel-like recesses: the whole design contained the essential elements of its

4.41 *Bramante's* Tempietto *in the* chiostro *of S. Pietro in Montorio,
Rome, of 1502, on the site of the martyrdom of S. Peter. It is based on
Early Christian* martyria *which were nearly always centrally planned,
and served as memorials. The Pantheon, therefore, was used as a
martyrium by the Church, and later became the burial-place of
distinguished men. So, the Tempietto is related to circular Antique
temples such as the 'Temple of Vesta', to the Pantheon, and to martyria.
Bramante therefore re-created Antique forms, and used a central drum
surrounded by an unfluted Doric peristyle and surmounted by a dome.
The severity of the Doric entablature and the Tuscan columns was felt to
be appropriate to the character of the Saint, and Bramante used Antique
shafts of granite with new marble capitals and bases. In the metopes are
representations of objects used in the Christian liturgy* (Batsford)

4.42 *Hypothetical section through nave and double aisles looking west towards the High Altar (the church was orientated thus) of the Constantinian Basilica of S. Pietro, Rome (fourth century AD): section (A)*

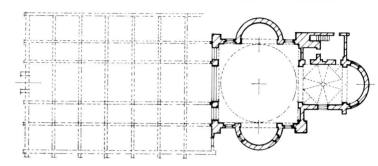

4.44 *S. Maria delle Grazie, Milan, by Bramante. (A)*

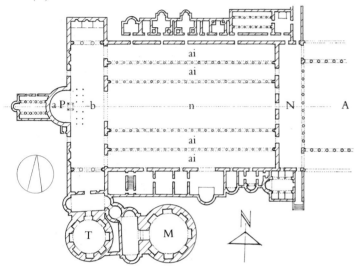

4.43 *Constantinian Basilica of S. Pietro, Rome (begun in c.333): plan showing the basilican arrangement that was to be the model for later*

T   Mausoleum of Honorius, later the tomb of S. Petronilla. It was the model for several chapter-houses of the mediaeval period
a   apse
b   bema (note the proto-transeptal arrangement)
ai aisle (double)
n   nave
N   narthex
A   atrium
P   Shrine of S. Peter
M   Second Imperial Mausoleum, later S. Maria della Febbre

mediaeval churches. Note that the shrine and High Altar were at the west end (A)

creator's great centralized plan for the rebuilding of S. Peter's in Rome.

Bramante and Pope Julius II determined in 1505 to restore, revive, and complete the choir of the Constantinian Basilica of S. Peter [4.42, 4.43], which Nicholas V had begun to rebuild in the 1450s. Bramante's elaborate geometry for the east end is modelled on his *Tempietto* and cloisters at S. Pietro in Montorio, and indicates that originally the idea was probably to create a suitable *martyrium*-type centralized form for the enclosure of the tomb of the Prince of the Apostles. It should be remembered that Bramante had added a centralized domed form with apsidal projections to the existing church of S. Maria delle Grazie in Milan [4.44], and that both the Church of the Holy Sepulchre and the Church of the Nativity in the Holy Land each had a *martyrium* combined with a basilica. However, the loss of the great domed church of Hagia Sophia in Constantinople to the Turks in 1453 probably acted as a catalyst to the idea of rebuilding the whole of the hallowed basilica rather than

just the choir, east end, and bema. The building history of S. Peter's is complicated and confused; it is generally assumed that Bramante proposed a huge centralized church based on a Greek-cross plan, but this assumption mostly derives from a half-plan in the Uffizi Gallery in Florence, and on a medal of 1506 which shows a rebuilt elevation of the church. Bramante was succeeded as Architect by Raphael, who, according to the evidence of Serlio, proposed a design based on a Latin cross. Bramante's dome was about the same diameter as that of the Pantheon, and was to have a similar stepped profile, but raised up on a colonnaded drum and surmounted by a lantern. Antonio da Sangallo the Elder's great church of S. Biagio at Montepulciano (1518–34) is a Greek cross on plan with a dome over the crossing; and was to have had two twin towers flanking the pedimented west front, so it is both a *martyrium* and very like Bramante's design for S. Peter's shown on the medal.

When Michelangelo succeeded Antonio da Sangallo the Younger as Architect to S. Peter's in 1547, he reverted

4.45 *The Giant Order was used by Michelangelo for the apses of S. Peter's Basilica in Rome, and the theme was continued by Carlo Maderno in the west front of 1606–12. Note that the tetrastyle arrangement of columns under the pediment in the centre is engaged and not prostyle.*

Above the main entablature is an attic storey crowned by statuary. On the left is an Ancient Egyptian obelisk erected by Fontana. Bernini then added the huge elliptical colonnades of the Tuscan Order from 1656 (AFK H8796)

4.46 *The Giant Order and the interior of S. Peter's, Rome, with its massive pilasters and piers, great coffered vault, domed crossing, and Baldacchino, from an engraving by Piranesi (Batsford)*

to a centralized plan, raised the dome to a more pointed section than Bramante's version, and introduced an heroic Giant Order of pilasters with an attic storey over for the scheme of the façades. The Latin cross returned when Carlo Maderno (c.1556–1629) added the nave and the west front, completed in 1612 [4.45, 4.46].

The early Renaissance saw a rediscovery of Antiquity, and Architects mixed direct quotation with a somewhat hesitant compositional technique. Even what we today call the High Renaissance was hardly easy in its use of Antique forms, but with Bramante the spirit as well as the letter of Antiquity was recalled in some of his remarkable buildings, notably the *Tempietto* and its great successor.

MICHELANGELO

During the sixteenth century in Italy, after the deaths of Bramante and Raphael, the imitation of Classical details gave way to a novel disposition of elements, and even the invention of new, non-historical, vocabularies of ornament. Michelangelo Buonarrotti's (1475–1564) design for the Medici Chapel (begun 1519), attached to the church of S. Lorenzo in Florence, is an example of the trend, with its wall surfaces treated as many-layered planes, its blind aedicules crushing the doors below (which have architraves and cornices but no friezes, so

4.47 *The Medici Chapel (New Sacristy) in S. Lorenzo, Florence, by Michelangelo, with tomb of Lorenzo de' Medici on the right. Note the sarcophagi with scrolled segmental pediment and figures of Dawn and Twilight, and the blank niches with large segmental pediments. The doors have cornices but no frieze, and the oversized consoles seem to have slipped downwards, almost crushed by the massive aedicules over. The idiosyncratic detail is characteristic of Mannerism (1520–34) (A)*

4.48 *The vestibule to the library of S. Lorenzo, Florence, by Michelangelo, of 1524–34. The aedicules are very odd, with their pilasters like inverted obelisks. Even more curious are the pairs of columns set in recesses and standing over consoles: these columns actually stand on an earlier wall, so their expression is probably logical, yet the effect is unsettling and strange, as we associate columns with structure, and not as elements in recesses. The capitals, with their elongated necks, are loosely Tuscan Doric, but the abaci are anything but Doric, and owe more to the Corinthian Order. This unexpectedness and this freedom with Classicism sum up the essence of Mannerism (A)*

their sense of compression is increased), and its deliberate distortion of academic Classicism [4.47]. Even more extraordinary is the stair to the library of S. Lorenzo, with its columns set in recesses, above pairs of consoles fixed to the dies of the pedestals, and the strange blind aedicules with the pilasters tapering towards their bases [4.48]. Such freedom, even licence, in which motifs are used in opposition to their original meaning, significance, or even content, is known as Mannerism [See Glossary]. Giorgio Vasari (1511–1574), in his account of Michelangelo, described the 'composite' nature of

Michelangelo's 'varied and original' ornament, and praised the latter's 'licence' for freeing design from 'measure, order, and rule', thus enabling craftsmen to break from the bonds and chains of usage.

After he settled in Rome Michelangelo designed the buildings on the Capitoline Hill from 1546 in which he introduced the historically important precedent of the Giant Order, uniting the storeys within the frame of the Order [4.50]. The lower storeys had smaller Orders which carried entablatures rather than arches, and the upper windows were aediculated, with segmental pediments: a Mannerist affection for complexity of plane and detail is demonstrated in these great buildings. The Giant Order, as mentioned above, also was an important element in the design of S. Peter's.

Michelangelo's inventiveness is demonstrated at the Porta Pia [4.51] in Rome of 1562: in the centre a broken segmental scrolled pediment is set within a triangular pediment, and the surrounds to windows and other openings became even more complex. Michelangelo's Mannerism was to offer Architects of the Baroque period many potent precedents.

SERLIO AND VIGNOLA

The second part of the sixteenth century saw not only much building, but a growing familiarity with rules, knowledge of precedents, and Antiquity. Much of this familiarity was achieved through printed sources.

Sebastiano Serlio not only published his treatise on Architecture, and in so doing codified the Orders and publicized the styles of Bramante and Raphael, but also established a French centre of Mannerism at Fontaine-bleau. Serlio's work was translated into Flemish, German, Spanish and French, and in 1611 an English version of the Dutch edition was published; his illustrations showed Antique and modern Architecture, including many elaborate and showy Mannerist features, which were copied indiscriminately and applied to what were really late-mediaeval buildings in France, Germany, and England [4.52].

Classicism was exported from Italy during the sixteenth century largely through two influences: the printed treatise and the important precedent of the church of *Il Gesù* in Rome, by Giacomo Barozzi da Vignola (1507–1573) and Giacomo della Porta (*c.*1533–1602) [4.53]. Certainly the influence of Serlio in northern Europe produced some very curious instances of applied ornament; while true Italian Classical Architecture appeared in Spain in the palace of Charles V in Granada of 1526, it did not occur in England or Germany until the second decade of the seventeenth century, with the works of Inigo Jones (1573–1652) and Elias Holl (1573–1646) respectively.

Vignola pursued the *Tempietto* theme in his S. Andrea, Via Flaminia, Rome [4.54, 4.55], of 1550–54, but it is a

4.49 Cortile *of Palazzo Marino in Milan, by Galeazzo Alessi of 1558, where decorative sculpture almost overwhelms the Orders. An example of Mannerism (Batsford)*

4.50 *The Palazzo Capitolino, Rome, by Michelangelo, with additions by Giacomo della Porta, from 1546. The most important innovation was the use of the Giant Order of Corinthian pilasters carrying the massive entablature in order to give the two-storey building the character of a mighty temple. Note the subsidiary Ionic Order on the lower level, and the aediculated windows on the second floor. The Antique statue of the Emperor Marcus Aurelius is on the left (Batsford)*

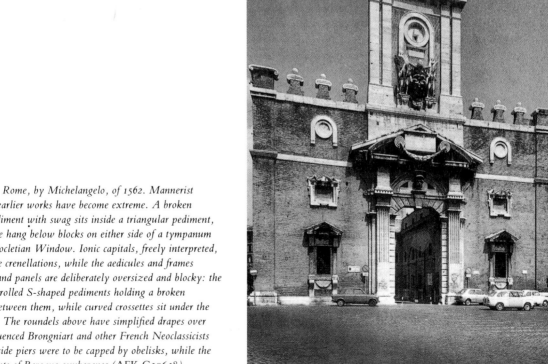

4.51 *The Porta Pia, Rome, by Michelangelo, of 1562. Mannerist tendencies present in earlier works have become extreme. A broken segmental scrolled pediment with swag sits inside a triangular pediment, while oversized guttae hang below blocks on either side of a tympanum which resembles a Diocletian Window. Ionic capitals, freely interpreted, become copings for the crenellations, while the aedicules and frames around the windows and panels are deliberately oversized and blocky: the panels have broken scrolled S-shaped pediments holding a broken segmental pediment between them, while curved crossettes sit under the ears of the architrave. The roundels above have simplified drapes over them that clearly influenced Brongniart and other French Neoclassicists 250 years later. The side piers were to be capped by obelisks, while the attic storey has elements of Baroque exuberance (AFK G19658)*

4.52 *Order upon Order. Five Orders piled up and superimposed on a late-Gothic gate-tower. Tuscan carries Doric, which carries Ionic, which carries Corinthian, and above is Composite. There is much strapwork and other ornament. This frontispiece is in the Schools Quadrangle in Oxford, completed in 1620, and is probably by John Akroyd (1556–1613) and his partner John Bentley, perhaps influenced by Sir Henry Savile. The sources are Italo-French Renaissance in origin (A)*

4.53 (ABOVE) *The west front of Il Gesù in Rome, the prototype of thousands of churches thereafter. It is a solution to the old problem of how to put a Classical façade on a clearstorey and nave with lean-to aisles. The church was designed by Vignola and begun in 1568, but the façade as built was modified by Giacomo della Porta from 1573. It is of two storeys, with superimposed Orders of pilasters and columns, and the roofs of the 'aisles' (they are actually chapels so we refer to this type of plan as wall-pier) are hidden behind scrolls. This device derives from Alberti's church of S. Maria Novella in Florence, but because Il Gesù was the Mother-Church of the Jesuits, the Vignola-della Porta design had far-reaching effects. Mannerist tendencies merge with the Baroque (Archivi Alinari)*

4.54 (BELOW) *Vignola's church of S. Andrea in the Via Flaminia, Rome, completed 1554, is the earliest example of the use of an elliptical drum and dome set on a rectangular base. Ellipses were to become important elements in Baroque design. S. Andrea's overall external appearance derives from Roman tombs (the suggestion of a temple-front should be noted). Vignola's later church of S. Anna dei Palafrenieri, begun in 1572, takes this idea a step further, and uses an ellipse for the actual* form *of the building (Archivi Alinari)*

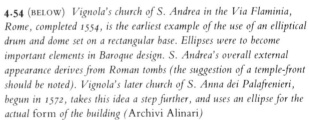

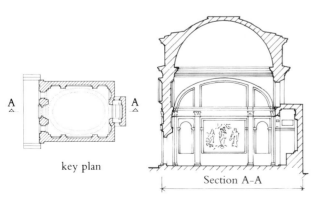

key plan

Section A–A

4.55 *S. Andrea, in the Via Flaminia, Rome, by Vignola. Key plan and section showing Antique style of dome and variant on Diocletian Window (A)*

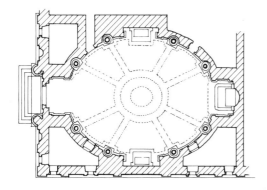

4.56 *S. Anna de Palafrenieri: plan (A)*

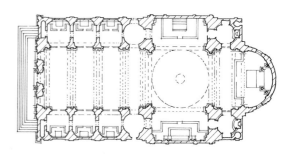

4.57 *Il Gesù, Rome, showing the wall-pier arrangement with side chapels instead of aisles (A)*

rectangle on plan, with an elliptical dome over it based on the Pantheon form; the upper part of the rectangular volume inside has blind Thermal Windows above the entablature. This is the earliest example of a church with an elliptical dome on a drum. Later, from 1572, Vignola was to introduce an elliptical plan with a dome over it at the church of S. Anna dei Palafrenieri in Rome [4.56]. The elliptical theme was to become a favourite of Architects of the Baroque period.

However, although these little churches with their ellipses were to be influential, *Il Gesù* was to be a precedent of immense importance, for it was the mother-church of the Society of Jesus, and was begun in 1568 [4.57]. The plan, with side chapels rather than aisles, shallow transepts with an altar in each arm, apse, and great dome, is derived from the type of S. Andrea in Mantua. Alberti had concealed the roofs of the lower

aisles at S. Maria Novella in Florence [4.31] behind giant scrolls, and Vignola and della Porta took up Alberti's theme at *Il Gesù*, designing two distinct storeys using vigorous modelling, superimposed Orders, and scrolls on either side of the upper storey. *Il Gesù* was to be the model for thousands of churches all over the world, was probably the most influential ecclesiastical design in the last half millennium, and is the type *par excellence* associated with the Counter-Reformation.

Vignola's *La Regola delli Cinque Ordini d'Architettura* of 1562, though modelled on Serlio's work, was more scholarly and had better illustrations, but was more limited in scope. It became the standard work on the Orders and their details, and went into over 200 editions over some three centuries. The importance of Vignola's work in the context of Architecture cannot be overstated.

PALLADIO

There can be no doubting the importance of Andrea Palladio (1508–1580) as an Architect of genius, whose works had a far-ranging influence, although he lived for almost all his life in the provincial city of Vicenza. It was not only his buildings, notably his *palazzi* and *ville* in and around Vicenza and his churches (S. Giorgio Maggiore and Il Redentore in Venice) [4.58, 4.59], which had international significance, but his publications, especially his *Quattro Libri dell' Architettura* of 1570: the latter stated the theoretical basis for his work, illustrated the Orders,

publicized his own buildings, and showed a good selection of buildings from Antiquity. Not only were the *Quattro Libri* more scholarly and accurate than Serlio's offering, but they covered more ground than Vignola had attempted. Palladio had studied and drawn Antique remains in Rome, and was influenced by the works of both Bramante and Vignola; he also provided illustrations for one of the finest editions of Vitruvius, published in 1556.

Palladio's first great building was the case he designed

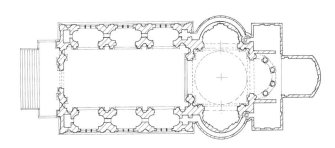

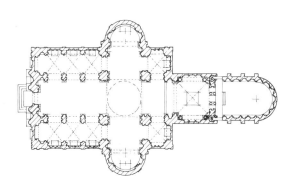

4.58 Il Redentore, *Venice. Note the sculptured effect of the wall-piers and the creation of shaped chapels* (A)

4.59 *S. Giorgio Maggiore, Venice. Note the monastic choir in the space beyond the High Altar* (A)

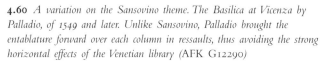

4.60 *A variation on the Sansovino theme. The Basilica at Vicenza by Palladio, of 1549 and later. Unlike Sansovino, Palladio brought the entablature forward over each column in ressaults, thus avoiding the strong horizontal effects of the Venetian library* (AFK G12290)

4.61 *The Palazzo Porto-Breganza, known as the Casa del Diavolo, Vicenza, by Palladio, of 1571. Here Palladio used the Giant Composite Order of Michelangelo on high pedestals, with swags between the capitals. Although it is only a fragment, the two bays show a pronounced Michelangelesque influence. Once again the entablature breaks forward over each column in ressaults (A)*

for the Town Hall in Vicenza (the so-called Basilica) consisting of an engaged Ionic Order on a Tuscan-Doric ground floor, with arches carried on smaller columns between the piers (the Serliana, Palladian motif, or Venetian Window) [4.60]. This theme derived from Sansovino's Biblioteca Marciano [4.30] of some 12 years earlier, although Palladio set the entablature back between the engaged columns, whereas Sansovino emphasized the horizontal entablatures, making the Serliana motifs subservient.

At the Palazzo Porto of 1552 Palladio was influenced by Bramante, but introduced sculpture over the pedi-ments of the windows of the centre and end bays, rather in the style of Michelangelo. His use of a Giant Order round the *cortile* is a reference to the atrium of Antiquity. The façade of the Palazzo Chiericati, begun in the 1550s, has superimposed Orders without arches, the three end bays on each side of the symmetrical five-bay front treated as *loggie*. Palladio's Palazzo Thiene, with its Mannerist textures and room plans derived from the shapes of interiors in Roman *Thermae*, merges contemporary architectural concerns with themes from Antiquity. Palladio proportioned his rooms in relation to each other, setting up cunningly contrived axes, symmetries, and balances in his interiors.

At the Palazzi Valmarano (1566) and Porto-Breganza (1571) [4.61] he used Giant Orders for the façades: the latter recalls Michelangelo's work at the Capitol in Rome. The powerful theme of a grave Antique Order recurs in Palladio's *ville*, for which he designed grand entrance porticos, in the mistaken belief that Antique villas had temple-like fronts. His sources were the vague

4.62 (ABOVE) *Villa Rotonda (Villa Capra), Vicenza, by Palladio, begun about 1550. This villa suburbana has four Ionic porticoes set at piano nobile level over a basement, and a central domed circular space. The prostyle hexastyle porticoes were thought by Palladio to indicate Antiquity, and they are, in fact, temple fronts (Batsford)*

4.63 (BELOW) *Teatro Olimpico, Vicenza, by Palladio, of 1580, completed by Scamozzi. This is based on the Roman scheme of a fixed architectural background with the stage in front of it. The auditorium is a half-ellipse with seats rising to a colonnade with niches round the back. The flat ceiling is painted to resemble the open real sky that would have been a feature of theatres in Antiquity. Behind the proscenium is an elaborate permanent set using false perspective effects (Batsford)*

4.65 (ABOVE) *The façade of Il Redentore in Venice, of 1576, also by Palladio, is similar to that of S Giorgio. Inside, however, the effects are different. In Il Redentore the nave is wide, and the aisles are replaced by chapels, the nave piers being altogether more massive. There is a dome over the crossing, and the transepts are apsidal, the apsidal form being echoed in the curved colonnade at the east separating the monastic choir from the nave. The spectator therefore seems to be looking through the apse itself. Above, the vaulted ceiling is illuminated by Diocletian Windows over the entablature carried on engaged Corinthian columns. In fact, this remarkable church uses a fully articulated Corinthian Order in a church, making a considerable departure from the massive piers with pilasters usual at the time (AFK G11103)*

4.64 (OPPOSITE) *The façade of the church of S. Giorgio Maggiore, Venice, by Palladio, of 1566, showing the Architect's solution to the problem of applying a Classical façade to a clearstoreyed nave with lean-to aisles. The nave is faced with an engaged temple front of the Composite Order on pedestals, complete with pediment and niches. The aisles are fronted using the expedient of a second, much wider and lower pediment, carried on Corinthian pilasters, which is the entire width of the church, but which is interrupted by the engaged columns of the nave 'temple' front, and is therefore subservient. Left and right, above the low wall, are Venetian crenellations (AFK G12009)*

descriptions in Pliny and Vitruvius. Good examples of prostyle hexastyle porticoes on high podia, rather like temple fronts set against plainer, massive walls, can be found at the Villa Malcontenta near Mestre (1560), and the celebrated Villa Capra (or Villa Rotonda) near Vicenza (c.1550), where there are four porticoes, one on each face [5.61]. The Villa Rotonda [4.62] was completed by Vincenzo Scamozzi (1552–1616); it has a circular, central-domed hall with finely proportioned rooms disposed around it and, of course, the porticoes with four flights of steps, giving the villa four identical elevations. The formal symmetry of the Villa Capra and its architectonic perfection made it an important model for the eighteenth-century Palladians in England.

Palladio's Teatro Olimpico [4.63] in Vicenza of 1580 (again, completed by Scamozzi) was strongly influenced by Antique theatres, and had a permanent architectural backdrop of elaborate 'streets' with false perspectives to give an illusion of great depth and size.

With the two great Venetian churches, S. Giorgio Maggiore (from 1566) [4.64] and *Il Redentore* (from

4.66 *Palladianism. The Queen's House, Greenwich, by Inigo Jones, begun 1616, in stark contrast to the overloaded ornament of Jacobean Architecture. Note the rusticated base and the* piano nobile *level given extra importance by means of the Ionic* loggia *(RCHME BB60/1916)*

1576) Palladio designed Classical façades for what was still basically a basilican west front, by overlaying two temple fronts: the nave end of S. Giorgio was finished with a tall, narrow, engaged temple front set on pedestals and capped with a pediment, while behind this front ran the lower part of what was apparently a wider pediment, the ends of which concealed the roofs of the aisles. This subsidiary wider pediment (broken at the top when the raking elements hit the tall engaged columns of the central engaged temple front) was 'carried' on a smaller Order of pilasters. Inside S. Giorgio, Palladio used a Corinthian Order of engaged columns and pilasters to give a much greater sense of modelling and articulation of the piers than earlier Architects had achieved, while his use of a domed crossing, apsidal-ended transepts, vaults, and Thermal Windows recalled Antiquity in a very powerful and original way.

At *Il Redentore* the temple front sits on a podium, but the subsidiary wider pediment is completely broken by this, and an attic storey, with subsidiary broken pediment, rises up above. The 'aisles' are side chapels, and the liturgical east end has a dome on a drum over the apsidal-ended vestigial transepts. Both churches have open screens, behind which are the monastic choirs; the architectural treatment is particularly successful in *Il Redentore*, with its segmental colonnade suggesting an apse beyond the crossing [4.65]. The Roman effect of the design is stunningly evocative.

Palladio's designs were free from the bustle of so much overloaded northern European work, influenced as it was by a somewhat indiscriminately eclectic use of Mannerist designs loosely interpreted from Serlio's publications. By their elegance, their serenity, and their evocation of Antique *gravitas*, Palladio's works held remarkable appeal for European sensibilities. Inigo Jones first imported the Palladian style into England in the first half of the seventeenth century [4.66], and it was revived and further disseminated through the influence of Richard Boyle, Earl of Burlington (1694–1753), who saw absolute and Antique standards in the master's works. Eighteenth-century aesthetic discernment in Britain was dominated for much of the time by Palladianism, and by the examples of Palladio's villas set in landscapes that were themselves evocative of Antiquity.

V

BAROQUE, ROCOCO, AND PALLADIANISM

Introduction; Bernini, Borromini,
ellipses, and western façades; some
French examples; Classical Architecture
in England; some German buildings;
Palladianism

*The belief in the absolute value of the Classical
conception of art, a prejudice established by the
Renaissance and revived at the end of the
eighteenth century . . . caused every departure from
that kind of art to be considered inferior. One
result has been that some of the great styles created
by Western civilisation bear names that at first
were terms of contempt: Gothic, Baroque, Rococo.*

GERMAIN BAZIN (1901–1990): *Baroque and Rococo.* London, 1964, p. 6.

INTRODUCTION

The Baroque (which is essentially of the seventeenth century) and the Rococo (which is firmly of the eighteenth century) styles are both developments and branches of Classical art and Architecture. 'Baroque' means irregularly shaped, whimsical, and odd, and was a term originally applied to a rough or imperfect pearl.

Classical Architecture implies a degree of clarity within precise boundaries, and perhaps a static quality, yet with a profound sense of order and of a continuity from Antiquity, and with a serenity, a balance, and a logic that expresses developed intellect.

Baroque Architecture, on the other hand, gives an impression of always being in movement: it is expansive, and full of contrast, violence, and passion. It is expressive, seems to burst beyond its own space, and exploits illusion, appearing to defy reason and even logic; but it is in reality very much under control. It is in motion, with entablatures that sway in and out, surfaces that undulate on plan and are deeply modelled, and its sense of theatre.

'Rococo' probably stems from the French *rocaille*, meaning shell- or pebble-work associated with grottoes and similar conceits. It is essentially a light, frothy, elegant style used in the eighteenth century, and suggesting marine-like plants, shells, and encrustations. It seems first to have appeared around 1700 at Versailles, but reached its apogee in southern Germany from the 1720s until around 1780, especially in church Architecture, where it can be found in many a riot of stucco, carving, and paint.

BERNINI, BORROMINI, ELLIPSES, AND WESTERN FAÇADES

As has been mentioned above, elaborate entablatures that curved on plan were known in Antiquity; the examples from Baalbek and Tivoli have proto-Baroque qualities. Vignola used ellipses, and during the seventeenth century ellipses occur in many church plans. With the works of Gianlorenzo Bernini (1598–1680) and Francesco Borromini (1599–1667) a new vehemence, overstatement, and disregard for convention or restraint can be found in church Architecture. Bernini's S. Andrea al Quirinale (1658–70) [5.1–5.2] and Borromini's S. Carlo alle Quattro Fontane (1634–43) [5.3–5.4] both exploit ellipses on plan, but in entirely different ways: the former contains an ellipsoidal space with chapels off this space set in the thickness of the encompassing walls (rather like a miniature and elliptical version of the Pantheon); the latter has an elliptical, central space that merges with parts of other ellipses, with the result that the Orders are placed on contraflexed curves on plan, so that wall surfaces bow inwards and outwards. Both churches exploit both the ellipse and the domed central space, but Bernini used a

5.1 *Bernini's elliptical church of S. Andrea al Quirinale, Rome, of 1658–70 expands on the elliptical theme and also recalls the Pantheon, with its chapels set into the thickness of the walls, and its great domed interior. It should be remembered that Bernini's Piazza, in front of S. Peter's in Rome, is also an ellipse (Archivi Alinari)*

5.2 *Exterior of S. Andrea al Quirinale, with entrance façade loosely based on the Palazzo Capitolino of Michelangelo, but with the subsidiary Ionic Order bursting out as a porch instead of remaining either framed, or a flat plane within the larger Order (Archivi Alinari)*

5.3 *S. Carlo alle Quattro Fontane by Borromini, begun in 1634, in which the ellipse is expressed in the dome, but is actually set over fragments of other ellipses that form the recesses of the chapels, the entrance chapel, and apsidal chapel. Thus, various ellipsoidal figures in plan merge. The result is that this* tour-de-force *of the Baroque, completed in 1667, seems to be in motion, rocking and swaying. The façade has two Orders superimposed, and there are subsidiary Orders for the aedicules, but the plan of the front consists of convex and concave curves. On the lower storey the plan is concave-convex-concave, but the first floor is concave-concave-concave, with a miniature elliptical pillbox set in the centre, reminiscent of the Khazna at Petra [2.69]. Gesticulating angels hold an elliptical frame aloft between two swaying entablatures. It is a dizzy composition, but Borromini's work had considerable influence (Archivi Alinari)*

5.4 *Interior of S. Carlo alle Quattro Fontane* (Archivi Alinari)

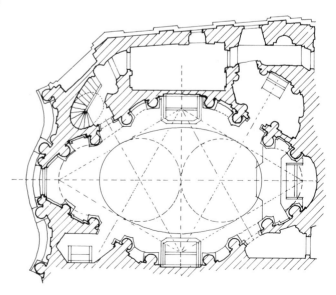

5.5 *S. Carlo alle Quattro Fontane, Rome, showing the geometry of vistas, ellipses, and circles. Note the centres from which circles and arcs are struck, and the relationships between the circles and the main ellipse (A)*

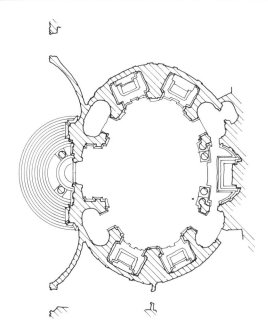

5.6 *S. Andrea al Quirinale, Rome. Plan showing an ellipse with short axis coinciding with that of the High Altar; and the main entrance (A)*

5.7 *The* Baldacchino *over the High Altar in S. Peter's, Rome, by Bernini, of 1624–33. This huge bronze canopy employs the twisted 'Solomonic' columns associated with the Temple of Solomon and with the Constantinian sanctuary over the tomb of S. Peter in the older basilica. Solomonic columns frequently were used in canopies over altars, in aedicules, and framing paintings or sculptures above altars set against walls. They represent not only the Biblical Temple but the entrance to Paradise, and are a mnemonic of these. Note the valancing hanging between the entablatures (Batsford)*

Giant Order of pilasters on his pedimented façade, with a smaller Ionic Order carrying a curved entablature as a porch, whereas Borromini set the whole front of S. Carlo in motion by using a concave-convex-concave plan for the Ionic lower storey, and a concave-concave-concave plan for the upper Corinthian façade, but with subsidiary miniature Orders for the aedicules, as on Michelangelo's Capitoline buildings.

Michelangelo had heralded the Baroque in the forms of the great drum and dome of S. Peter's in Rome, but Roman Architects at the start of the seventeenth century, bored, perhaps, by the way Architecture had evolved at the end of the sixteenth, rediscovered Michelangelo and Mannerism, and took their themes even further. One of the first true Baroque masterpieces was Bernini's massive Baldacchino in S. Peter's, begun in 1624 [4.46, 5.7] luxuriant in its detail and employing curves and twists, even in its Composite Order. The same Architect's colonnades in front of S. Peter's, begun in 1656, use severe Tuscan columns carrying an Ionic entablature, but are arranged on a vast elliptical plan [4.45].

S. Agnese in Agone, in the Piazza Navona [5.8, 5.9], begun in 1652 by Carlo Rainaldi (1611–1691) on a Greek cross plan, was transformed by Borromini, who took over as Architect from 1653 to 1657. The central space is an octagon in a square, over which is a drum and dome;

5.8 *S. Agnese in Agone in the Piazza Navona in Rome, begun by Carlo Rainaldi in 1652, worked on by Borromini (1653–7), and completed by Rainaldi. The plan has a central octagon with niches in the corners, with choir and entrance chapels and deeper north and south transeptal chapels, which gives the effect of an ellipse with its long axis parallel to the façade. In the centre of the façade is an engaged temple front set in a wall, concave on plan, with two towers of considerable inventive virtuosity flanking the composition. The top stages of these towers are circular on plan with projecting paired columns, set on square bases. The effect is stunningly Baroque (Batsford)*

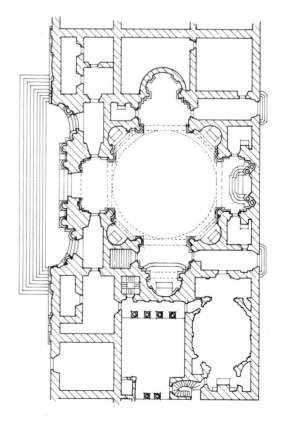

5.9 *S. Agnese in Agone, Piazza Navona, Rome. Plan showing the concave front, and centralized space (A)*

5.10 (ABOVE, LEFT) *Church of S. Susanna, Rome, by Carlo Maderno, of 1597. A more elegant version of the* Il Gesù *theme, with satisfying proportions and a more positive vertical emphasis. Here Mannerism starts to herald the Baroque (Batsford)*

5.11 (ABOVE, RIGHT) *SS Vincenzo ed Anastasio, Rome, by Martino Longhi, of 1646, powerfully modelled and indubitably Baroque in its vehemence, passion, and power (Archivi Alinari)*

5.12 (RIGHT) *S. Maria della Pace by Pietro da Cortona, of 1656–9, with its great concave front, out of which pushes the pedimented façade, out of which again spring two convex curved walls linked to an open-bed segmental pediment on a Composite Order, while a Tuscan semicircular portico completes an extraordinarily vivid and plastic composition (Batsford)*

5.13 *Pietro da Cortona's church of S. Maria in Via Lata, Rome, of 1658–62, a more restrained front than S. Maria della Pace, employing a variety of Serliana in the upper storey* (Batsford)

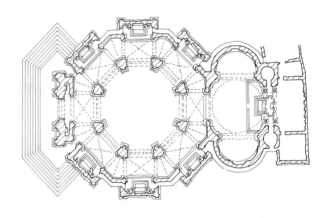

5.14 *S. Maria della Salute, Venice: plan* (A)

the side chapels, with their apsidal ends lying on an axis parallel to the façade, give an illusion of an elliptical plan, while the front, with its concave plan flanked by twin towers, proved to be an important precedent.

Most Baroque, liturgical western façades are similar to the composition of that of *Il Gesù* [4.53], but with more heavily modelled planes, a profusion of columns, and a riot of pediments (segmental, triangular, open, broken and scrolled). *Il Gesù*'s west front, though, was essentially Mannerist, and displays a curiously uneasy relationship between horizontal and vertical elements. More successful, perhaps, was Carlo Maderno's S. Susanna in Rome of 1597 [5.10], with its arrangement of two storeys of Orders (six engaged columns rather than pilasters on the lower storey, with pilasters above), and the scrolls linking the narrower upper façade to the wider front below. The emphasis was more decisive and vertical than that of the front of *Il Gesù*. Only a few years later, when Martino Longhi's (1602–1660) church of SS. Vincenzo ed Anasta-

sio in Rome was built in 1646–50 [5.11], the Mannerist motifs, including the mixing of segmental and triangular pediments, had been further transformed. The modelling was deeper, the columns fully experienced as such, above and below, the verticality unhesitant, the scrolls merged with other sculpture; the assured rhetoric of fully developed Baroque had arrived. Nevertheless, the basic elements of the composition are those of the façade of *Il Gesù*, and the descendants of that design were many. The invention displayed in Roman Baroque churches was remarkable [5.12, 5.13].

5.15 *Longhena's great church of S. Maria della Salute, Venice, from 1630. Another centrally planned church, it is in fact an octagon with a great octagonal clearstorey supported by massive buttresses in the form of scrolls above which rises a drum and dome with lantern. Chapels illuminated by Diocletian Windows project from the central body of the church, and the entrance façade facing the Grand Canal is a variation on the triumphal arch that is also used in the arrangement of bays around the interior* (A)

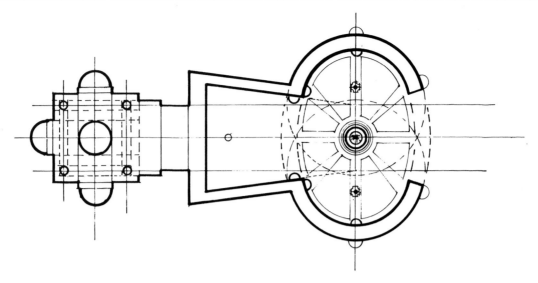

5.16 *S. Peter's, Rome, as built, with the Bernini elliptical piazza (A)*

5.17 *Theatinerkirche of S. Kajetan, Munich, a great Baroque church (based on S. Andrea della Valle), begun by Barelli and Zuccalli in 1663, and completed by the Walloon dwarf Architect, François Cuvilliés, in 1767. This is a variant of the two-storeyed west front of Il Gesù and S. Susanna, but with twin towers capped by cupolas supported by console-buttresses. Note the dome over the crossing (A)*

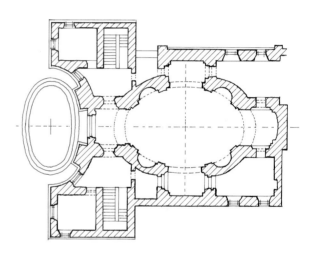

5.18 *Dreifaltigkeitskirche, Salzburg, showing ellipses in the plan (A)*

5.19 *The Karlskirche, Vienna, by J. B. Fischer von Erlach, from 1715 to 1738. This remarkable building is a synthesis of many important ideas. The most obvious is the Temple in Jerusalem, which is shown in Mannerist prints as a Pantheon-like structure with a porch flanked by two large columns. The spiral columns, which are mnemonics of the Temple although they are based on Trajan's column in Rome, record events in the life of S. Carlo Borromeo, and signify the Plus Ultra of the world beyond the Pillars of Hercules, so they are gateways to Paradise, to a New World, and emblems of Habsburg supremacy. In the centre is the prostyle hexastyle temple front, looking back to Roman Antiquity and the Temple of Concord in the Forum in Rome. There are also references to the Pantheon in the portico and dome behind (which is elliptical and therefore connected with works by Borromini and Bernini in Rome).*

The wide front recalls both Borromini's S. Agnese in Agone and the wide porch of the Solomonic Temple, which Perrault had illustrated, while the curious towers recall works of Borromini and Guarini. Fischer von Erlach also referred to the domes of François Mansart's Église des Minimes, of the Dôme des Invalides in Paris of 1693–1706 by J. Hardouin-Mansart (the latter building being associated with the iconography of King Louis XIV), and of S. Paul's Cathedral in London. The spiral columns also remind us of the minarets added to the great church of Hagia Sophia in Constantinople (and therefore are references not only to Constantine and the lost Eastern Roman Empire, but to the recent invasion of Europe by Ottoman Turks). Thus the Holy Roman Emperor is identified with Solomon, with the Roman Emperors, and with the Plus Ultra of Charles V (Batsford)

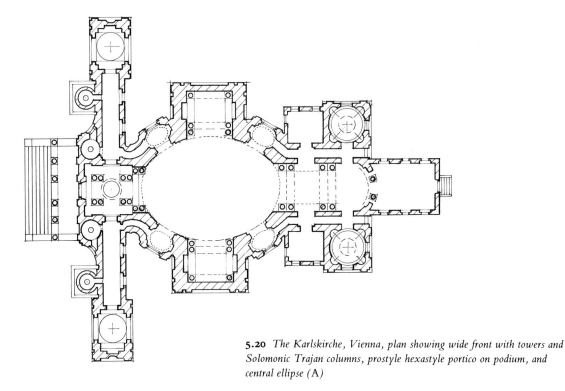

5.20 *The Karlskirche, Vienna, plan showing wide front with towers and Solomonic Trajan columns, prostyle hexastyle portico on podium, and central ellipse (A)*

A centralized plan recurs in the extraordinary church of S. Maria della Salute in Venice, by Baldassare Longhena, begun in 1630 [5.14, 5.15]. The plan is basically octagonal and the octagonal clerestorey is linked to the radiating chapels by means of vast buttresses in the form of scrolls; a triumphal arch motif reappears on the entrance façade, and Diocletian Windows are much in evidence in the chapels. In time motifs from Antiquity were used with later inventions, such as theatrical illusionist effects, large scrolls, and swaying, undulating planes, alive with ornament.

Both illusion and perspective are invoked in Bernini's *Piazza* of S. Peter [5.16], for the ground rises to the great front by Maderno, and the straight arms joining the elliptical *piazza* to the façade are not parallel, but converge as they progress from the west front: the result is that of an illusion of greater length [4.45]. Bernini employed similar tricks of perspective at the Scala Regia in the Vatican, which narrows and lowers as it rises: this has the effect of making the stair seem much longer and grander than it is. Light further increases the dramatic tension.

However, as the Baroque style found its way over the Alps it produced some interesting variants. Often, the two-storey *Gesù*-type front acquired flanking towers, as at Salzburg Cathedral (1614–28) by Solari, and at the Theatine church in Munich, begun in 1663 by Barelli and Zuccalli, but completed by François Cuvilliés [5.17]. The Munich church towers have scrolled buttresses at the tops of the three-staged supporting polygonal cupolas; these scrolls resemble those of S. Maria della Salute, but have serrated edges, like gear-wheels.

The concave front with flanking towers of S. Agnese in Agone is found again, in variance, at the Dreifaltigkeitskirche in Salzburg [5.18] (1694–1702), by Johann Bernhard Fischer von Erlach (1656–1723), but combined with an elliptical plan, the long axis of which runs through the centre of the composition, and at the same Architect's Karlskirche in Vienna of 1715–38 [5.19, 5.20]. At the Karlskirche a mighty elliptical dome sits over the central space and its radiating chapels, and the long axis of the ellipse is again on the centre-line of the façade. The strange towers have scrolls at the tops, over the attic storey above the second stages. In the centre of the façade is a prostyle hexastyle portico, a clear reference to Antiquity, and to the Pantheon in particular; the Antique allusions are reinforced by the two spiral columns (recalling Trajan's column in Rome), which feature scenes from the life of S. Charles Borromeo.

Ellipse and theatre recur in the church of the Benedictine Abbey of Weltenburg by C. D. and E. Q. Asam (begun 1714): the central ellipse [5.21] has small chapels off it, and the longer axis passes through the centre-line of the high altar and western door. A statue of S. George on horseback charges out of the sun, slaying the dragon, while a figure rushes off to the right: the group, rather like a scene from a Händel opera, is held within an aedicule with twisted columns set under a segmental arch.

At the pilgrimage church of Vierzehnheiligen [5.22, 5.23] (1742–72), by Johann Balthasar Neumann (1687–

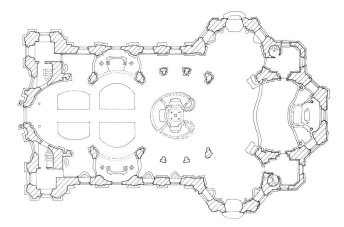

5.23 *Vierzehnheiligen: plan, showing interpenetrating circles, ovals, and ellipses (A)*

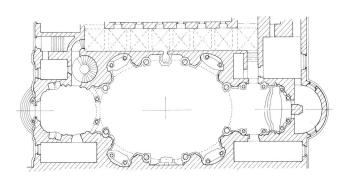

5.21 *Benedictine Abbey-church of Weltenburg (A)*

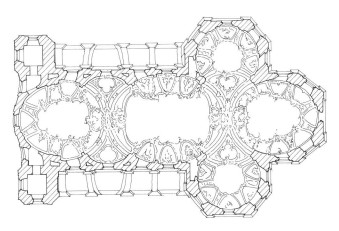

5.22 *Vierzehnheiligen, Franconia: ceiling plan (A)*

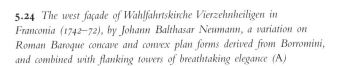

5.24 *The west façade of Wahlfahrtskirche Vierzehnheiligen in Franconia (1742–72), by Johann Balthasar Neumann, a variation on Roman Baroque concave and convex plan forms derived from Borromini, and combined with flanking towers of breathtaking elegance (A)*

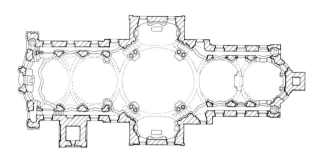

5.26 *Abbey-church, Neresheim (A)*

5.25 *Interior of Vierzehnheiligen. The nave consists of one large ellipse joined to two ovals, with circular transepts, a development of Borromini's ideas. All the decorative effects are Rococo, that frothy, light and elegant surface decoration developed in the eighteenth century, and everything seems to be in motion, with swaying, nodding entablatures and gesticulating figures. The Rococo decorations were by Franz Xaver (1705–1764) and Johann Michael (1709–1772) Feichtmayr, and Johann Georg Üblhör (1700–1763) (A)*

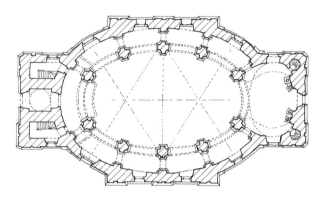

5.27 *Wallfahrtskirche Steinhausen of 1727–35, by Dominikus Zimmermann: plan showing the elliptical form (A)*

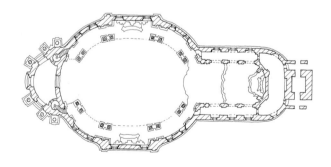

5.28 *Wallfahrtskirche 'Die Wies' of 1744–54, by Dominikus Zimmermann (A)*

1753), the plan is cruciform, but the nave and chancel consist of *five* interlocking ovals or ellipses, three of which have their long axes on the centre-line of the church, and two of which lie at right angles to the main axis. The transeptal arrangement consists of one of the two ellipses at the crossing, with intersecting circles at either end. Twin towers and a west front that bows outwards complete this extraordinary architectural ensemble [5.24]. The enchanting Rococo decorations were almost entirely the work of F. X. and J. M. Feichtmayr and J. G. Üblhör, and the *Gnadenaltar* in the centre of the largest ellipse in the middle of the nave, an extraordinary Rococo *tour de force* that resembles a sedan chair (designed by J. M. Küchel), was made into something rich and strange, as though it had been immersed in the sea. Even the Rococo capitals, vaguely Corinthian in form, have sprouted upwards over the fasciae of the entablature, and downwards over the shafts. It is as though the entire interior of this white, gold, purple, and pink building, with its vestigial aisles, had been made of Meissen porcelain; it is one of the loveliest things on earth. Yet it is unquestionably Classical, derived from a great architectural language, with a vocabulary and a syntax extended and graciously expanded as only a great language can be [5.25]. Ellipses occur at Neumann's Neresheim [5.26], at Dominikus Zimmermann's Steinhausen (1727–35), and elsewhere [5.27, 5.28]; used as main elements (as in the *Piazza* of S. Peter in Rome, or in the church of S. Andrea al Quirinale [5.1, 5.2], both by Bernini), or in combination with other ellipses, circles, or figures (as in Neumann's Vierzehnheiligen), they are one of the motifs exploited to the full by Baroque and Rococo Architects, especially in Central Europe, notably in Southern Germany and Bohemia.

SOME FRENCH EXAMPLES

While the Baroque churches of Rome and the Rococo interiors of central Europe offer some of the most breathtaking and complex architectural experiences possible, a brief word is necessary concerning the design of palaces, a building type that required a specific architectural solution.

The east front of the Louvre (1665–74) [5.29] in Paris, goes far beyond anything that Italian Architects had

5.29 *The east front of the Louvre in Paris by Le Vau, Le Brun, and Perrault, of 1665–74, an astonishingly 'modern' and Classical building for its date, with a colonnade of coupled Corinthian columns (held between the pedimented centrepiece and the end-pavilions with their in antis columns) set on top of a plainer podium that is punctuated by segmental-headed windows with eared architraves. This demonstrates how France was developing a clear, uncluttered architectural language which, while owing something to Bernini and Bramante (House of Raphael and Belvedere Court in the Vatican), looks forward to the Neoclassicism of the next century (Batsford)*

5.30 *The Dôme of the Invalides by J. Hardouin-Mansart, of c.1677–91: a great central space carries the dome, and the overall plan is a Greek cross with chapels filling the angles, creating a square plan. Note the severe, Classical treatment of the front, which, although having a Corinthian over a Doric Order, is very much more restrained than Roman Baroque examples (A)*

5.31 *Church of the Val de Grâce in Paris by François Mansart and Lemercier, begun 1645 and completed 1666. The full-blown Baroque front with massive scrolls (which not only help to support the front, but also act as buttresses over the aisles) is a variation on the Il Gesù theme. The mighty dome with lantern crowns this stunning Baroque composition (A)*

5.32 *Order upon Order: the church of S. Gervais, Paris, possibly by Salomon de Brosse of 1616–23, but more likely to be by J.-C. Métezeau (1581–1652) (Giraudon, Paris, G.9474)*

achieved in terms of the exploitation of the freestanding column in the façade of a large building. The Architects were Le Vau, Le Brun, and Claude Perrault (1613–1688), but it was probably Perrault who was mostly responsible for the design. Bernini's work was the main influence on Perrault, who hid the roofs behind a balustrade, and who modelled the front without any great projecting wings or centrepiece; thus the design marked a departure from the elaborate style of French château Architecture that had prevailed to that time. The smooth, ashlar face of the ground floor became, in effect, a podium in which segmental-headed windows were set, and on which the colonnade of paired Roman Corinthian columns rests. The paired columns, of course, offer a wider intercolumniation in which to place the fenestration, and there were

precedents in the engaged columns used by Bramante and others, but Perrault used fully articulated freestanding columns, giving the façade something of the air of a Roman temple; this temple theme was enhanced by bringing the centre forward on four pairs of columns, carrying an entablature and pediment. This great façade, which terminates in plain projecting wings, must have looked shockingly new and plain when it was first built and when compared with French palatial Architecture of the first half of the seventeenth century; it evoked Antiquity, severity, gravity, and serenity, yet it had majesty, and in fact looks almost like a harbinger of Neoclassicism. It impressed Wren sufficiently for him to use the twinned columns on the west front of S. Paul's Cathedral in London (mixed with Borrominiesque

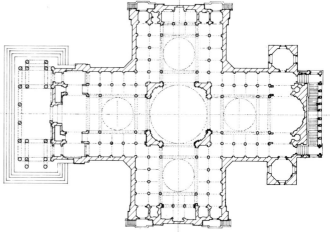

5.34 *Soufflot's final plan for the church of S. Geneviève (now the Panthéon), Paris (A)*

5.35 *The west prostyle hexastyle portico of the Panthéon in Paris by Jacques-Germain Soufflot, begun 1756. The windows were blocked by order of Quatremère de Quincy after the Revolution, when the building became a national tomb for the great of France. Wren's dome of S. Paul's was the model for that of the Panthéon, while the great portico suggests an Antique temple (Batsford)*

towers, it is true), and the segmental-headed windows at the new wing for Hampton Court Palace.

Jules Hardouin-Mansart (1646–1708) also created, in the great domed church of S. Louis des Invalides (c.1677–91) [5.30], a mixture of severe Antiquity, elegance, and grandeur, quite unlike Italian, English, or German Architecture of the time. Earlier French church façades, such as those of the Sorbonne (1635–42), by Jacques Lemercier, and the Val-de-Grâce (1645–66) [5.31], by François Mansart and Lemercier, have affinities with Roman types, but S. Gervais (1616–23) [5.32], probably by J.-C. Métezeau, is far more Classical, with its super-imposed Orders (Roman Doric, Ionic, and Corin-thian), the columns of which are not engaged, but stand before the façade proper, the topmost storey of which is crowned by a segmental pediment. By the time G.-N. Servandoni (1695–1766) added the west front to S. Sulpice in Paris (from 1732) [5.33] the effect was entirely un-Baroque, with two superimposed five-bay *loggie* set between two austerely Classical towers, while the Panthéon [5.34] (from 1756), by Soufflot, reverted entirely to Antiquity with its great prostyle hexastyle pedimented Corinthian portico [5.35, 5.36]. Nevertheless, the variations on the *Gesù* theme were powerfully inventive in French examples well into the eighteenth century.

Of course the palace of Versailles, as it had developed in the seventeenth century under the direction of Jules Hardouin-Mansart and others, set standards for the grand axial plan, by which great house, town, park, and even country, were united in one scheme. The master-plan for Rome under Sixtus V, Scamozzi's layout for Palmanova, and the axial planning of Italian *palazzi* and French *hôtels* all proved to be potent models.

5.36 *Corinthian Order for the Panthéon (A)*

CLASSICAL ARCHITECTURE IN ENGLAND

The political and cultural isolation of England after the break with Rome in 1533–4 led to knowledge of Italian Renaissance Architecture being acquired from Northern European sources. The triumphal arch motif appeared first at Somerset House in the Strand (1547–52), and later at Burghley House near Stamford, when superimposed Orders were used to great effect. However, the sources for much late-Tudor Renaissance Architecture were Shute's book on the Orders of 1563, French designs by Philibert de l'Orme, and, of course, Serlio. There are several English examples of frontispieces adorned with superimposed Orders [4.52], while a Giant Order of pilasters appears at Kirby Hall, Northamptonshire, of 1570–73 [5.37]. Until the advent of Inigo Jones's Palladianism, though, the elaborate style derived from Northern Europe, and especially from the publications of Shute, Vredeman de Vries, and Wendel Dietterlin.

The direct influence of Italy is found in the Architecture of Inigo Jones, notably the Queen's House at Greenwich [4.66] and the Banqueting House in Whitehall [5.38]. At Wilton House, Wiltshire, the south front of 1636 by Isaac de Caux (with Jones's advice) incorporates many Italian features, including the central window.

John Webb (1611–1672) designed the first pedimented temple portico for a country house in England at The Vyne, Hampshire, of 1654. Webb's very grand King Charles II block at Greenwich Palace (1664–69) has an engaged, pedimented temple front in the centre and two wings with Giant Orders of Corinthian pilasters at each end, one of the best of the palatial seventeenth-century façades in England [5.39].

With Sir Christopher Wren (1632–1723), the Baroque style arrived in England, but it was a Baroque filtered through France. Wren had visited Paris in 1665–66, when he saw 'esteem'd Fabricks' which influenced his future work. After the Great Fire of 1666, Wren was appointed Surveyor-General, and supervised the design of the City churches. In many of these schemes

5.37 *Kirby Hall, Northamptonshire. The Giant Order of pilasters derived from Philibert de l'Orme's S. Maur of 1541–4, and was illustrated in his work on Architecture of 1567. Jacques Androuet Ducerceau (1510/12–c.1585) also illustrated this Order. Such decoration is a form of Grotesque (A)*

5.38 *Palladianism. The Banqueting House, Whitehall, by Inigo Jones, of 1619–22, a development of the Vicenzan palazzi of Palladio, with its patterns of superimposed pilasters and columns. This treatment had no precedent in England (RCHME No BB66/1735)*

5.39 *King Charles II block at Greenwich of 1664–69 by John Webb, an uncommonly grand composition in which the Giant Order plays no small part (AFK H20758)*

Wren combined the Baroque concerns for centralized planning with some grandly Antique effects, while his inventiveness in the designs of the steeples rarely faltered [5.40].

His designs for S. Paul's Cathedral owe something to French precedents, notably Lemercier's Val-de-Grâce, and Michelangelo's S. Peter's in Rome, but the version as realized incorporates the doubled columns of Perrault's east front of the Louvre; the two storeys of Inigo Jones's Banqueting House; transepts that derive from da Cortona's S. Maria della Pace in Rome, mixed with Mansart's designs for the Louvre; western towers evolved from Borromini's and Rainaldi's S. Agnese in Agone; and a dome that is a felicitous marriage of ideas derived from Michelangelo and from French exemplars.

Wren's Trinity College Library, Cambridge (1676–84) has superimposed Orders, yet, although Sansovino's S. Mark's Library in Venice is an obvious influence, in many respects the detail seems more French than Italian [5.41]. Hampton Court Palace's south and east wings of 1689–94 have some segmental-headed windows based on Perrault's work at the Louvre, but Wren's great buildings at Greenwich (1696–1716), with their Baroque domes and colonnades (again employing twinned columns) are even finer, and, with the earlier Architecture of

5.40 *S. Lawrence, Jewry, London, of 1671–7 by Wren. The east wall shows a grandly Antique temple effect (Batsford)*

5.41 (ABOVE) *The Library at Trinity College, Cambridge, by Wren, of 1676–84, in which echoes of Sansovino's library in Venice can be discerned (AFK H8242)*

5.42 (BELOW) *Greenwich Hospital, with Jones's Queen's House in the centre of the composition, completed by Wren from 1696. Wren's work includes the colonnades (note the paired columns) and the twin domes. This is one of the finest Baroque compositions in England (AFK H11649)*

5.43 *Castle Howard, designed in 1699, and commenced on site in 1700, by Vanbrugh and Hawksmoor. This is one of the great monuments of English Baroque Architecture* (AFK H17559)

Webb and Jones, comprise one of the greatest monumental symmetrical compositions of the period [5.42].

The plan of the Invalides in Paris influenced Wren at the Greenwich and Chelsea Hospitals, and the layout of Versailles was no doubt lurking at the back of his mind when he designed these remarkable ensembles. Versailles was to be a model for some of the later Baroque palaces.

William Talman (1650–1719) was responsible for the south and east wings of Chatsworth House in Derbyshire. The south front, with its Giant Order of Ionic pilasters, owes something to Bernini's third project for the east front of the Louvre (1665). Although Talman's work at Chatsworth is grand and Baroque, it is overshadowed by the stupendous compositions of Castle Howard, Yorkshire, of 1699 [5.43], by Sir John Vanbrugh (1664–1726) assisted by Nicholas Hawksmoor (1661–1736). At Castle Howard the precedents of Webb's work at Greenwich, Talman's at Chatsworth, and Wren's at Greenwich combine with French exemplars such as Vaux-le-Vicomte and Marly. At Blenheim Palace, Oxfordshire (1705–16), Vanbrugh and Hawks-

moor combined the grand centre-block, courtyard, and wings (based on Palladian and Versailles precedents) with elements from Antiquity (a Roman ruin illustrated by Perrault in his 1673 edition of Vitruvius), suggestions of Borromini's distorted skylines, and echoes of Bernini's Piazza of S. Peter. Blenheim combines contrasting heavy masses of masonry, Giant and subsidiary Orders, and a busy, romantic silhouette that harks back, perhaps, to early Renaissance houses of the Elizabethan period [5.44].

Hawksmoor's London churches also mix several themes: S. George's, Bloomsbury, attempts to recreate the Mausoleum at Halicarnassus on top of the tower, while the noble body of the church has an Antique Roman temple front and an interior that suggests something of the massiveness of Roman Imperial buildings [5.45].

At S. Alphege, Greenwich, Hawksmoor used the Roman Imperial motif of an arch rising into a pediment, while at S. George-in-the-East and S. Anne, Limehouse, he combined Baroque exaggeration and changes of plane with Gothic lanterns composed of Classical details. Christ Church, Spitalfields, has a vast Serliana as the portico, a wide triumphal arch motif without overt Orders above, and a broach spire over the whole [5.46].

5.44 (ABOVE) *Blenheim Palace, Oxfordshire (1705–16), by Vanbrugh and Hawksmoor, an even more massively Baroque composition, with towers over which are attic-storey belvederes that incorporate Antique and Baroque themes from Perrault and Borromini. Yet Blenheim also has echoes of Elizabethan and Jacobean Architecture in the romantic skyline (AFK H5615)*

5.45 (ABOVE) *Church of S. George, Bloomsbury (1716–31) by Nicholas Hawksmoor, showing the prostyle hexastyle Corinthian portico, and the extraordinary steeple that attempts to re-create the stepped pyramidal form of the Mausoleum of Halicarnassus on the tower based on Pliny's description (AFK H1768)*

5.47 *Temple of the Four Winds of 1724–26 at Castle Howard, by Vanbrugh (RCHME AA 53/11413)*

5.46 (OPPOSITE) *The Serliana or Venetian Window arrangement as a portico. Christ Church, Spitalfields, London, by Nicholas Hawksmoor, of 1714–29. The motif recurs above in the tower (Batsford)*

At Castle Howard Vanbrugh designed the Temple of the Four Winds (1724–26): it is based on the Villa Capra near Vicenza, and so, with its four identical porticoes and dome over the central body, is Palladian in inspiration [5.47]. The mausoleum at Castle Howard, however, of 1728–42, was designed by Hawksmoor, and has a majestic clarity reminiscent of Bramante's *Tempietto*; but it is vast in size. The Tuscan columns are elongated and carry a Doric frieze: there is only one triglyph over each intercolumniation, and the effect is solemnly grand, powerful, and forbidding [5.48].

James Gibbs (1682–1754) used the circular temple theme at his Radcliffe Camera in Oxford, but with an engaged Order on a rusticated base, and references to Michelangelo and S. Maria della Salute, among other precedents [5.49]. It is important to recognize that the *Tempietto*, the domes of S. Paul's, S. Peter's, the Val de Grâce, the Invalides, the Radcliffe Camera, and the Mausoleum at Castle Howard are all related in their

5.48 (ABOVE) *The Mausoleum at Castle Howard, Yorkshire, by Nicholas Hawksmoor, designed 1728–9 and built 1731–42, based on Bramante's* Tempietto *and on Hawksmoor's first proposals for the Radcliffe Library in Oxford. The blending of Antiquity with Modernity is again expressed. Hawksmoor's intercolumniation is 1½ diameters, which has no Antique precedent, however, and this gives the building a stern and forbidding air, enhanced by the fortress-like plinth designed by Daniel Garrett (AFK H8911)*

5.49 (BELOW) *A further variation on the rotunda theme is provided by James Gibbs's Radcliffe Library in Oxford of 1737–48, with the paired Corinthian engaged columns set on a rusticated plinth, giving a richer effect, and mixing Baroque, Antique, and Renaissance motifs (A)*

5.50 (BELOW) *Church of S. Martin-in-the-Fields, London, of 1720–26 by James Gibbs, with temple front and spire (RCHME BB71/5193)*

5.51 *The Clarendon Building, Oxford, by Hawksmoor, of 1712–15. This marvellously grave and massive building suggests Antiquity in its brooding way. Note the pediments and the oversized keystone in the segmental arches set in the wide frame around the panels (A)*

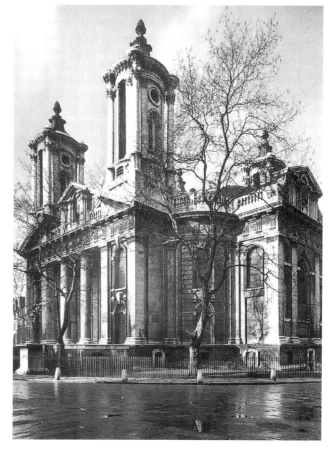

5.52 *S. John's Church, Smith Square, Westminster, by Thomas Archer (c.1668–1743) of 1713–28, a remarkable Baroque composition with four identical towers, which gave it the nickname 'Queen Anne's footstool'. Perhaps more than Wren, and certainly more than Hawksmoor, Archer was influenced by Bernini and Borromini (AFK H223)*

geometry and handling, yet they are all distinctly different as well: such were some of the infinite possibilities of the Classical language of Architecture. Gibbs, of course, was responsible for other distinguished buildings, including S. Mary-le-Strand of 1714–17 (which combines a three-stage steeple derived from Wren's inventions with a powerfully Roman Baroque body) and S. Martin-in-the-Fields [5.50] of 1720–26 (with its temple front, tower, and steeple emulating Gothic form in Classical detail, and two-storey fenestration system on the sides to accommodate the gallery). Gibbs, of course, published influential works dealing with design, rules, and methods of drawing Architecture, and provided patterns for doorcases and window surrounds that were widely copied, as with the 'Gibbs Surround'.

However, the sense of overpowering massiveness [5.51] found in works by Vanbrugh and Hawksmoor (both of whom knew well the language of Antiquity), the deliberate exaggeration of features such as keystones and aedicules, and the employment of Mannerist, Baroque, and other devices led to a reaction, which will be described below. There was another reason for the reaction too: the Baroque was associated with Roman Catholicism, and was acceptable during the reign of the Stuart Queen Anne [5.52]. Gibbs was a Catholic, a Tory, a Scot, and very likely had Jacobite sympathies: his Architecture, so obviously tainted with Papist Roman precedent, was hardly to be endured or encouraged by the Whigs after 1714, and so it proved. He was sacked from his Surveyorship to the Commissioners for Building Fifty New Churches in 1716.

SOME GERMAN BUILDINGS

One of the greatest of all European palaces was that in Berlin, designed by Andreas Schlüter (c.1659–1714), and totally destroyed in 1950 by the East German authorities acting on the orders of the Soviet Union after the Second World War: it owed a considerable debt to Bernini, notably his abortive scheme for the Louvre. Schlüter was also responsible for the Zeughaus, which still survives in the Unter den Linden. Two of his greatest contemporaries were J. B. Fischer von Erlach (1656–1723) and Johann Lukas von Hildebrandt

(1668–1745). The latter's Upper Belvedere in Vienna (1720–4) has exotic pavilion roofs derived from French precedents, but the detail owes much to Italian Mannerist and Baroque examples. Fischer von Erlach's Schönbrunn Palace in Vienna was strongly influenced by French Classicism, and demonstrates how the Classical language of Architecture could

5.53 *The pavilion principle of composition: Schloss Nymphenburg, Munich. Late-seventeenth and early-eighteenth century (A)*

5.54 *The extraordinary Zwinger Palace in Dresden, by Matthäus Daniel Pöppelmann (1662–1736), built 1711–22. This Baroque extravaganza consists of two-storey pavilions linked by single-storey galleries. The pavilions are decorated by Balthasar Permoser* (A)

be used in a long range, using a Giant Order on a plinth, repetitive elements, and emphases in the centre and ends of the composition. Very different was the system of pavilions used in Schloss Nymphenburg, Munich, designed by Barelli and Viscardi (1663–1728, with later alterations by others [5.53]).

Even more extraordinary is the series of galleries with two-storey pavilions – part grandstand, part pleasure-palace, part nymphaeum, part gallery, part orangery – known as the Zwinger in Dresden, designed by M. D. Pöppelmann (1662–1736), and built 1711–22, with sculptures by Balthasar Permoser. Here, broken segmental pediments are turned back to front, and sway apart; encrustations of figures and other decorations are piled up over every surface; and the most marvellous invention is displayed on the gate and other pavilions. Even the Italian Baroque designers seem ponderous in comparison with this Saxon masterpiece [5.54].

Enchanting, too, is Frederick the Great's one-storey palace of Sanssouci at Potsdam, designed by the King and G. W. von Knobelsdorff (1699–1753) from 1745. It has terminal atlantes on the outside, similar to those of the Zwinger, but the central hall, with its Corinthian columns, has a Classical simplicity in which a pro-

nounced French influence may be detected. Some of the rooms, however, are still deliciously Rococo [5.55, 5.56].

Also at Potsdam, the Neues Palais of 1755–66 owes something to the design of Castle Howard, and a further English influence is obvious at Knobelsdorff's Opera House on the Unter den Linden, begun in 1740 [5.57]. Those English influences are significant, and are representative of a general reaction against Baroque and Rococo that led back first to Italian sixteenth-century exemplars [5.58] and then, as we will see, to a search for the purity of Antiquity, and even to primitive stereometrically simple forms.

5.55 *Sanssouci, Potsdam, by Knobelsdorff, of the 1740s. The elliptical Marmorsaal from the outside, showing the terms (pedestals like inverted obelisks merging with heroic male and female figures supporting the entablature)* (A)

5.56 (LEFT) *The Marmorsaal in Sanssouci by Knobelsdorff, of 1745–6, showing the coupled columns. This interior is inspired by the Antique source of the Pantheon, and also suggests the Perrault coupled columns. Antiquity and Modernity merge* (A)

5.58 (ABOVE) *The French Church in the Gendarmenplatz, Berlin, of 1701–8, by J.-L. Cayart (1645–1702), with drum and dome of 1780–85, by Karl von Gontard (1731–91), a building mixing the clarity of Franco-Prussian Classicism with a Neo-Palladianism influenced partly by England: the shades of the Villa Capra are apparent* (A)

5.57 *Georg Wenzeslaus von Knobelsdorff's (1699–1753) Opera House on the Unter den Linden, Berlin, of 1740–3, the first great Neo-Palladian building in Germany. It has a temple front, and indeed was conceived partly as a temple, with a ceremonial hall serving as vestibule and dining-room. It was partly based on Colen Campbell's Wanstead of c.1714–20* (A)

PALLADIANISM

Palladianism is a type of Architecture distinguished by a style and composition derived from the buildings and publications of Andrea Palladio. Inigo Jones introduced Palladio's Architecture to England in the reign of King James I and VI [4.66, 5.38, 5.59] while Jacob van Campen (1595–1657) and Elias Holl were the leading exponents of Palladianism in the Netherlands and in Germany.

There is one great house in England that stylistically stands between the grander Baroque palaces and the Palladian country houses. That is Burley-on-the-Hill (1696–1705), by the Second Earl of Nottingham, Henry Dormer, and John Lumley. The main house is connected by quadrants to two lower blocks which, in turn, are joined to two wings by means of great sweeping colonnades: they are Palladian-villa-scale versions of the Bernini colonnades in Rome, and form a *cour d'honneur*, the grandest of such compositions to be found anywhere in England. So Palladian villa design, complete with *piano nobile*, combines with Baroque bravura at Burley-on-the-Hill.

The true Palladian Revival took place in the first half of the eighteenth century, and began in Venetia (Il Venéto) and in England. In the latter it was led by Colen Campbell (1676–1729) and Lord Burlington, and was not only a reaction against the Baroque of Hawksmoor, Vanbrugh, Wren, and others, but a revival of the style of Inigo Jones, which the Commonwealth and the Baroque were perceived to have interrupted.

Campbell's Wanstead House of *c.*1714–20 was the first great eighteenth-century 'Palladian' mansion, and its building coincided with the establishment of the Hanoverian dynasty. It demonstrated immediately its anti-Baroque credentials by its austere horizontality, its prostyle hexastyle portico standing on a high podium, clearly derived from Palladio's notion of the Antique villa, and Architecture that owed so much to Palladio and Jones. In 1719 Burlington sacked Gibbs as his Architect, and appointed Campbell to remodel Burlington House in Piccadilly.

Burlington's adoption of the Palladian style commenced with the publication of Campbell's *Vitruvius Britannicus* (1715–25) and Giacomo Leoni's version of the *Quattro Libri* (1715–20): it also, significantly, coincided with the beginning of the Hanoverian Succession, and so was associated with Whiggery and with a desire to resume a style that had been interrupted in its development by the Civil War, the Commonwealth, and Baroque flirtations. It is perhaps not fanciful to see, in the

5.59 *Palladianism. Palladio also reconstructed the primitive Tuscan Order as described by Vitruvius, and published his interpretation (2.37). This was the source for the remarkable portico of the church of S. Paul, Covent Garden, by Inigo Jones, of 1631–3. Note that this Order has widely spaced columns, an architrave, but no frieze or cornice: instead there is a wide overhanging eaves and a pediment carried on brackets which are elongated mutules (A)*

5.60 *Palladianism. Chiswick House, west London, by Lord Burlington, of c.1723–9, a villa inspired by Palladio's Villa Capra at Vicenza, although the dome and room beneath are octagonal instead of circular. Note the Diocletian or Thermal Window in the octagon (AFK H16670)*

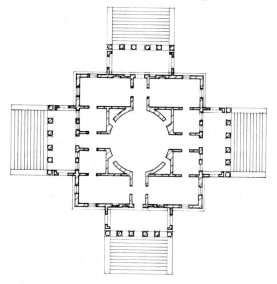

5.61 *Palladio: Villa Capra, near Vicenza (A)*

adoption of Palladianism, a seeking to legitimize the Succession by association and continuity with the pre-Cromwellian period. The Baroque style was associated with the Counter-Reformation and with Continental Absolutism, so Palladio, Jones, and the Palladian style seemed to offer untainted exemplars worthy of emulation.

Many books appeared under the aegis of Burlington, who paid for the publication (1730) of several unknown Palladio drawings of *Thermae* as well as an edition of works by Inigo Jones (1727) by William Kent (c.1685–1748). Burlington saw Palladianism as a means of returning to the principles of the Architecture of Antiquity. His villa at Chiswick (c.1723–29) [5.60] is loosely based on Palladio's Villa Capra [4.62, 5.61] and on Scamozzi's Vettor Pisani Villa, Lonigo (1576–9), and contains a sequence of rooms employing circles, apses, an octagon, and a rectangle, clearly derived from Palladio's Palazzo Thiene in Vicenza, which itself owed much to Roman Antiquity, especially the *Thermae*. Campbell's Mereworth Castle [5.62] in Kent (1722–25) is even closer to Italian precedents, and is, in some ways, an improvement on the

5.62 (ABOVE) *Mereworth Castle, Kent, by Colen Campbell, of 1722–25* (RCHME AA50/10360)

5.63 (BELOW) *Palladianism. Lord Burlington's Assembly Rooms in York of 1731–2 which reconstruct the so-called 'Egyptian' Hall of Vitruvius as interpreted in a drawing by Palladio* (AFK G18333)

Villa Capra. Burlington's Assembly Rooms in York of 1731–2 [5.63] are an almost exact copy of Palladio's reconstruction of a so-called 'Egyptian Hall' (i.e. one with an internal peristyle and clerestory) as described by Vitruvius. Kent's Holkham Hall in Norfolk (1734–65), with its great hexastyle portico, symmetrical wings, and fully expressed *piano nobile* [5.64] is a good example of a Palladian country house, as is Campbell's Houghton Hall (1721–6) [5.65], the cubic central hall of which is modelled on Jones's Queen's House at Greenwich: Houghton has Venetian windows in the towers [5.65], which were to have been crowned with pediments, but which Gibbs altered to stone domes. Holkham Hall was designed as a house in the Antique style, in which a collection of paintings and Classical sculpture could be set off to advantage. At the entrance hall of Holkham, set behind a prostyle hexastyle portico on a podium, Kent devised a room of stunning and severe Classical grandeur [5.66], employing references to the screen in S. Giorgio Maggiore, coffered Roman vaults, the frieze of an Antique Roman temple, and a Vitruvian peristyled

5.64 *Holkham Hall, Norfolk of 1734–65, by William Kent (RCHME DD50/71)*

5.65 *Houghton Hall, Norfolk, of 1721–6, by Colen Campbell (A)*

5.66 *Entrance Hall at Holkham Hall (RCHME BB66/3688)*

interior. At Stowe, of course, he designed gardens, and buildings to adorn them, which evoked Arcady itself and the landscapes of Poussin and Claude.

Other Palladian compositions include Kent's Horse Guards, Whitehall, (1748–59) and James Paine's (1717–1789) Kedleston Hall in Derbyshire (1759–60), which had a central block with wings linked by curving elements (like Palladio's design for the Villa Mocenigo), but also included a Pantheon-like saloon and a hall with an internal peristyle on the main axis. Kedleston was completed, in *c.*1760–70, by the Adam Brothers, who replaced the bowed front on the south façade with a triumphal arch, and remodelled Paine's hall and saloon to resemble elements of Diocletian's Palace at Spalato, thus rendering a Palladian design less Palladian and more Antique [5.67–5.69].

Sir Edward Lovett Pearce's (*c.*1699–1733) Parliament House in Dublin [5.70], with its brilliant E-shaped Ionic portico and colonnade, Knobelsdorff's Berlin Opera House, Friedrich Wilhelm von Erdmannsdorff's (1736-1800) Schloss Wörlitz (1769–73), and Castle Ward, Co. Down [5.71], are further fine examples of Palladian Revival Architecture.

Sir William Chambers (1723–1796) based his style on a scholarly interpretation of Palladianism, the best example of which is his Somerset House in London (1776–96), probably the grandest official building ever erected in the capital. His Casino at Marino, near Dublin, (1758–76) combines a Greek cross on plan with scholarly attention to Classical detail using a Roman Doric Order. Chambers's *A Treatise on Civil Architecture* of 1759 became a standard and influential work on Classical

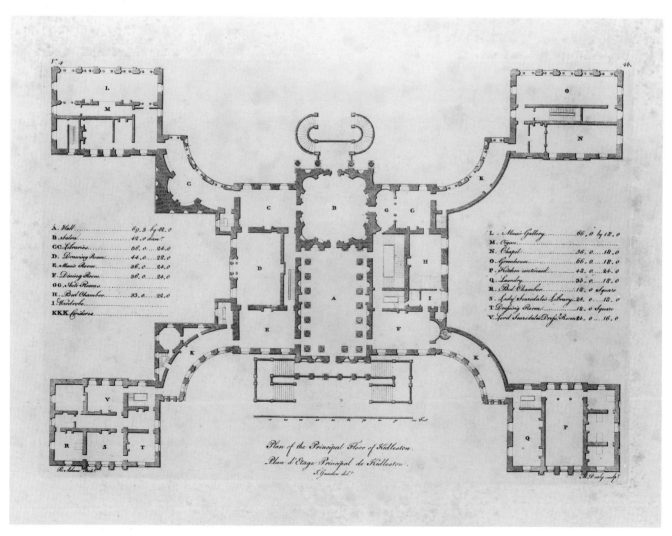

5.67 *Plan of Kedleston Hall, Derbyshire, showing the composition, with wings, based on Palladian precedent. The two pavilions and wings at the top were not built (A)*

5.68 (ABOVE) *South front of Kedleston, showing the basic Palladian composition with the variation on the triumphal arch, by the Adam Brothers, in the centre (*AFK G8585*)*

5.69 (BELOW) *The hall, Kedleston, showing the Corinthian columns and the grave, Antique effect (*Batsford*)*

5.70 (ABOVE) *The Bank of Ireland (formerly the Parliament), Dublin, by Sir Edward Lovett Pearce (d.1733), of c.1728–39, an essay in Palladianism and in form the precedent for the British Museum (A)*

5.71 (BELOW) *Palladianism. Castle Ward, Co. Down, a grand house built 1760–73 to designs by an unidentified Architect. Note the engaged Ionic Order with pediment set on the rusticated plinth treated as a basement (A)*

5.72 *The Four Courts, Dublin, by James Gandon (1743–1823), of 1786–1802, incorporating the south and west sides of a quadrangle designed by Thomas Cooley. A severe Antique grandeur is suggested by the domed rotunda, while variations on the triumphal arch theme lead to the two courtyards. Note that the hexastyle portico is prostyle (A)*

5.73 *Royal Crescent, Bath, by Wood the Younger (AFK H4241)*

Architecture. His pupil, James Gandon (1743–1823), also combined Palladian compositional methods with scholarly Classical detail, as at the Custom House in Dublin (1781–91) (where elements from Wren's Chelsea and Greenwich Hospitals are also quoted, with parts of Somerset House), and the Four Courts in Dublin [5.72] (with Thomas Cooley (c.1740–1784)), which unites a severe Neoclassical drum and dome, Antique hexastyle pedimented portico, and three relatively plain blocks. Gandon published, with J. Woolfe, two further supplements to *Vitruvius Britannicus*, in 1767 and 1771. His work is probably more eclectically Classical than purely Palladian, although his compositional method owes much to English Palladian Architecture.

Generally, Palladian town houses had rusticated bases, applied upper Orders, and a balustrade or parapet. Three superimposed engaged Orders are found at the Circus in Bath (1754) by the Woods of Bath, while at Royal Crescent (1767–75), by the younger Wood (1728–1781) [5.73], a Giant Order of engaged columns rises two storeys from the ground floor over a basement. At Bath, the Woods consciously evoked Roman plan-forms, such as the amphitheatre, while adhering to Palladian uniformity, to combine individual houses in one grand composition. John Wood the Elder (1704–1754) was the first English Architect after Inigo Jones to try to make an English square a uniform Palladian composition (although Henry Aldrich (1648–1710) had designed Peckwater Quadrangle, Christ Church, Oxford (1707–1714), some twenty years earlier than Queen Square in Bath), and Robert Adam reintroduced the principle of the unified palatial façade to London, at the Adelphi (1768–72).

VI

NEOCLASSICISM AND AFTER

Neoclassicism and Rome; Cordemoy
and Laugier; the rediscovery of Greece;
the Greek Revival; the move away from
Neoclassicism

*From the innumerable beautiful monuments of
[Greek art] which remain, it is the worthiest
object of study and imitation; it therefore demands
a minute investigation, consisting . . . in
information as to its essential; an investigation in
which not merely facts are communicated for
instruction, but also principles for practice.*

JOHANN JOACHIM WINCKELMANN (1717–1768): *The History of Ancient Art,*
first published in Dresden in 1764, Book IV, Ch. 1, para. 2.

NEOCLASSICISM AND ROME

The published works of Giovanni Battista Piranesi (1720–1778) attracted further attention to the Architecture of Roman Antiquity, inflating its scale and exaggerating its impact. Certainly this Architecture was revered, and the superiority of Antiquity became an eighteenth-century article of faith, supported not only by the images of Piranesi, but by the archaeological discoveries in Rome itself and in the partially preserved towns of Herculaneum, Stabiae, and Pompeii.

CORDEMOY AND LAUGIER

When the Abbé Jean-Louis de Cordemoy (1631–1713) published his *Nouveau Traité de Toute l'Architecture* in 1706 he was not only writing about the Orders, but was attacking the Baroque styles, and arguing for a cleansed and purified Architecture which, by implication, looked to Antiquity rather than to more recent times (even sixteenth-century Architecture in Italy) for appropriate precedents. What Cordemoy was also striving for was the removal of all Mannerist and Baroque affectations, distortions, and effects: he inveighed against engaged columns, pilasters that were purely ornamental, and anything that was not 'true' to the Orders. In fact, he proposed that the Orders should be used as functional elements, that columns should be there for support only, and that the principles of Antiquity should be reappraised.

The problem with Cordemoy's notions, and indeed the whole veneration for Roman exemplars, was that the latter were not 'pure', that there were buildings erected during the Empire that were unquestionably proto-Baroque, and that Roman use of the Orders can hardly be seen as 'Primitive', rational, or always necessary. One could hardly examine great buildings like the *Thermae* of Diocletian or Caracalla and see them as 'pure' or free from very stylized use of the Orders.

When Marc-Antoine Laugier (1713–1769) published his *Essai sur l'Architecture* in 1753 he presented an image of the Primitive Hut with its tree-trunks, beams, and pitched roof (all of timber) as the only begetter of Architecture, and he saw early Doric as directly descended from the Primitive Hut; first as a timber prototype, and then as a stone temple: from that source, Laugier argued, all Architecture had evolved. Interestingly, Bramante designed columns with branches lopped off on the shafts at the cloisters of S. Ambrogio in Milan, a deliberate allusion to Antiquity, to Vitruvius, and to the timber origins of the Orders (1492).

So, Laugier took Cordemoy's arguments, gave the Orders a rational and far more primitive origin than the Orders of Roman Antiquity, and showed that in their earliest forms they did indeed do a job, rather than merely decorate the structure. Laugier, in short, established that the column should be used and expressed as such, not used engaged or for decoration, and that something more primitive and more true to its origins than a mere copy of Roman Antique buildings was necessary. Laugier, in fact, promoted certain architectural ideals and principles that struck chords at a time when archaeology was becoming ever more important as a source of correct Antique details and motifs. Laugier was read all over Europe: his is the great architectural text of the Enlightenment, and it is perhaps worth pointing out that he was closely involved with Freemasonry, that columns and the Orders play no small part in Masonic iconography and systems, and that the Enlightenment was permeated with Masonic ideas.

With Jacques-Germain Soufflot's (1713–1780) Parisian church of Ste Geneviève [5.35, 5.36], begun in 1756, we find the first fruits of Laugier's ideas, and the beginnings of French Neoclassicism. Soufflot used a dome loosely modelled on that of S. Paul's Cathedral in London, but with a peristyle of Antique columns expressed all round the drum, a Greek cross as the plan, and a grave, hexastyle portico recalling the best of Roman Antiquity. Laugier said that Ste Geneviève was the first expression of perfect Architecture: inside, the load-bearing Corinthian columns are fully expressed as such, carry straight entablatures, and give a completely different effect from that of earlier Baroque interiors with engaged columns, pilasters, and mighty piers. Soufflot combined regularity, monumental Roman detail, and elegance; and the columns, being more slender than piers, contribute to the sense of lightness judiciously mixed with gravity. Later, when Ste Geneviève was designated as the Panthéon in the 1790s, through the influence of Quatremère de Quincy (1755–1849), the windows were filled in to give the building the character of a mausoleum: the blocking of the windows was nothing whatsoever to do with safety factors, as some have claimed.

THE REDISCOVERY OF GREECE

Laugier and J.-J. Rousseau (1712–1778) both saw virtues in the primitive. From the 1750s the search for archaeological precedents and for 'purity' led back in time to the beginnings of Classicism, beyond Rome, to Greek Doric. Soufflot had visited Paestum to see the Greek temples there in 1750, Piranesi drew them, and Richard Payne Knight (1750–1824) found them 'Picturesque' in 1777, which established them in the realms of respectability. Johann Wolfgang von Goethe (1749–1832) was stupefied by them in 1787, and John Soane (1753–1837) had seen them in 1780. However, the real champion of Greek Architecture was Johann Joachim Winckelmann (1717–1768), who published his *Reflections* on the imitation of Greek precedents in paintings and sculptures in 1755: Winckelmann's description of the noble simplicity and quiet grandeur of Greek art struck home, while his *Observations on the Architecture of the Ancients* of 1764, produced after a visit to Paestum in 1758, helped to draw attention to the necessity, as he saw it, of imitating the Greeks.

However, although there were substantial remnants of Greek Architecture in Italy and Sicily, Greece and Asia Minor (as part of the Ottoman Empire) were not the easiest places to visit. The Society of Dilettanti was responsible for organizing and financing the expedition that was to make Greek Architecture, its Orders, and its details as familiar as those of Rome. Robert Wood (c.1717–1771), who was to become a member of the Society, toured the Greek islands in 1742–43, but in 1749 the Earl of Charlemont (1728–1799) visited a number of sites in company with Richard Dalton (c.1715–1791), who made detailed drawings of Greek antiquities. These stimulated further interest, and in 1748 James Stuart (1713–1788) and Nicholas Revett (1720–1804) determined on a project which would establish a methodology of architectural archaeology for Greek Architecture on the lines of Antoine Desgodetz's *Édifices Antiques de Rome* of 1682. Stuart and Revett became members of the Dilettanti in 1751, and the Society helped to fund their expedition from 1751 to 1754. The work of surveying, measuring, and drawing the remains of Greek buildings was slow, painstaking, and often fraught with danger, but the first volume of *The Antiquities of Athens* was published in 1762. The rest of the work was extremely slow in coming out: Volume II appeared in 1789, and the third, fourth, and fifth volumes were published in 1794, 1814, and 1830 respectively, largely the work of younger men. So this great source book of the Greek Revival took 82 years to appear in its entirety and, as a result, its impact on Architecture was spasmodic and gradual.

The 1750s saw other, less accurate, publications on Greek Architecture by Julien-David Le Roy (*Ruines des plus beaux monuments de la Grèce*) in 1758 and Robert Sayer (*Ruins of Athens*) in 1759. Robert Wood brought out his *Ruins of Palmyra* in 1753 and *Ruins of Balbec* in 1757, both of which added to the store of knowledge of buildings of Classical Antiquity, while Robert Adam's (1728–1792) *Ruins of the Palace of the Emperor Diocletian, at*

Spalatro, Dalmatia, was published in 1764. So, in the middle of the eighteenth century the Primitive had been extolled, Greek Architecture was being discovered, and Antique Architecture generally seemed to offer more real, more pure exemplars than the second- or third-hand works of the Italian Renaissance, even when the last contained a strong dose of the Antique, as in Palladio's work.

THE GREEK REVIVAL

In terms of buildings, Stuart's Doric Temple at Hagley [6.1] of 1758 is the first Doric Revival building in Europe, while Revett's church at Ayot St Lawrence in Hertford-shire, with its Order based on that of the temple of Apollo at Delos, dates from 1778–9, and is the first Greek Revival church. Stuart designed several Greek buildings for the gardens at Shugborough in Staffordshire in the 1760s, but the greatest Greek Revival Architecture was put up in the next century. H. W. (1794–1843) and W.

(c.1771–1843) Inwood's S. Pancras church in London (1819–22) is an eclectic mix of elements from the Erechtheion, the Tower of the Winds, the Choragic Monument of Lysicrates, and other Athenian buildings culled from *The Antiquities of Athens* and other source books. The invention of the tower applied to a temple, with two rows of windows (one above and one below the gallery) on its long sides, was ingenious, for congregational worship and side windows were not features of Greek temples [6.2, 6.3].

The Greek Revival had an enormous impact on Architecture, and there are many works of Architecture of the highest quality in which Greek themes are well to

6.1 *The Doric Temple at Hagley, Worcestershire, probably the first Greek Doric Revival building in Europe* (AFK H7384)

6.2 *S. Pancras church, London, by H. W. and W. Inwood, 1819–22, an exquisite and scholarly work of the Greek Revival. The prostyle hexastyle Greek Ionic portico is based on the Order of the Erechtheion, while the tower is an ingenious mix of elements from the Tower of the Winds and the Choragic Monument of Lysicrates (AFK H4905)*

6.3 *Caryatide porch with sarcophagus at S. Pancras church, London.*
Note the arrangement of windows on the right to accommodate the balcony
inside (AFK H15197)

6.4 *Corn capital and tobacco capital designs by Benjamin Latrobe for the United States Capitol, Washington DC* (Dictionary of Ornament, Macmillan, 1986)

the fore. Gilly and Schinkel in Berlin, von Klenze in Bavaria, Wilkins, Smirke, Playfair, Thomas Hamilton, C. R. Cockerell, Decimus Burton, Thomas Harrison, Alexander Thomson, and Soane in Britain, Ledoux in France, Ehrensvård in Sweden, and many other Architects produced Neoclassical buildings in which Greek elements were well to the fore.

Benjamin Henry Latrobe (1764–1820), who was a pupil of S. P. Cockerell, designed a number of buildings in an advanced Neoclassical style, including Hammerwood Lodge, East Grinstead, which employs a primitive 'Paestum' Order. He emigrated to Virginia in 1796, and introduced a severe Neoclassicism to the United States, giving it an American identity, beginning with his Bank of Pennsylvania of 1798. He invented 'native Orders' for the Federal Capitol in Washington (from 1814) contrasting the corncob and tobacco leaves [6.4]. Corncob finials, rice plants, the bald eagle, and stars (representing the States), began to appear in American Classical design.

Robert Adam did not adopt Grecian Architecture in its entirety, although he used Greek motifs in many of his designs, judiciously mixing them with a large repertory of decorative elements taken from many sources, mostly Roman, or from Pompeii or Herculaneum. His assured use of differing room shapes in his planning derives from his studies of Roman *Thermae*. His work is lighter and

more elegant than that of the earlier Palladians or the later Greek Revivalists.

Neoclassicism, then, included turning to the buildings of Greek and Roman Antiquity to provide exemplars, motifs, and stimuli for new Architecture: this might be termed the archaeological approach, and demonstrated the desire to use more original and uncorrupted sources for Classical Architecture than those of the Italian Renaissance, Mannerist, and Baroque periods. Neoclassicism was partly a reaction against what was seen as Baroque and Rococo excess. It also embraced the idea that the further back one looked to primitive forms (the Primitive Hut) produced by Man in his primitive state, the more uncorrupted and less decadent would the Architecture be. The severity, sturdiness, robustness, clarity, and 'primitiveness' of Greek Doric seemed to rise to the demand, and therefore scholarly examinations of Greek Architecture were necessary in order to provide the vocabulary and language of Greek, as opposed to Roman, Classical Architecture. Neoclassicism does not imply mere copying, for, as has been pointed out, the congregational form of worship in an Anglican church of the early nineteenth century was quite different from the function of a Greek temple, so considerable invention had to be employed in order to adapt scholarly quotations from Ancient Greek buildings to a modern church.

Adam, too, was not the only Architect to mix his elements in an eclectic way: Adam, of course, produced exquisite interiors that were at once serene, elegant, and full of imaginative virtuosity, but he employed both quotation and interpretation, and mixed his Greek, Pompeian, and Roman motifs (or motifs derived from those sources) quite freely. Very different in character, yet mixing Greek, Roman, and primitive elements, is Great Packington church in Warwickshire by Joseph Bonomi (1739–1808) and the fourth Earl of Aylesford (1751–1812) of 1789–80: the building is severely, almost aggressively plain on the outside [6.5], employing semicircular lunettes and Diocletian Windows in the brick walls, with no dressings or ornament, and the effect is Roman, primitive, forbidding, and Antique, with a strong hint, in the lunettes, of the *loculi* in *hypogea* or columbaria, both favourite devices used by French Neoclassicist Architects in designs for tombs and cemeteries. Inside [6.6], Doric columns and fragments of entablature based on the temples at Paestum appear, almost as vestigial memories, in the corners of the central groin-vaulted space. To have primitive Doric carrying a square groin vault, mixed with lunettes and Thermal Windows gives a grave air to the building: a primitive,

6.5 (ABOVE) *The church of S. James, Great Packington, Warwickshire. View from the south-west showing the plain exterior with Diocletian Windows and lunettes* (RCHME BB77/810)

6.6 (BELOW) *Interior of Great Packington church showing the primitive Greek Doric Order carrying the groin vaults* (RCHME BB77/812)

6.7 (ABOVE) *'Egyptian Architecture in a Nordic Landscape' by Carl August Ehrensvärd, showing how primitive Doric was thought to be 'Egyptian' in the 1780s (Statens Konstmuseer, Stockholm, Teckning och Grafik NMH 179/1866)*

6.8 (BELOW) *Design for a Mausoleum to the Memory of James King Esq drowned June 9, 1776. Design by (Sir) John Soane in which a rusticated base, pyramids, and a Pantheon-like structure occur in the same composition (SJSM)*

6.9 *The Barrière de la Villette in Paris by C.-N. Ledoux of 1785–87. It is a severe square surmounted by a drum carried on pairs of primitive baseless Tuscan columns supporting plain arches directly on the abaci. A simplified Doric entablature crowns the composition. The very stark pedimented portico has square stripped Doric columns, combining elements of the Greek Doric Revival with an even more basic language. Here is primitive Neoclassicism at its most sophisticated (A)*

no-nonsense feel, yet a type of composite and almost painful allusion to Greek and Roman Antiquity.

Yet even Paestum was not primitive enough for some Neoclassicists. Carl August Ehrensvård (1745–1800) in Sweden, for example, produced a very stumpy version of Doric in some of his designs, that he thought of as 'Egyptian', though they were nothing of the sort. His design for a dockyard gate at Karlskrona of 1785, and his 'Egyptian Architecture in a Nordic Landscape [6.7] are examples of this ultra-primitive Doric. James Playfair (1755–94) used primitive, stumpy, unfluted Doric columns carrying a horizontal slab within a semicircular arch (a sort of primitive-Greek-mullioned form of the Diocletian Window) at Cairness House in Aberdeenshire (1791–97), in which building he also designed an 'Egyptian' billiard room with primitive architraves and bogus hieroglyphs. Of the same period are countless designs mixing pyramids with domes, sphinxes, Greek

6.10 *The Albert Dock Warehouses in Liverpool of 1843–45 by Jesse Hartley (1780–1860). These are among the most Sublime of all nineteenth-century examples of commercial and industrial Architecture, with their cast-iron unfluted primitive Greek Doric columns, massive undecorated brick walls, repetitive elements, and avoidance of ornament, all worthy of Ledoux at his most uncompromising (A)*

6.11 *Newgate Gaol, London, by George Dance, of 1768–85. Here, Sublime Terror is suggested in a grim Architecture that speaks of its purpose (*Architecture Parlante*); the message being one of punishment and retribution, and that prisoners cannot get out (RCHME BB64/359)*

and Roman quotations, and much else [6.8]. The search for the primitive was leading beyond the Orders to an Architecture that was ever older: that was the Architecture of Ancient Egypt. In the last part of the eighteenth century the primitive began suggesting the stripping of all decoration, quotation, and even the Orders from buildings. Architects turned to stereometrically pure forms: the square, the circle, the cube, the sphere, the cylinder, the cone, the pyramid, and the obelisk began to appear, unadorned, in many schemes, notably those of Gilly and Weinbrenner in Germany, Bonomi and Soane in England, Latrobe in the United States, and Boullée, Ledoux, and many young French Architects [6.9]. Sometimes the Piranesian tendency to exaggerate scale occurs in Neoclassical designs, notably in those of

Boullée, while blank walls, primitive shapes, overpowering mass, and dark, cavernous vaults suggest the awe and terror of the Sublime [6.10, 6.11]. Neoclassicism is essentially restrained, and is often somewhat chilly in its imagery and severity. It is characterized by the clarity of the disposition of elements, the way in which junctions are handled, and the rigid definition of the parts of the building. Greek, Egyptian, and Roman elements can sometimes be found in the same compositions.

THE MOVE AWAY FROM NEOCLASSICISM

During the nineteenth century taste gradually moved away from the cold and primitive images of Neoclassicism. There were many great Greek Revival buildings, but the Sublime Terror of George Dance's (1741–1825) Newgate Gaol of 1768–85 [6.11], recalling the *Carceri* designs of Piranesi in its sense of oppression, bare Antiquity, and crushing weight; the chilly purity of Thomas Hamilton's (1784–1858) Greek Doric High School in Edinburgh; and the forbidding masterpieces of William Wilkins's (1778–1839) Grange Park in Hampshire from 1809, and Monck, Gell, and Dobson's Belsay

Hall in Northumberland of 1807–17 [6.12, 6.13] were all strong meat. Although Greek Revival buildings continued to be built, taste perceptibly changed to more opulent and showy styles, prodded, perhaps, by Napoleonic and Regency fashions. It is odd that Roman temples were not revived in their rectangular form until relatively recently, but the reason for this seems to have been the Renaissance models, and especially the Palladian theme, of planting 'temple-fronts' in the form of porticoes on to buildings. Roman temples were first revived in their circular forms. The *Tempietto* of S. Pietro

6.12 (ABOVE) *Belsay Hall, Northumberland; view from the south-east.* *An example of a country house using the severe Greek Doric Order* (RCHME BB78/6768)

6.13 (BELOW) *Staircase hall at Belsay, showing the elegant and manly Greek Revival style* (RCHME BB78/6781)

6.16 *Interior of the Pelham Mausoleum at Brocklesby Park, Lincolnshire, where the Pantheon quotations are more overt in the coffered ceiling and arrangements of recesses for sculpture. In the centre is the statue of Sophia Aufrere carved by Nollekens, but the funerary monuments are Italian, dating from the 1760s (Country Life)*

6.14 *Severe and astylar is Robert Adam's tomb of David Hume in Calton Hill Cemetery, Edinburgh, of 1778. This deceptively 'simple' drum, crowned by a Doric entablature with paterae in the metopes, is based in its form on the drum of the tomb of Caecilia Metella outside Rome, but the entablature is derived from that of the celebrated sarcophagus of Lucius Cornelius Scipio Barbatus (third century BC) (A)*

6.15 *Yet another variation on the circular temple theme occurs in the Pelham Mausoleum at Brocklesby Park in Lincolnshire, designed by James Wyatt, of 1786–94, where the effect is lighter and more elegant than that of Hawksmoor's Castle Howard Mausoleum because of the wider spacing of the fluted Roman Doric columns, and the use of a frieze hung with swags rather than treated with triglyphs and metopes. Wyatt's charming building is an interpretation of the Temples of Vesta at Tivoli and Rome (Country Life)*

6.17 (OPPOSITE) *The Pantheon theme. Belle Isle, Windermere, Westmorland, by John Plaw (c.1745–1820), of 1774–75, a house with an Ionic portico. A much larger version, but with the drum embellished with superimposed Orders, can be found at Ickworth in Suffolk (begun 1796), and another spectacular version was built at Ballyscullion, Co. Londonderry, both on elliptical plans, and both to designs apparently by Francis Sandys. Both Ballyscullion and Ickworth were based on designs by Mario Asprucci (A)*

6.18 *The Mussenden Temple, a Belvedere at Downhill, Co. Londonderry, by Michael Shanahan, a version of a circular Roman temple, built 1783–85 (A)*

6.19 *The Befreiungshalle, near Kelheim, Bavaria, begun by Friedrich von Gärtner in 1836, but completely redesigned by Leo von Klenze from 1844, and completed by him in 1846. It is a rotunda with 18 buttresses on which stand sculptures by Johann Halbig representing the German States. Above is a Doric colonnade of 54 marble columns. The building has a grave, monumental appearance, worthy of a tomb, and indeed it recalls the grander mausolea of Antiquity to mind (A)*

in Montorio in Rome is an early example, and variants, such as the great dome of S. Paul's Cathedral in London, the Panthéon in Paris, the Castle Howard Mausoleum in Yorkshire, the Radcliffe Library in Oxford, and the Barrière Monceau, are all derived from early precedents. The greatest of all Roman circular temples was, of course, the Pantheon itself, but there are numerous instances of eighteenth- and nineteenth-century buildings based on a combination of the *Tempietto* and Pantheon themes [6.14–6.19].

Roman too was the inspiration for the Arc de Triomphe [3.3], begun in 1806 to designs by Chalgrin, but the church of the Madeleine, started in 1804 to designs by Vignon, marks an interesting departure, for this is essentially a Roman rectangular temple [6.20]. The

Roman temple on a high podium reappeared at Birmingham Town Hall [6.22], begun in 1832 to designs by J. A. Hansom (1803–1882), and at Todmorden Town Hall [6.24] of 1860–75, by John Gibson (1817–1892). Grandly Roman, too, are George Basevi's (1794–1845) Fitzwilliam Museum (1836–45) in Cambridge, and many other major Classical buildings of the nineteenth century [6.23]. S. George's Hall in Liverpool, begun in 1841 to designs by H. L. Elmes (1814–1847), combines the temple theme with Graeco-Egyptian elements, while the interior has pure Greek Revival parts, but also grander rooms that are free interpretations of parts of the *Thermae* of Caracalla [6.25, 6.26]. C. R. Cockerell's (1788–1863) University Library at Cambridge, and Ashmolean Museum and Taylorian Institute at Oxford

6.20 *The Roman Temple theme. The church of the Madeleine in Paris (Temple de la Gloire), begun in 1806 to designs by A.-P. Vignon. This grand octastyle Corinthian temple recreates a peripteral version of a Roman temple on its podium. Curiously, although the Orders are associated with Classical temples, the rectangular temple form was not revived until the eighteenth century, and there are several spectacular examples dating from the nineteenth century* (AFK G5428)

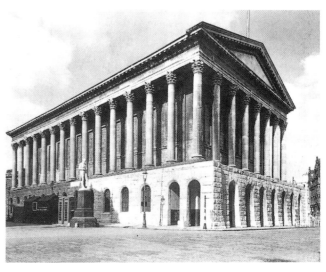

6.22 *The Roman Temple theme: Birmingham Town Hall. An octastyle peripteral temple of the Roman Corinthian Order on a podium, designed by J. A. Hansom (1803–1882) and his partner E. Welch, in 1830–34. It was supervised by Charles Edge from 1836 to 1849. The design is closely based on the Temple of Castor and Pollux in the Roman Forum (AFK H3938)*

6.21 *Detail of the Roman Corinthian Order of the Madeleine in Paris, by A.-P. Vignon. Note the modillions, coffers, and elaborate frieze (A)*

6.23 *The Roman Temple theme. The National Gallery building, Berlin, in the form of a Roman Corinthian temple on a high podium, with prostyle octastyle portico, designed by Friedrich August Stüler (1800–1865), who had been a principal assistant of Schinkel from 1827. The building is based on a plan devised by King Friedrich Wilhelm IV of Prussia, and the structure was erected by Johann Heinrich Strack (1805–1880) in 1866–76. The basic idea of the building is related to Gilly's proposed monument to Frederick the Great (A)*

6.24 (ABOVE) *The Roman Temple theme: Todmorden Town Hall of 1860–75 by John Gibson (1817–1892), who had been a pupil of J. A. Hansom in Birmingham. The very festive Corinthian Order is engaged and set on a podium (A)*

6.25 (BELOW) *S. George's Hall, Liverpool, from 1839. Severely Neoclassical from the outside, with its Roman temple front, long rows of columns (some square on plan), the building is grandly opulent inside (RCHME CC73/2985)*

6.26 *Interior of S. George's Hall, Liverpool, showing the pronounced Roman influence based on the* Thermae of Caracalla. *In spite of its allusions to Antiquity, the interior is more exuberant than the relatively severe exterior, and signals a Victorian taste for greater opulence than the sparse, cold language of Neoclassicism could offer* (RCHME BB/2849)

both employ the Antique Greek Ionic Order from Bassae mixed with arcuated elements [2.21].

In the 1820s, '30s, and '40s Charles Barry (1795–1860) introduced an astylar Italian *palazzo* style with his Travellers' (1830–32) and Reform (1838–41) Clubs and Bridgewater House (1846–51); this style was used on a great many buildings, including London Bridge Railway terminus (1841–44) by Henry Roberts (1803–1876), and the Headquarters of the Belfast Bank (1845) by Sir Charles Lanyon (1813–1889) [4.26]. A revival of interest in opulence as an antidote, perhaps, to the austerities of Neoclassicism, led, not surprisingly, to renewed studies of Italian Renaissance Architecture. The Barry *palazzo* style was one aspect, but even those chaste façades, capped by a *cornicione* and with aediculated windows, proved to be rather understated. Soon the Venetian verve of Sansovino at S. Mark's Library was being quoted in a number of instances, including Sydney Smirke's (1798–1877) Carlton Club [6.27] in Pall Mall of 1854–6, and Parnell and Smith's Army and Navy Club in Pall Mall of 1848–51. That is not to say the Italianate style did not continue for many years in the stucco-faced terraces of Kensington, prompted no doubt by Osborne House (1845–53) by Thomas Cubitt and the Prince Consort [6.28]. Sixteenth-century Italian styles mingled with seventeenth-century French motifs appear in Scott's Foreign Office of 1868–73, while Roman Baroque was revived at Brompton Oratory.

6.27 (ABOVE) *A variation on the Sansovino theme. The Carlton Club, Pall Mall, London, by Sydney Smirke, of 1854–56, closely modelled on the Library of San Marco in Venice (RCHME BB85/3068)*

6.28 (BELOW) *Osborne House, Isle of Wight, of 1845–51, a palace in the Italianate style, designed by Thomas Cubitt (1788–1855) and Prince Albert (1819–1861). Note the campanile-like towers, the Barryesque aedicules, and the arcading on the right based on Palladio's Basilica at Vicenza (RCHME BB452/772)*

6.29 (ABOVE) *Chelsea Town Hall of 1885–87, by J. McK. Brydon, in a Free Classical style ('Wrenaissance') influenced by the work of Wren* (A)

6.30 (BELOW) *Municipal Chambers, Glasgow, by William Young, of 1883–88. An opulent pile of French, Flemish, Venetian, and Spanish Renaissance styles* (RCAHMS GW/1890)

6.31 *William Young's New (now Old) War Office in Whitehall, London, of 1898–1906, a mixture of Palladian, Mannerist, and Baroque features (RCHME CC73/2589)*

6.32 *Stockport Town Hall (1904–08) by Sir Alfred Brumwell Thomas, an essay in Edwardian Baroque (Batsford)*

In Scotland the Classical tradition was still strong: there were Alexander Thomson (1817–1875) in Glasgow (mixing Graeco-Egyptian elements with liberal quotations from Schinkel [2.29]), the Hamiltons, Playfair, Sellars, and other robust Classicists. And it was Classicism that was to be brought south from Scotland by people like R. Norman Shaw (1831–1912), John Brydon (1840–1901), William Young (1843–1900), and J. J. Burnet (1857–1938). Baroque elements appear on Shaw's New Scotland Yard (1887–90) mixed with themes from Loire Châteaux, but with Brydon's Chelsea Town Hall (1885) [6.29] and his Government offices at Whitehall (1898) architectural devices, strongly influenced by Wren, were revived. Young's City Chambers in Glasgow (1883) [6.30] quoted from Sanmichele and Sansovino, among other sources, but at the War Office in Whitehall of 1898 [6.31] he used Palladian, Mannerist, and Anglo-French quotations, with a strong hint of Wren.

By the turn of the century the Baroque Revival was in full swing in the hands of Architects such as John Belcher (1841–1913) and Sir Alfred Brumwell Thomas (1868–1948). Yet even as early as 1866 Joseph Poelaert, in his Palais de Justice in Brussels, created a mighty pile of Baroque compositions, and Cuthbert Brodrick (1822–

1905) in his Leeds Town Hall of 1853–9 mixed Roman, Italianate, French, and English Baroque themes.

There were Baroque revivals in Germany, Austria, France, and the United States. Berlin's Cathedral by Raschdorff, the New Hofburg in Vienna, the Paris Opéra, and the Capitol in Washington all show distinctly Baroque tendencies, but in England the Baroque Revival was closely associated with an interest in the work of Wren, giving it the rather awful name of the Wrenaissance. Wren quotations can be found in Brumwell Thomas's Belfast City Hall (1899–1906), his Stockport Town Hall [6.32], and at Belcher's Ashton Memorial (1906) near Lancaster, to name but three great examples of late-Victorian and Edwardian Baroque.

As had been the case in the eighteenth century, there was a reaction against this florid and theatrical style. Neoclassicism emerged in various guises. J. J. Burnet's extension to the British Museum (1905–14), using an engaged Ionic Order, consciously rejects Laugier's (and Smirke's) insistence on the detached column, and mixes in some judicious battered Egyptianisms with his modern Greek. Scotland's loyalty to Classicism enabled Scottish Architects such as Burnet, Norman Shaw, William Young, and John McK. Brydon to bring that style south to England when the time was ripe, towards the end of the nineteenth century. Sir Edwin Lutyens (1869–1944) also used the Wren style (the so-called 'Wrenaissance') at the offices of *Country Life* in Tavistock Street, Covent Garden, of 1904, directly quoting from Hampton Court Palace. At Heathcote (1906), near Ilkley in Yorkshire, Lutyens produced a Palladian Baroque villa in which he also drew on Sanmichele, Vignola, Wren, Vanbrugh, and Hawksmoor for this essay in the 'High Game'. But after Burnet's extension to the British Museum, a more austere Classicism found favour, notably in Smith and Brewer's National Museum of Wales of 1910, Swales, Atkinson, Burnet, and Burnham's Selfridge's in Oxford Street of 1908–9 [6.33], and Burnet's own Kodak House, Kingsway, of 1911, which eschewed the Orders altogether and, with its coved Egyptianesque cornice, seems to be using the same stripped language of Perret and others on the Continent [6.34].

Peter Behrens, in the office block for the AEG in Berlin (1908–10), used a stripped Classical style, while Henry Bacon built a plain rectangular box surrounded by a chaste peristyle of purist Greek Doric for his Lincoln Memorial in Washington (1911–12). Very different was the work of Auguste Perret in France: it often uses Classical proportion, and suggests a Classical arrangement without overt quotation. Behrens, Perret, and some of their contemporaries *paraphrased* Classical elements, but their

6.33 *Selfridge's in Oxford Street, London, 1908–09. Photograph by Barnet Saidman (Batsford)*

6.34 *Kodak House, Kingsway, London, by John James Burnet (1857–1938). Designed in 1911, and built the following year, Kodak House admits to its steel frame, but it is still Classical. There is a two-storey podium on which sits a Giant Order, but it is an Order with a base and no capitals. This capital-less language was used by the Ancient Egyptians (as at the mortuary temple of Queen Hatshepsut), and the Egyptian theme is further pursued in the coved cornice. The attic storey is not original, but works well (Duckworth & Co. Ltd., 2974–363)*

work is Classical nevertheless. Stripped Neoclassicism recurs in the work of J. C. C. Petersen and I. Bentsen in 1919 for proposals in Copenhagen, and also in J. F. M. Hoffmann's Austrian Pavilion and Behrens's Festival Hall, both at the Cologne Werkbund Exhibition of 1914.

With I. J. Tengbom's Concert Hall in Stockholm (1923–6) comes a tendency to interpret and elongate the Orders, something that occurs in the work of several Architects of the era. This can also be seen in P. L. Troost's Haus der Kunst (1933–7) in Munich [2.26], a primitivist Neoclassicism that was matched by several German Architects in the 1920s and '30s. A concern for the simple purity of form re-emerges at A. V. Shchusev's Lenin Mausoleum in Moscow, which is very Egyptian in its inspiration, and in K. Fisker's Danish Pavilion at the 1925 Paris International Exposition. Sigurd Lewerentz, in his designs for funerary buildings (Malmö, 1926, and Enskede, 1922–5, for example), exploited both the

Orders, blank walls, and stereometrically pure forms to create a dignified and solemn Architecture. E. G. Asplund, too, interpreted Classical Architecture, and during the 1920s and '30s Classicism was pre-eminent in Scandinavia.

Speer, Kreis, and others looked to Schinkel and von Klenze as well as to Roman Antiquity (the Pantheon and triumphal arches in Rome, both inflated to Boullée-esque scales). Vast buildings designed within a Classical system were not confined to National Socialist Germany, but were erected in quantities in various Eastern European countries, in the post-War era, under Stalin and his associates. Even Communist China adopted an official Architecture that owes not a little to European Classicism and Neoclassicism, and examples were still being erected in the 1970s (e.g. the Memorial Hall of Chairman Mao in Beijing, which although hardly subtle or refined, betrays its origins).

VII

EPILOGUE

Now . . . it has become the fashion to declare the Modern Movement dead . . . there may be, once again, some point in discussing architectural language. . . . From such speculations the classical language of architecture will never be far absent. The understanding of it will surely remain one of the most potent elements in architectural thought.

SIR JOHN SUMMERSON (1904–1992): *The Classical Language of Architecture.*
London, 1988, p. 114.

Looking back on the twentieth century from its last decade, it is difficult to enthuse about the vast majority of buildings erected in Britain since the Second World War. In spite of the polemics and claims for the so-called Modern Movement as *the* style (or non-style) of the era, there were very few examples of it until after 1945. At the beginning of the century the Baroque Revival was in full swing, but a more severe Neoclassical manner, sometimes stripped of all but the most elemental mouldings, emerged before 1914, and continued after 1918. Classicism, in one guise or another, was undoubtedly the most significant architectural language in Europe and America, and where there were Western influences, until 1945. The single most devastating blow given to the acceptability of Classical Architecture was the fact that Classicism was favoured in the Third Reich, that Adolf Hitler himself was deeply interested in it, and that talented Architects in Germany (such as Troost, Kreis, and Speer) produced many remarkable designs under the aegis of the Führer.

This association was almost fatal to Classicism, in spite of the fact that there were very distinguished Classical buildings designed during the inter-War years in the Scandinavian democracies (by Lewerentz, Asplund, Aalto, Rafn, Petersen, Bentsen, and many others),[1] in France (the Palais de Chaillot is only one example), in the United States, and in countries untainted by 'National Socialism'. The Hitler connection gave the Modernists a weapon which they did not fail to use. A curious aspect of this dismal and dishonest affair is that since Classicism was the favoured style of many democracies in the 1920s and 1930s, why can it not, therefore, be 'Democratic' rather than 'Fascist'? Even more peculiar is the fact that Lenin's Mausoleum in Moscow of 1924–30 (by Alexei Shchusev) is in the most severe stripped and impeccable Neoclassical manner, worthy of a Gilly or a Ledoux in their most 'primitive' moods; in fact the building owes much to the square-columned arrangement of Egyptian temples, so it belongs firmly in the Neoclassical canon. Classicism was also the dominant architectural language of the Stalinist era throughout Eastern Europe after 1945: the former *Stalinallee* in Berlin, and similar developments in Magdeburg, Dresden, and throughout the Soviet Union and its satellites all suggest (if the association with Hitler and Classicism is used to damn that language) that Classical Architecture can also be a style associated with

7.1 *Thiepval Memorial on the Somme (1927–32), by Sir Edwin Lutyens, showing the transformation of the triumphal Arch so that the subordinate sides become triumphal arches themselves. Monumental blocky masses make this one of the most Sublime memorials ever created: it is a brilliant variation on the simple two-axis arch* (Commonwealth War Graves Commission)

the extreme left, that is Soviet Communism and centralised Socialism. Those who promoted the Modern Movement in the post-1945 era cannot have it both ways: they cannot condemn a language for its association with Hitler on the grounds that it is 'right-wing' if it is also a language widely used by *both* Western democracies *and* Stalinist régimes in Eastern Europe. Unbelievably, in Britain during the 1900s and early 2000s, commentators are still equating Classicism with Naziism, particularly in the 'debate' (if it may be so called) over HRH the Prince of Wales's intervention in architectural matters, and his apparent championing of Classical and traditional forms. Charity restrains a naming of those 'professionals' and 'critics' who have adopted such ludicrous poses.

In recent years various labels have been attached to certain architectural trends, including 'Post-Modernism' and the 'Classical Revival', but it seems increasingly improbable that anything that can be called Classical Architecture is being realised; indeed, it is debatable

if there is any real Architecture being conceived and built at all. Much of the 'Classical' stuff is anything but Classical, and owes more to the fairground, to commercial vulgarity, or to the 'Modern Movement' with a few illiterate nods to Classicism stuck on. One of the most worrying things of all is that much of the new 'Classicism' consists, in fact, of applied motifs from pattern books on façades that are unrelated to what is happening behind; rooms uneasily placed behind fenestration that would be unacceptable to any real Classicist; and a sense of buildings becoming skin-deep, with badly proportioned and uncomfortably designed spaces behind hesitant sub-Palladian-Revival or indifferently understood Georgian elevations. This is a sorry state of affairs, and has nothing to do with real Classicism.[2]

Neoclassical Architecture in the late-eighteenth and early-nineteenth centuries was infinitely varied, often brilliant, frequently stripped to its bare minimum, and usually displayed a scholarly notion of proportion, detail, and composition. Twentieth-century Classicism, especially in Scandinavia, Germany, Austria, France, and the United States, often explored further the ideas of simplicity and stripped Architecture which the Neoclassicists of the period 1770 to 1830 had developed. Wagner, Loos, Behrens, Kreis, and others were actually building in an earlier tradition, while in Britain, Architects such as Reginald Blomfield (1856–1942) (with his Menin Gate at Ieper); Lutyens (with his Sublime memorial at Thiepval [7.1]); Sir John Burnet (with his splendidly assured extension to the British Museum); and Thomas S. Tait of John Burnet, Tait, & Lorne (with his masterly S. Andrew's House at Calton Hill in Edinburgh, of 1936–9) demonstrated that the language of Classicism was very much alive, offered an enormous vocabulary, and could be explored to marvellous effect in the hands of competent and imaginative designers. Compared with the feeble and unarchitectonic use of applied decoration which passed as Classicism in the 1990s, the achievements of those early twentieth-century masters are all the more worthy of our respect.

The purpose of this book, then, is to attempt to provide an introduction to Classical Architecture, with definitions of terms, illustrations, and a brief narrative of its most significant features, in order to help to foster an understanding of the vocabulary and language of such Architecture.

---

1. *See* Paavilainen, Simo, *Nordic Classicism 1910–1930* (Museum of Finnish Architecture, Helsinki, 1982).

2. There are honourable exceptions. Robert A. M. Stern, Julian Bicknell, John Simpson, Robert Adam, Demetri Porphyrios, and a few others, on both sides of the Atlantic, are designing buildings that draw on the Classical tradition, and Quinlan Terry has added a Greek Revival library to Wilkins's Downing College, Cambridge (1989–93). Perhaps the most extraordinary (and polychrome) buildings in which Classicism plays a part are those inventions of John Outram, including the Judge Institute of Management Studies, Cambridge (1993–5).

GLOSSARY

There are numbers of architects who can reproduce the beauties of antiquity . . . but where is the one who . . . can produce a work answering its purpose, and suitable to place and period, in the same manner and with the same freedom as did the architects of old when they produced the works which are still the marvel of the world? These architects were familiar with the alphabet and grammar of Architecture. Ours of today, ignorant of the first principles . . . collect and collate the choicest bits . . ., glue them together and imagine they have made a whole. In fact, our buildings are but mere odds and ends brought together . . . generally without care. At the best, this is not architecture; at the worst, it is charlatanism.

EDWARD WELBY PUGIN (1834–1875): Letter in *The Times*, 19 December 1871.

Illustrations by the author unless indicated otherwise.

AARONS ROD   A staff entwined with leaves, or a rod with a serpent coiled around it. The **caduceus** [Fig. 1].

Fig. 1 *Aaron's Rod (if unwinged), or Caduceus (if winged)*

ABACISCUS   Synonymous with **abacus**, but more usually a square compartment enclosing part of a design or the whole of a **mosaic pavement**.

ABACUS (pl. **ABACI**)   The slab at the top of a **capital**, crowning the **column**, and supporting the **entablature**. Vitruvius confined the term to Ionic and Corinthian capitals, and called the **Doric** abacus **plinthus**, which indeed corresponds to the plinth-block under many later column-bases of other Orders. The **Tuscan** abacus, in the versions of Palladio and Serlio, is square on plan with flat, plain, unmoulded sides, but in the versions of Scamozzi and Vignola has a plain crowning **fillet** with **cavetto** moulding under it. The Greek Doric abacus is a simple square block, unmoulded and unchamfered, but the Roman Doric version, while also square on plan, has plain sides surmounted by a **cyma reversa** moulding (plain or enriched) over which is a fillet. The Greek Ionic **abacus** is much thinner than the Doric or Tuscan, with an **ovolo** edge sometimes enriched, sometimes plain: in some cases (Temple of Apollo Epicurius at Bassae) it is deeper, with concave sides on plan; usually, however, it has straight sides, although, in the case of corner capitals with volutes at forty-five degrees, it follows the plan shape of the capital. Roman Ionic abaci usually have fillets over cyma reversa mouldings (the latter plain or enriched), although the ovolo-fillet-cavetto section also occurs. Usually the **Corinthian** and **Composite** abacus (both Greek and

Roman) has four concave faces, segmental on plan, joining in points or, more often, chamfered where the concave sides meet. The four-concave-sided abacus on plan is also found in the Roman Ionic Order where there are eight volutes present instead of the usual four. In the centres of each of the four faces of the Corinthian abacus is a floral or other ornament, and the vertical section consists of ovolo, fillet, and cavetto moulding, plain or ornamented. In the Tower of the Winds, Athens, also known as the Horologium of Andronikos Cyrrhestes, the capitals have one row of **acanthus** leaves and a row of pointed forms resembling palm-leaves: the abacus is, unusually for the Corinthian type, square on plan, although in vertical section it still has the ovolo, fillet, and cavetto moulds (*see* **Orders** and under the names of **Orders**). [2.1–2.13, 2.15–2.34, 2.36–2.41, 2.43–2.57, 2.60–2.62].

ABUTMENT   The solid part of a pier from which an arch springs, or the extremities of a bridge. Abutments must be strong enough to resist the natural tendency of an arch or an arcade to collapse by opening outwards. Any solid structure which receives the thrust of an arch or vault [Fig. 9].

ACANTHUS   A genus of herbaceous plants, especially the species **Acanthus spinosus**, Bear's Breech, or Brank-Ursine, native to the shores of the Mediterranean, and prized among the Greeks and Romans for the elegance of its leaves. A stylized version of the thick leaf of this spiny plant, said to have been modelled first by Callimachus, is used to decorate the lower part of capitals of the Corinthian and Composite Orders but the disposition of the leaves is different for each of these Orders. The acanthus is also found as a decorative feature elsewhere in Classical Architecture. In some instances (the Arches of Titus and Septimius Severus in Rome, for example), the leaves of the Composite Order resemble parsley, while those of the Temple of Vesta in Rome look more like the leaves of the laurel. The acanthus seems to have been used in important Architecture for the first time on the **acroteria** of the Parthenon and in the decoration of the Erechtheion [2.20, 2.30–2.32, 2.51–2.57, 2.59–2.62, 2.65].

ACHIEVEMENT   Representation of Armorial ensigns, etc.

ACORN   With fir cones and pineapples, a common pendant or terminal, usually on gate-piers [Fig. 2].

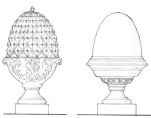

Fig. 2 *Acorn (right) and pine-cone (left) both as finials or terminating features*

ACROTERIA   Pedestals or plinths at the apex and lower extremities of pediments: they can support statuary or ornaments or can be quite unadorned. **Acroteria** or **acroters** can also refer, incorrectly, to the statues or ornaments on the plinths, while the singular (**acroterium, acroterion**), is applied to the ridge of a building, and is also erroneously used to describe the pieces of wall between pedestals and balusters. **Acroterium** can be interchangeable with **fastigium** in the sense of the blocks [2.1, Fig. 27].

ADYTON, ADYTUM   An inner sanctuary, or holy of holies. An inner room of a temple.

AEDICULE   An opening or niche framed by two columns or pilasters carrying an entablature and pediment (segmental or triangular). A niche framed in such a manner is said to be **aediculated** [Figs. 3, 4].

AEGIS   A shield or breast-plate.

AEGICRANE   Head or skull of ram or goat, usually associated with festoons or swags like a **bucranium** [Fig. 17].

AEOLIC   An early form of the Ionic capital: it has an elongated **abacus** carried on two volutes with palmettes filling the gap between them [2.14].

AETOMA, AETOS   The **tympanum** of a pediment.

AGORA   An open space in a Greek city which doubled as market-place and general rendezvous: it was often surrounded by colonnades.

AISLE   Lateral portions of a basilican building parallel to the nave, choir, and chancel, and separated from the central portion of the building by **arcades** or **colonnades** carrying the clerestory. Aisles are usually lower than the central, main body of the edifice (*see* **basilica** [4.42, 4.43]).

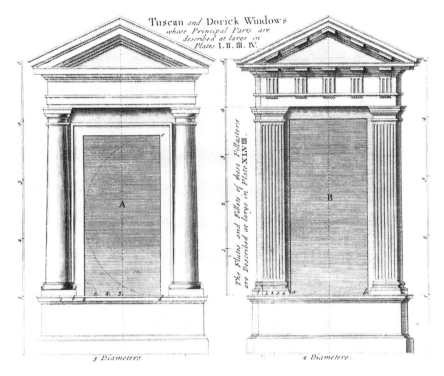

Fig. 3 *Tuscan and 'Dorick' aedicules. Note that the Doric version has pilasters instead of columns, and the mutules are emphasized in the manner of Vignola. Both aedicules rest on podia or pedestals. From Langley*

Fig. 4 *'Ionick' and Corinthian aedicules. The Ionic version has a pulvinated frieze and triangular pediment, while the Corinthian has a segmental pediment. Both examples have plain modillions, and both are set on pedestals or podia. From Langley*

ALA (pl. **ALAE**)   **Cellae** on either side of the central **cella** of a Tuscan temple, so that there were one large central and two smaller compartments set behind a portico [3.1].

ALBARIUM   **Opus albarium** or **tectorium** was a coating applied to sun-dried brick, coarse stone, or other rough walls. The finest stucco was made of powdered marble.

ALCOVE   A large niche or an ornamental building in a garden, usually with a seat.

ALTAR   An elevated table on which to place or sacrifice offerings to deities.

ALTAR TOMB   A tomb-chest or memorial resembling an altar on which there are often recumbent effigies.

AMBITUS   A space round a tomb, or a **loculus** for a body, or recess for an urn: it was often decorated and sealed in.

AMBO   An elevated lectern or pulpit.

AMMONITE ORDER   A variety of Ionic in which the capital volutes are modelled on a fossil genus of Cephalopods, consisting of whorled chambered shells, also called snake-stones. The Order is peculiarly English, and many examples occur in Brighton and in South London [Fig. 5].

Fig. 5 *Ammonite Order. An example of c.1825 from the Old Kent Road, London, made of stucco*

AMORINO (pl. **AMORINI**)   Alternative term for Cupid.

AMPHI-PROSTYLE A Classical building with a prostyle portico at each end and no columns along the sides. In compounds such as amphi-prostyle or amphidistyle the **amphi** means that the same architectural features are used at the front and back [Fig. 65].

AMPHITHEATRE A Classical Greek theatre was semi-circular on plan, with concentric rings of seats rising steeply from the stage. An amphitheatre was elliptical on plan (like the Colosseum in Rome), and was essentially two theatres with the stages joined together to form an arena or pit. Amphitheatres had no Greek precedents.

ANACTORON A sacred building or a sacred part of a building, used chiefly in connection with the Mysteries (various kinds of secret worship in Classical Antiquity which rested on the belief that, besides the general modes of honouring the deities, there was another, revealed only to the select few, or initiates). A hall.

ANATHYROSIS A system of close fitting of the drums of a column at the edges only. Within the edge-ring was a rough surface, then a shallow circular depression with a deep hole in the centre for the reception of the **empolia**, or wooden blocks which contained the **poloi**, or timber dowels that connected the drums. Anathyrosis was also employed in the vertical and horizontal joints of the stones of which walls were built.

ANCHOR An ornament like an arrow-head, used with an egg design to enrich mouldings: it is also known as a dart [2.20, 3.11 and illustrations of the **Orders**]. An anchor is also a symbol of Hope, as a disguised form of the Cross. An anchor fouled with rope is a symbol of death.

ANCON (pl. **ANCONES**) The console ornament cut on the keystone of an arch, and supporting a bust or other feature. As a feature of a keystone the ancon is wedge-shaped, that is narrower at the bottom than at the top. The term is also used to denote a **truss**, **console**, **shouldering piece**, or **crossette** employed in the dressings or **antepagmenta** of apertures, serving as an apparent support to the cornice above at the topmost corners of the apertures. In this sense, an Antique ancon was often not in contact with the flanks of the **architrave**, but placed at a small distance from them, and was frequently wider at

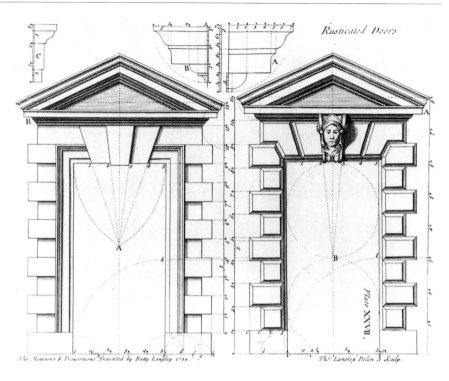

Fig. 6 *Rusticated doorways. Note the ancon on the right used as a keystone, and the fact that it tapers. From Langley*

the top than at the bottom, like an ancon on a **keystone**: indeed the term ancon seems most properly to apply to this tapering type of form, as opposed to a **crossette** *or* **console**, which has parallel sides. Vitruvius called ancones **prothyrides**. An ancon is also the corner of a quoin of a wall [Figs. 6, 23, 24, 52, 55, 62].

ANDRON An apartment reserved for men, especially a dining-room, in a Greek house.

ANGLE CAPITAL In the **Ionic Order**, the corner capitals often have the corner volutes 'pulled out' at an angle of 135 degrees with the planes of the front and returning entablatures [2.16, 2.17, 2.21].

ANGLE MODILLION A modillion at the mitring of a cornice, generally regarded as an abuse of true Classical detail, and therefore to be avoided.

ANGOULÊME SPRIG The barbeau (cornflower).

ANNULET A small flat **fillet** encircling a column. It is used under the **echinus** of a Doric capital several times, and is also called a **shaft ring**. The term has also been applied to the fillets separating **flutes** in columns, and is also called a **list** or **listella** [Fig. 26].

ANTA A species of pilaster used in Classical Architecture to terminate the side walls of temples. The anta capital (and usually the base) differs from the capitals of the columns with which it is associated. When the **pronaos** or **porch** in front of the **cell** is formed by the projection of the walls terminated by **antae** with columns between the antae, the portico is said to be **in antis**: the columns in an in antis arrangement, therefore, do not stand in front of the outer face of the antae. A jamb (*see* **Orders**, [Figs. 26, 65]).

ANTEFIX An ornamental vertical element fixed at regular intervals above the cornice of a Classical building at the lower edge of the roof to cover the ends of the **harmi** or joint-tiles. Antefixa are usually ornamented with the **anthemion** or other motifs. The term is also sometimes given to ornamental heads below the eaves through the mouths of which water is cast away [2.1, Fig. 27] (*see* **Orders**).

ANTEPAGMENTA Moulded **architraves** around an opening. More accurately the antepagmenta are the jambs of a door- or window-opening, moulded like an architrave, while the top part of the architrave (or **lintel**), returning at the ends (with similar mouldings to those of the jambs) down upon the antepagmenta, is called the **supercilium**. The singular is **antepagment** or **antepagmentum**. An antepagmentum can also mean an **anta** or a **pilaster** [Figs. 11, 23, 62].

ANTHEMION The honeysuckle or **palmette** ornament found above **acroteria**, in **cornices**, on **antefixa**, on the neckings of some Ionic capitals, and elsewhere in Classical Architecture [Fig. 7].

Fig. 7 *Anthemion and palmette*

ANTICK **Grotesque** ornament.

ANTIQUITY The word refers to the Classical civilizations of the Graeco-Roman world.

ANTITHEMA The backing of steps, architrave, and frieze, usually separate blocks from those of the front.

APODYTERIUM A dressing-room, especially in baths.

APOLLINE DECORATION Male head surrounded by sunrays, or the Sunburst [Fig. 61]. Male figure with lyre or chariot. Associated with Versailles.

APOPHYGE The curve given to the top and bottom of the shaft of a column where it expands to meet the edge of the fillet above the base and beneath the **astragal** under the capital: it is also known as the **apothesis** and the **apophysis** [2.22].

APPLIED COLUMN An **engaged column**: one attached to a wall.

APRON Panel below a window-sill, plain or ornamented.

APSE The semicircular or polygonal recess usually found at the end of the nave of a basilican building. Apses are frequently covered with a half-dome. The term **apsidal** means shaped like an apse. An **apsidiole** is a subsidiary apse. An apse is also called an **apsis** (*see* **basilica**).

APTERAL A Classical building of a temple form without columns at the sides.

ARABESQUE Capricious ornament found in Classical Architecture, usually involving the combination of flowing lines of branches, leaves, and scroll-work, fancifully intertwined. It does not contain human or animal figures, and it is therefore not to be confused with **Grotesque** ornament [Fig. 8, 5.37].

Fig. 8 *Arabesque*

ARAEOSTYLE A wide spacing of columns (three-and-a-half diameters or more, up to five diameters), usually only appropriate to the **Tuscan Order**, but occasionally found in Hellenistic architecture.

ARCADE A range of arches carried on piers, pilasters, or columns, either freestanding [2.11] or attached to a wall to form a decorative rhythmic pattern: in the latter case it is referred to as a **blind arcade**. The term is applied to the arches on piers or columns that divide a nave from an aisle, in which case it is called a **nave arcade**.

ARCH A construction of blocks of material disposed in a curve or curves, and supporting one another by mutual pressure: an arch so formed over an opening is capable of carrying a superimposed weight. Each block is called a **voussoir** (usually in the shape of a truncated wedge), and the block in the centre is called the **keystone**. The solid extremities on or against which the arch rests are called **abutments**. The lower or under curve of each stone is called the **intrados**, and the upper curve the **extrados**. The distance between the piers

or abutments is the **span** of the arch, and the vertical distance between the level line of the **springing** to the intrados is the **height** of the arch. The springing or **impost** is the point at which an arch unites with its support. The simplest arches are the **semicircular** and **segmental** arches, the former with its centre on the springing line and the latter with its centre below the springing line. A **relieving** or **discharging arch** is one built into a wall to transfer the load of a wall from a lintel [Fig. 9].

ARCHITRAVE The lowest of the divisions of an **entablature** that rests directly on the **abaci** of columns. Architraves in the Doric Order are plain, but in the more elaborate Orders are often divided into three **fasciae**. In their simplest form the architraves as structural beams resting on columns are called **trabes compactiles**. The term also refers to the lintels, jambs, and mouldings surrounding a window, door, panel, or niche. It can also be applied to the ornamental mouldings round the exterior curve of an arch. (*see* **Orders**, [Figs. 11, 26, 2.37]).

ARCHITRAVE CORNICE An **entablature** with no frieze.

ARCHIVOLT A group of concentric mouldings around a Classical arch: an **architrave** that is curved to frame an arched opening. It is not to be confused with the **soffite** of an arch (*see* **Arch** [Fig. 9]).

ARCUATED A system of construction based on the **arch** rather than on columns and beams.

ARENA The central elliptical part of an amphitheatre.

ARRIS A sharp edge at the junction of two surfaces, e.g. the **flutes** of a Greek Doric column meeting in a sharp **arris** [Fig. 26].

ARROW Found, with quiver, in trophies, or associated with Cupid. A jagged arrow is an attribute of Jupiter, associated with thunder and lightning.

ARTISAN MANNERISM The use of Classical motifs in a way not like their original disposition, evolved by craftsmen rather than Architects.

ASHLAR Cut stone worked to even faces and right-angled **arrises**, laid on horizontal courses with vertical joints. When the resulting façade is smooth and

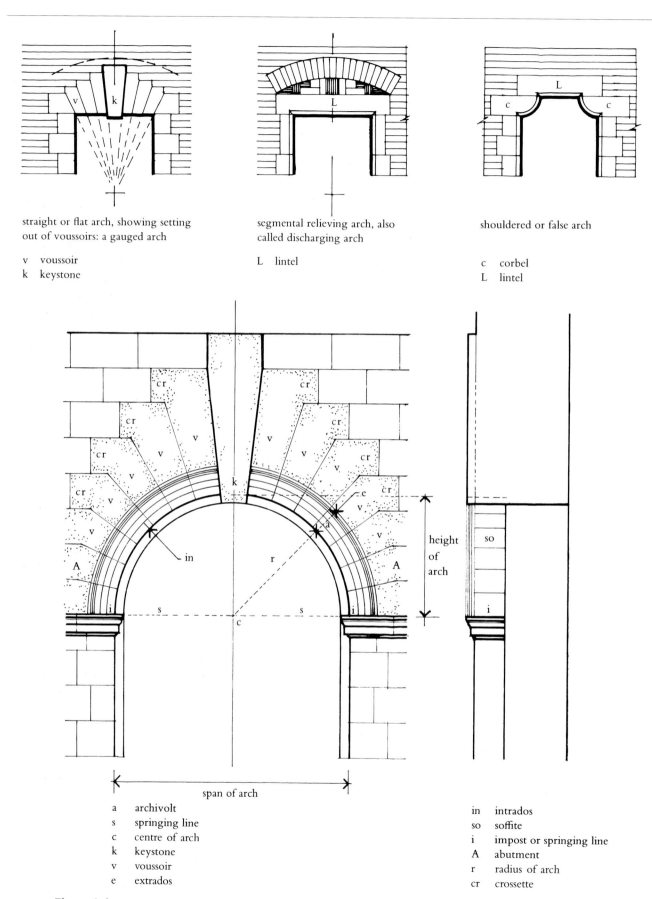

straight or flat arch, showing setting
out of voussoirs: a gauged arch

v   voussoir
k   keystone

segmental relieving arch, also
called discharging arch

L   lintel

shouldered or false arch

c   corbel
L   lintel

span of arch

a   archivolt
s   springing line
c   centre of arch
k   keystone
v   voussoir
e   extrados

in   intrados
so   soffite
i   impost or springing line
A   abutment
r   radius of arch
cr   crossette

Fig. 9 *Arches*

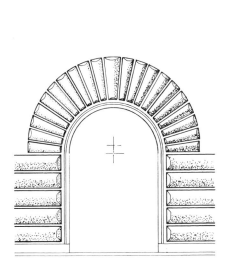

Fig. 10 *Florentine arch*

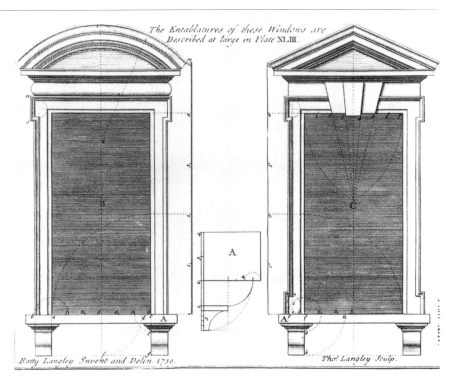

The Entablatures of these Windows are Described at large in Plate XLIII.

Batty Langley Invent and Delin. 1750.

Tho? Langley Sculp.

Fig. 11 *Window surrounds. Both have eared architraves. That on the left has a segmental pediment and a pulvinated frieze, and both sills are carried on brackets. From Langley*

finished finely, it is called **plain ashlar**; when the surface is cut regularly, with parallel incisions like miniature flutes, it is called **tooled ashlar**. Other finishes are **random tooling**, or irregular texturing using a broad implement; **chiselling** or **boasting**, created with a fine, narrow tool; and **pointed**, if the surface is finished with a very fine narrow tool. When the face of ashlar projects beyond the joints the finish is known as **rustication**. The Romans called ashlar **opus quadratum**, from the regular squared forms of the blocks (*see* **rustication** [Figs. 53, 54]).

Fig. 12 *Asiatic base (Ionic)*

ASIATIC BASE   An Ionic base developed in Asia Minor and consisting of a lower drum decorated with horizontal reeding, usually two scotias with separating astragals, and an upper **torus** decorated with reeds [Fig. 12].

ASSER (pl. **ASSERES**)   **Trabiculae** are the main beams resting on the **mutuli** of a temple. On top of the trabiculae are the **asseres** laid over the main beams and spanning over them at right angles.

ASTRAGAL   A small moulding with a semicircular profile, a bead, sometimes called a **roundel** or a baguette. It is found as a ring separating the capital from the shaft of a Classical column, and may be ornamented. It can also be the bead that separates the **fasciae** of **architraves**, and in such a position is usually ornamented with **bead-and-reel**. The name, meaning 'knucklebones', however, implies enrichment with bead-and-reel (*see* **Orders**).

ASTYLAR   Without columns or pilasters.

ATLANTES, ATLANTIDES   Heroic male figures or half-figures supporting a structure, and usually shown straining against a weight. **Telamon** appears to have been an alternative name for **Atlas**, and so **atlantes** are also termed **telamons** or **telamones**, but these are usually straight male figures used instead of columns, and not shown in an attitude of vigorous struggle (*see* **canephorae**, **caryatides**, **telamones**).

ATRIUM   An open court surrounded by a colonnaded covered walk, found in Roman domestic Architecture and in front of Early Christian churches. The open garth received light and rainwater, the latter collected in a cistern [4.43].

ATTACHED COLUMN   Engaged column.

ATTIC   The **storey** over the main **entablature**, not to be confused with a garret. An **attic storey** is closely related to the architectural arrangement below the entablature (as in a **triumphal arch**) [2.68], and if it contains accommodation it has ceilings square with the side walls, and is quite distinct from a roof-space.

ATTIC BASE   The base of a Classical column consisting of two **torus** mouldings separated by a **scotia** with **fillets** (i.e. two large convex rings between which is a concave moulding). This is found with all Orders except the Greek Doric and the Tuscan (*see* **Orders** [Fig. 51]).

ATTIC ORDER   An Order of low pilasters placed over some other Order of columns or pilasters.

ATTRIBUTES   Motifs associated with mythological, saintly, or legendary figures. Club equals Hercules, Trident equals Neptune, Spear equals Pallas, wheel equals S. Catherine, etc.

BACCHIC ORNAMENT   Decoration featuring vines, panthers, dolphins, rams, Maenades, and Thyiades, and much drunken revelry.

BALCONY   A platform projecting from the surface of a wall of a building carried on brackets, consoles, or columns, or cantilevered. It is usually placed before windows or openings, and is protected by a railing or a balustrade.

BALDACCHINO, BALDACHIN, or **BALDAQUIN**   A canopy over an altar, carried on columns, supported on brackets, or suspended. Also known as a **ciborium** [4.46, 5.7].

BALECTION   *See* **bolection**.

BALNEAE   Plural form of **balneum**, meaning a bathing establishment.

BALTEUS   The wide step in theatres which allowed spectators to walk without disturbing those already seated. The term is also used to describe the strap which appears to bind the **cushion** or **coussinet** of the Ionic capital.

BALUSTER   A small colonnette or post, forming part of a balustrade and supporting a handrail or coping. It can be square, polygonal, or circular on plan, and its profile can be elaborate. Balusters are also known as **columellae** (*see* **balustrade** [Fig. 13]).

BALUSTRADE   A parapet composed of balusters with a coping or rail, usually found with pedestals or some stronger element at the ends of runs of balusters [Fig. 13].

Fig. 14 Tuscan gateway, with plain or banded columns and pilasters. A combination of columnar and trabeated and arcuated forms derived from Roman exemplars. From Langley

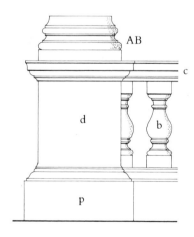

d   die or dado, the middle part
    of a pedestal
p   plinth
b   baluster
c   cornice
AB Attic Base

Fig. 13 *Balustrade*

BAND   A **face** or a **fascia**. A flat, low, square-profiled moulding encircling a building or running across its façade. The strips from which modillions or dentils project are therefore termed **modillion** or **dentil bands**. A banded column is one where the shaft is broken by the addition of plain or rusticated blocks of stone: this is sometimes known as a bandel column [Fig. 14].

BANDELET   Any narrow flat moulding such as the **taenia** between the Doric **frieze** and **architrave**.

BANDEROLE, BANNEROL, or **BANNER**   A narrow streamer or flag with a cleft end.

BANISTER   A vulgar term for a **baluster**: the plural, **banisters**, signifies a **balustrade**.

BARLEY-SUGAR COLUMN   A Classical column twisted like a stick of barley-sugar, also known as a **Solomonic** (from its supposed use in the Temple of Solomon in Jerusalem) or **twisted** column [5.7].

BAROQUE   A florid form of Classical Architecture prevalent during the seventeenth and eighteenth centuries, which developed from Mannerism. It is characterized by exuberance, movement, curvaceous forms, theatrical illusionist effects, and by cunningly contrived and complex spatial inter-relationships [5.1–5.24].

BARREL VAULT A vault with a semicircular or segmental uniform concave ceiling and no vaults or ribs. It is like an elongated continuous arch (*see* **vaults** [Fig. 69]).

BASE The base of a column is that part of it between the shaft and the pavement or the pedestal. The Greek Doric Order has no base; the Tuscan base has only a single **torus** with a **fillet**; the Roman Doric Base has a **torus**, an **astragal**, and a fillet; the Ionic base has a single large torus over two slender **scotiae** separated by two astragals (although there are many other variations); the Corinthian base has two **tori**, two **scotiae**, and two astragals; the Composite base has a double astragal in the middle. The commonest type of base, however, is the Attic base, consisting of two **tori** and a **scotia**, the top torus being smaller than the bottom, and the torus separated from the scotia by a fillet on the top of one and the bottom of the other. The **Attic base** can be used on all Orders except the Greek Doric and the Tuscan, and even then it occasionally occurs on impure Tuscan Orders. Base-blocks are plinth-blocks. **Bases** can also be built-up skirtings with plain bands and separate mouldings above. A base-course is a plinth. A base means a **basis**, a **support**, or a **pedestal**. The circular Ionic and Corinthian column-base is called **spira**, and can be confined to a single torus moulding, but can be extended to include the square plinth under the base proper, or the base of an **anta**, or its continuation as a wall-base or skirting. Greek Ionic bases can sometimes be extremely elaborate, with many horizontal **flutes** called **reeds**, torus, or scotia mouldingss, and fillets (*see* **Asiatic Base**, **Orders**).

BASEMENT The lowest storey of a building, whether partly above or below ground.

BASILICA A building divided into a nave flanked by two aisles, the former being wider and taller than the latter, with an apse at the end of the nave. Nave and aisles are divided from one another by means of colonnades or arcades above which is a clearstorey [4.43].

BASIS *See* **base**.

BASKET OF FRUIT OR FLOWERS Known as corbeil, this is a common form of ornament, usually associated with festoons.

BASKETWEAVE A pattern found in Rococo decorations, especially porcelain and stucco.

BATSWING Radiating flutes or fluted paterae [Fig. 15].

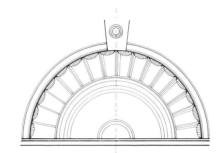

Fig. 15 *Batswing*

BATTER An inclined face, applied to walls or openings that are sloping, thicker at the bottom than at the top.

BAY A principal structural compartment or division of the architectural arrangement of a building, marked by pilasters, piers, or columns, or by the main vaults of the roof. It is incorrect to speak of the façade of a plain Georgian house as of 'five bays wide' if those 'bays' are not structural: 'five windows wide' would be more correct (*see* **laurel**).

BAY-LEAF GARLAND **Torus** moulding enriched with bound bay leaves [Fig. 16].

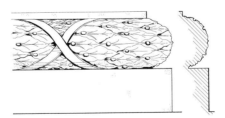

Fig. 16 *Bay-leaf garland*

BAY WINDOW A window forming a bay or recess off a room, projecting out from the main wall in a rectangular, polygonal, or semicircular form. A bay, segmental on plan, is called a bow, and is associated with Architecture of the Regency period. A bay window on an upper floor, cantilevered or corbelled out above the naked of the wall below, is called an oriel.

BEAD A small convex or semicircular moulding, often enriched. Any moulding with a convex section, an **astragal** [3.11].

BEAD-AND-REEL Enrichment of an **astragal** resembing a string of beads and reels [2.20, 3.11].

BEAK MOULDING A moulding forming an **ovolo** or **ogee** with or without a **fillet** under it, followed by a hollow. It is found in the capital of an **anta** of the Doric Order.

BED MOULDING The mouldings in the Orders under a **corona**, between it and the **frieze**, or any moulding under any projection.

BEE A feature of Renaissance and Neoclassical ornament. A symbol of order and industry.

BELETION *See* **bolection**.

BELL The shape of a Corinthian capital. Bells hanging from many eaves are associated with **Chinoiserie**. A term for guttae.

BELLFLOWER *See* **husk**.

BELVEDERE A turret, lantern, or room built above a roof or on an eminence for the enjoyment of an agreeable view. A summer-house or **gazebo**.

BEMA A raised platform used as a sanctuary. The proto-transept of the building type based on the Constantinian basilica of S. Peter in Rome [4.42, 4.43].

BIEDERMEIER South-German and Austrian style of furniture and decoration from 1816 to around 1860, derived from French Neoclassical and English Regency taste.

BIFRONT Figure with two heads or faces looking in opposite directions. Janus.

BILECTION *See* **bolection**.

BIPEDALES Large tiles used in bonding courses measuring two Roman feet each way, running at intervals through the wall.

BLACKAMOOR Negroid heads or figures used in decoration.

BLIND Blank, as in blind arcade, where an arcade is engaged or fixed to a blank wall for ornamental purposes.

BLIND STOREY A heightened parapet or a fake storey, employed usually to conceal a roof or give an appearance of an **attic storey**.

BLOCKING COURSE   The plain course of stone surmounting a **cornice** at the top of a Classical building, which weights the cantilevered cornice-blocks and stabilizes them. A projecting course without mouldings at the base of a building.

BOAST   To boast is to shape a stone into a simple form. Often stone carvings are boasted and built into position unfinished to be carved *in situ* at some later date. Any projection left rough on the face of a stone for the purpose of later enrichment is referred to as **boasted** or **bossage**.

BOCAGE   Densely designed leaves and flowers as backgrounds to figures, common in Rococo decorations.

BOISERIE   Wainscoting. The term is commonly applied to seventeenth- or eighteenth-century panelling elaborately decorated with shallow-relief carvings.

BOLECTION MOULDING   A moulding that projects beyond the surface of a panel or frame, usually found in doors or in the panelling of rooms. It is used to cover the joint between the parts with different surface levels (*see* **panel mouldings**).

BOLSTER, or **PILLOW**   The return side of an Ionic capital resembling a baluster on its side, or a cushion (*see* **Orders**).

BONNET TOP   Scrolled pediment.

BOSSAGE   Projecting stones laid in a wall to be carved later. **Rusticated** work. Can also be applied to **boasted** work.

BOULEUTERION   A meeting-place for the senate in a city-state: a debating-chamber.

BOULLE   *See* **Buhl**.

BOULTIN   A moulding also called the egg or quarter-round.

BOW   A projecting part of a building, semicircular or segmental on plan, as in bow-window or bay-window.

BRACKETING   The wooden frame to support large cornices. A bracketed cornice is one where the modillions have become transmogrified into large brackets, usually found in Victorian work.

BRICK   In Antiquity bricks were often sun-dried (**later crudus**), but later they were baked (**later coctus** or **testaceus**). Burnt bricks used as facing to Roman concrete were called **tegulae.**

BOYS AND CROWN   A crown supported by putti or Cherubs.

BRITANNIC ORDER   A version of the Corinthian Order invented by Robert Adam, which incorporated the lion and unicorn instead of the corner volutes and the crown instead of the central helices.

BUCRANE, BUCRANIUM   A carved representation of an ox-head or an ox-skull, (or aegicrane if ram or goat), garlanded, found in the **metopes** of the Roman Doric **frieze**, often alternating with **rosettes** or **phialai** [2.40, 2.52, Fig. 17].

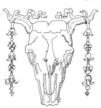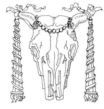

Fig. 17 *Bucranium*

BUHL WORK   Also known as **boule** or **boulle**, it consists of thin fretwork patterning of one or more metals (usually brass but sometimes other metals) inlaid on a ground, with polished tortoiseshell veneer surrounding the metal.

BULL'S EYE   A circular aperture for the admission of light or air. It is more often called **oeil-de-boeuf**, and is commonly elliptical in form.

CABLE MOULDING   A moulding resembling twisted rope.

CABLING   Convex mouldings set within the flutes of Classical columns or pilasters, nearly filling up the hollow flutes to about one third the total height of the shaft. Flutings thus treated are said to be cabled [Fig. 51]. They are not known in Ancient Greek Orders.

CABRIOLE LEG   Carved leg with feet in shape of claws, paws, or hoofs, based on the Monopodia of Roman tripods.

CADUCEUS   Winged staff entwined with serpents [Fig. 1].

CAEMENTICIUM   Also known as **structura caementicia**, **opus structile**, or **caementum**, it denotes concrete.

CAISSON   Sunken panel of various shapes, symmetrically disposed in ceilings, vaults, or soffites generally.

CALDARIUM   That part of **thermae** containing the hot water.

CALOTTE   Low segmental dome, like a skull-cap, on a circular base set directly on **pendentives** or **squinches** with no drum.

CALYX   Ornament resembling the botanical form.

CAMARA or **CAMERA**   A roof or ceiling of brick, stone, or concrete of vaulted construction.

CAMPANULAE   Bells, or the **guttae** of the Doric Order (*see* **Doric Order**).

CANALIS   The wide shallow concave channel edged by small mouldings between the **echinus** and **abacus** of the Ionic capital (*see* **Capital, Ionic Order**).

CANDELABRA   Ornament resembling the Classical candelabrum.

CANEPHORAE   Figures of young persons bearing baskets on their heads (not capitals and **abaci**) used instead of **caryatides** or columns (*see* **atlantes, caryatides**).

CANNON   Often found in trophies, or the form used in bollards or parts of furniture of the Neoclassical style.

CANOPIC JAR   Ornament in the form of Ancient Egyptian jars, with humanoid lids.

CANTHERIUS   A rafter.

CAP   A capital, a cornice, or an uppermost crowning member. The cornice on a pedestal is called the cap of the pedestal.

CAPITAL   The upper part or head of a column or pilaster set over the shaft. Each of the Five Orders has a distinctive capital. The **Aeolic** capital is an early form of the Ionic. Capitals of the Tuscan and Roman Doric Orders are similar, and consist of an **abacus, ovolo, neck,** and **astragal**: the Roman Doric Order has more elaboration of the mouldings, and the necks are sometimes enriched with **rosettes**; the Greek Doric capital has a plain abacus, a cushion-like **echinus** under which are **annulets**, and a groove called the **hypotrachelium** below; the Ionic capital has coiled or scrolled elements known as **volutes**, sometimes placed between the abacus and the ovolo moulding, and sometimes springing separately from the ovolo (front and side faces of volutes normally are not the same, except when four volutes are set diagonally (i.e. 135 degrees to the plane of the entablature), or when angle volutes are used at corners); the Corinthian capital (about one-and-a-sixth diameters high) is a bell-shaped object with two rows of eight **acanthus** leaves (*acanthus spinosus* in Greek work and *acanthus mollis* in Roman) rising above the astragal – from between the leaves of the upper row rise eight **stalks** or **caulicoli** each surmounted by a **calyx** from which emerge volutes or **helices** carrying the 'corners' of the concave-sided abacus and the central ornaments (a variation has one row of acanthus leaves with palm leaves above, no caulicoli or volutes, and a moulded **abacus**, square on plan, as at the Tower of the Winds in Athens); and the Composite capital (a Roman Order) has two rows of acanthus leaves over an astragal with, instead of the caulicoli, eight Ionic volutes set at the corners (i.e. at 135 degrees to the plane of the entablature) and egg-and-dart and bead-and-reel between them. The Composite Order is a late Roman form, is not described by Vitruvius, was identified by Alberti, and was designated by Serlio as the fifth and grandest of all the Orders.

CAPREOLUS   A rafter in a roof or similar structure, but it also seems to imply a support or a strut.

CAPRICE   Decorative vignette of the Rococo period showing architectural ruins and emblematic figures.

CARDO   The main north-south street of a Roman camp, fortress, or town.

CARTOUCH, CARTOUCHE   A **modillion**, usually internal, or under the **eaves** of a building, as opposed to modillions of the standard Classical cornice. The term is more commonly applied to a decorative tablet or frame for inscriptions in the form of a scroll or curling piece of parchment [Fig. 18].

CARYATIDES   Figures of females used instead of columns for the support of an entablature, with astragal, ovolo (usually enriched with egg-and-dart and bead-and-reel), and abacus on top of the head [6.3]. The term is also given to any support carved in the form of a human figure, but is not, strictly speaking, correct. Male figures, usually heroic in scale and proportion, and 'bent' under the weight of what they are carrying are called **atlantes**: if the male figures are unbowed and straight, they are called **telamons** or **telamones**. Figures of young persons with **baskets** on their heads instead of **astragal**, **ovolo**, and **abacus**, also used instead of columns, are called **canephorae**. **Herms** are portions of figures *on* pedestals, whether carrying a weight or not, while **terms** [5.55] *are*

Fig. 18 *Cartouche commemorating Sir Walter Curl, Bart. (died 1678) in the south transept of the church of S. Peter, Soberton, Hampshire*

pedestals (often inverted obelisks or parts of obelisks) which merge into the torsos and busts of humanoid or other figures. The word 'caryatid' derives from the belief by Vitruvius that the female figures of the Erechtheion represent Carian prisoners (*see* **atlantes**, **canephorae**, **telamones**).

CASE OF A DOOR   A doorcase, meaning the whole of an elaborate Classical frame to a doorway, usually of timber [Fig. 23].

CASEMENT   A **scotia** or deep concave moulding. Window with opening-lights hinged at the sides.

CASINO   A small country house, or a lodge in a park. A summer-house or decorative building.

CASTELLATED   With battlements and turrets.

CATACOMB   An underground public cemetery with **loculi** for the entombment of bodies.

CATAFALQUE   A temporary or permanent structure, decorated and usually draped, representing a tomb or a **cenotaph**, and used in funeral ceremonies. Catafalques are also the altar-like structures on which coffins are placed in mortuary chapels, etc.

CATENARY   Festoon of chain-links, often used on prisons.

CAULICOLI, CAULICOLAE, CAULCOLES   In the Corinthian capital the eight stalks that spring from the upper row of **acanthus** leaves (*see* **Corinthian Order**).

CAVAEDIUM   The **cavum aedium**, or main room of a Roman house, also called the **atrium**, and partly open to the sky by means of the **compluvium**, with an **impluvium** or tank of water in the centre.

CAVETTO   A hollow moulding, principally used in cornices, with as profile the quadrant of a circle.

CAVUM AEDIUM   *See* **cavaedium**

CELL   Part of a temple enclosed within the walls, otherwise the **naos** or **cella**.

CEMETERY   A sleeping-place, or any place where the dead are interred or deposited.

CENOTAPH   An empty tomb, or a monument to commemorate a person or persons buried elsewhere.

CERQUATE   Arrangement of oak leaves and acorns.

CHAÎNES   Vertical strips of masonry (often rusticated) of blocks of alternating width resembling **quoins** associated with door- or window-surrounds.

CHAINS   Symbols of enslavement, usually associated with the Vices, or used in association with marine decorations, or with prisons.

CHAIR RAIL   The upper moulding of a **dado** around a room to prevent the backs of chairs from damaging the walls or their coverings. It corresponds to the cornice of a pedestal.

CHAMFERING   A finish in which right-angled edges are cut off at 45 degrees often to prevent damage, or in association with decoration, such as rustication.

CHANDELLE   Decoration of lower parts of fluted columns or pilasters with plain or enriched beading. A form of **cabling**.

CHANNEL   The same as **canalis**.

CHAPITER, CHAPTREL   A capital. An impost.

CHARGED   A frieze is charged with an ornament on it, so the term implies the dependence of one part of a work of Architecture upon another.

CHERUB An infantile male figure, winged, usually associated with clouds, funerary monuments, etc, in Baroque sculpture. Cherubs are usually podgy, and may be given to overt displays of grief. They must be distinguished from **putti** (sing. **putto**) (little boys, otherwise indistinguishable from Cherubs) who are wingless.

CHEVRON The zigzag. Very fluid chevron forms are called **Bargello**.

CHIMERA Creature with mane, head, and legs of a lion, the tail of a dragon, the body of a goat, and the wings of an eagle.

CHINOISERIE A style of art, decoration, and Architecture that evoked Cathay, reaching its finest flowering in the eighteenth century. It is associated with the **Rococo** [Fig. 20]. A **Chinese fret** or lattice incorporates diagonal members [Fig. 19].

Fig. 19 *Chinese Fret (Chinoiserie)*

CIBORIUM A domed canopy on columns and arches set over an altar [4.4].

CINCTURE A ring, **list**, or **fillet** at the top and bottom of a column dividing the shaft from the capital and base (*see* **Order**).

CINERARIUM LID A Neoclassical capping for gate-piers, sarcophagi, etc.

CIPPUS A small, low **column**, sometimes without base or capital.

CIRCUS A circular, elliptical, or rectangular space with semicircular ends in which horse- or chariot-races were held. The term later signified any circular space surrounded by buildings, as in the Circus in Bath.

CIVIC CROWN A garland of acorns and oak-leaves used in architectural ornament.

CLASSICAL ARCHITECTURE Architecture based on the precedents of the Architecture of Ancient Greece and Rome, or that Architecture of Antiquity itself. In the eighteenth century a scholarly return to Classical principles was led by William Kent, Lord Burlington, and Colen Campbell, who revered the works of Palladio and Inigo Jones: this movement was known as Palladianism, and dominated significant Architecture for most of the century. Studies of the buildings of Antiquity, notably those of Rome, Greece, Spalato, Palmyra, Herculaneum, and Pompeii led to the Neoclassical movement, of which the Greek Revival was an important element.

CLAW Claws can appear at the bases of **herms**, **terms**, and **cabrioles**, and are any terminating figure resembling a claw.

CLEARSTOREY, CLERESTOREY Any window, row of windows, or openings, in the upper part of a building, notably

Fig. 20 *The Chinoiserie Tea-Pavilion, in the gardens of Sanssouci at Potsdam, designed by King Friedrich II of Prussia and Johann Gottfried Büring. It was erected 1754–7*

above the nave arcades and aisle roofs in a basilican building.

COADE STONE   Artificial cast stone manufactured in London from the 1770s onwards, and used for decorative keystones, quoins, statuary, etc.

COCKLE STAIR   A winding stair.

COFFER   Flat ceilings were often constructed by placing small beams at right angles between or on the main beams. The **soffite** was then formed by covering the square compartments with frames closed by flat lids. The sunken square compartments, often emulated in stone, concrete, or plaster, are called coffers.

COIN MOULDING   A repeated series of overlapping discs [Fig. 21], not unlike **guilloche** [Fig. 41].

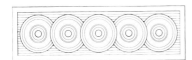

Fig. 21 *Coin moulding*

COLOSSEUM   The huge amphitheatre built by Vespasian in Rome.

COLLARINO   The cylindrical part of the capital of the Tuscan and Roman Doric Orders, lying between the **annulets** under the **ovolo** and the **astragal**. It is termed the **neck**, and is the **hypotrachelium** of Vitruvius (*see* **Orders**).

COLONNADE   A row of columns with entablature. If four, the range is called **tetrastyle**; if six, **hexastyle**; if eight, **octastyle**; if ten, **decastyle**, etc. When a colonnade stands before a building it is called a **portico**, and if it surrounds a building it is called a **peristyle**. Colonnades are further described in terms of the spaces between columns: **intercolumniation** is the distance between columns measured from the lower parts of the shafts in multiples of the diameter of a column. The main types of intercolumniation as defined by Vitruvius are: **pycnostyle**, where columns are 1½ diameters apart; **systyle**, where they are 2 diameters apart; **eustyle** where they are 2¼ diameters apart; **diastyle** where they are 3 diameters apart; and **araeostyle** where they are greater than 3 diameters apart (up to a maximum of 5), the last only used with the Tuscan Order.

In Classical Architecture, two columns between **antae** would be described as **distyle in antis**; a front portico of four columns standing before the antae is **prostyle tetrastyle**; and a building with four columns standing before the antae at the front and rear is described as **amphi-prostyle tetrastyle**. A circular building with columns all round it is **peripteral circular**, while the term **peripteral octastyle** means a rectangular building surrounded by columns, with eight at each end forming porticoes. **Pseudo-peripteral** means that columns are joined (**engaged**) to the walls and are not freestanding. To say that a colonnade is **dipteral** means that there are double rows of columns, so **dipteral octastyle** means a building surrounded by two rows of columns, with a **portico** of sixteen columns at each end, eight columns wide [Figs. 64, 65].

COLONNETTE   A small column.

COLOSSAL ORDER   An Order where the columns or pilasters rise from the ground or a plinth more than one storey, also known as **Giant Order**.

COLUMBARIUM   A dovecote, or building with holes or **niches** in the walls, such as a structure for the reception of urns or ash-chests containing cremated remains, so called from the resemblance to the niches for pigeons or doves.

COLUMELLAE   *See* **balusters**.

COLUMEN   The ridge-beam of a gabled roof resting in front on the tympanum of the primitive Tuscan Order. It was therefore supported on a wall or on other timbers resting on the **trabes compactiles** or architraves resting on the widely spaced columns, and was cantilevered out over the line of the colonnade to the same projection as the **mutuli**, or secondary beams. The rafters, or **cantherii** were supported on the **columen** and on the mutuli at the sides, producing a very deep pedimented space with overhanging roof at the ends.

COLUMN   An upright, usually circular on plan, but also polygonal or square, supporting a lintel. It consists of a base, shaft, and capital, except in the case of the Greek Doric Order which has no base. It must not be confused with a pier, which is more massive, and must not be called a **pillar**.

COLUMNA ROSTRATA   A Rostral column, usually on a pedestal, decorated with the

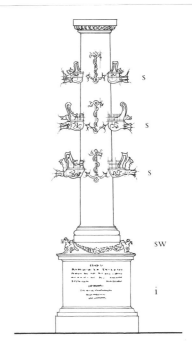

s   ships' prows with battering rams
i   inscription on die of pedestal
sw   festoons or swags between birds
     (sometimes eagles)

Fig. 22 *Rostral Column, or Columna Rostrata*

bows of warships and celebrating naval victories. It was a Roman form, and was revived in the Neoclassical period [Fig. 22].

COLUMNIATION   An arrangement of columns.

COMEDY and **TRAGEDY MASKS**   Emblems of the theatre.

COMPACTILIS   A term meaning fastened together, as **trabes compactiles**, or rafters.

COMPARTMENT CEILING   A panelled or coffered ceiling.

COMPLUVIUM   The opening in a roof to allow sun and rain to enter, as in the atrium of a Roman house.

COMPOSITE ORDER   A Roman Order, mixing features of Ionic and Corinthian Orders. It is the grandest of all the Orders. It resembles the Corinthian Order except that the capitals have Ionic volutes and **echini** instead of the Corinthian **caulicoli** and scrolls (*see* **Orders**).

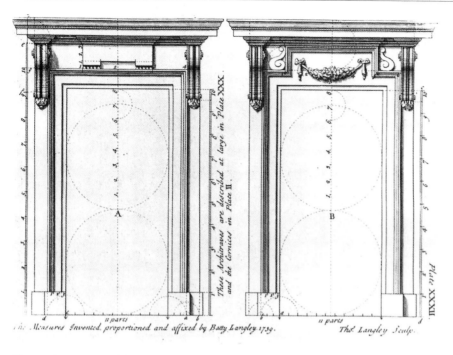

Fig. 23 *Doorcases. Both have consoles. Above the architrave on the left is a suggestion of a Doric detail, with the guttae set under the raised panel. On the right is a swag, and there are two scrolls. Note the system of proportion. From Langley*

CONCH, CONCHA The half dome of an **apse**, or a niche with a semi-dome over it. A shell is sometimes carved or formed over the half-domed niche, hence the term.

CONCRETE, STRUCTURA CAEMENTICIA, CAEMENTICIUM, OPUS STRUCTILE were names for Roman concrete. Broken stones or bricks were laid in courses and each course, when laid, was filled with liquid mortar made from lime and volcanic dust.

CONGE The **echinus** or quarter-round, and the **cavetto**. The former is the swelling conge, and the latter the hollow conge.

CONGELATION Representation of water or icicles in rustication and grottoes.

CONSOLE An s-shaped bracket or corbel, ornamented, with a greater height than projection in the vertical position (also called **ancones**, **trusses**, or **crossettes**). Consoles can be placed vertically, with the smaller scroll at the base, and can support a bust or urn, or, if placed on either side of a doorcase, the cornice over. If laid horizontally (the larger scroll nearer the wall or vertical face) it becomes the expression of a cantilever to carry a balcony. Consoles also occur as keystones, in which case they are definitely called ancones. Horizontal consoles under cornices are called **modillions**. A console is also known as **parotis** [Figs. 23, 24, 62 see also 2.53, 2.54, 2.56, 2.58, 2.59].

CONTRACTURA The diminution of the shaft of a column with its height, usually associated with **entasis**.

COQUILLAGE Shell-work, as in grottoes.

CORBEIL A carved basket with sculptured flowers and fruit. The bell of the Corinthian capital. Baskets on the heads of **canephorae**.

CORBEL A projecting stone or timber support, or cantilever, which can be a **modillion**. Corbelling is the bridging of an opening or the roofing of a space by means of a series of overlapping horizontal courses, without using the principle of the arch.

CORINTHIAN ORDER A lavish Order of Architecture used by the Greeks and Romans, and the most festive of the Greek Orders, associated with Beauty. The distinctive feature is the capital, which is about one-and-one-sixth diameters high, and very ornate, with **acanthus** leaves and **caulicoli**, each of which is surmounted by a **calyx** from which emerge **volutes** or **helices** supporting the **abacus** and the central foliate ornaments on each face of the abacus. Originally only the capital differentiated the Corinthian from the Ionic Order but in Roman work the Corinthian entablature became rich in carved ornament. The **architrave**, for example, had many decorated mouldings, while the **frieze** was enriched with acanthus scroll and figured ornament. Cornices had sculptured coffers on the soffites, and elaborately ornamented modillions. Much **egg-and-dart**, **bead-and-reel**, **dentil**, and florid decoration was in evidence. Shafts were fluted or plain, but in the Greek version of the Order they were fluted. Abaci have moulded concave faces, meeting at points, or with chamfered 'corners' over the volutes. A simpler form of the capital, found at the Tower of the Winds in Athens, has one row of acanthus leaves over which is a row of palm leaves, but with this version the abacus is square on plan [2.32]. The term **Corinthian** also seems to suggest an arrangement with more than four columns associated with the **cavum aedium** or **cavaedium**, or inner court of a house, and supporting the roof which allowed rain to drain through the open centre (**compluvium**) into the tank or pool (**impluvium**).

CORN Corn and corn-cobs sometimes appeared in Neoclassical forms of the Corinthian Order [6.4].

Fig. 24 *Truss, console, or crossette. To draw it, divide the desired height into 11 equal parts, and divide the upper 3 into 7 parts. Make ne the perpendicular line of the projection of the upper volute 8 of those parts out from the wall. Divide the 3rd and 4th larger vertical parts together into 7 parts, making the projection of the lower volute equal to 8 of those parts: the truss will also be 8 of those parts wide. The centre of the upper eye is 4.5 and the centre of the lower is 3.5 relevant parts in from the furthest projections. Each eye is 1 relevant part in diameter, and the larger circumference of the outer eye is 1.5 relevant parts in radius. Set out the diagonal square in each smaller eye, and subdivide this square as shown, so points 1–8 are the centres to describe the volute. The face of the truss has fillets each 1 lower part wide, the central astragal and its 2 fillets is 1 part wide, and the cyma recta mouldings are each 2.5 parts wide. From Langley*

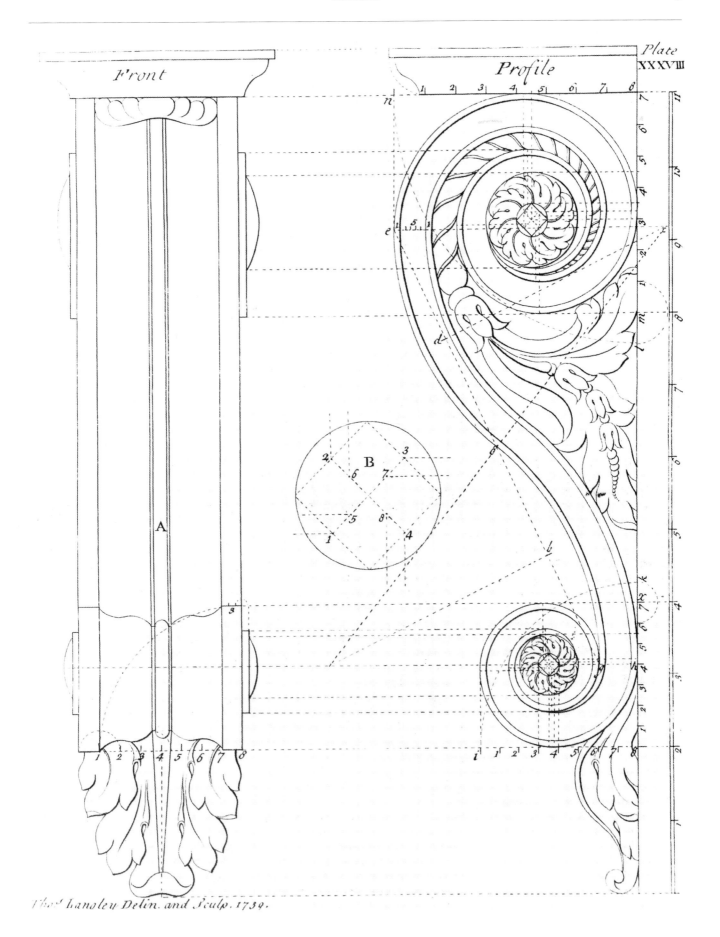

Front

Profile

Plate XXXVIII

Thos. Langley Delin. and Sculp. 1739.

CORNICE The moulded projection which is the crowning feature, consisting of several members, of an entablature. It also can crown a wall, a moulding, or pedestal. A cornice can be any horizontal moulding, although it is primarily the topmost of the three main divisions of an entablature. It is also the moulding at the junction of a wall and ceiling, and, in such a position, is similar in profile to a cornice on an entablature. If a cornice is used on a pedestal it is called the **cap** of the pedestal. An **encased cornice** was one faced with terracotta, which implies an earlier timber model (*see* **Orders**).

CORNICIONE The large elaborate crowning entablature of an Italian *palazzo*, imported by Barry and used on several buildings in the astylar Italianate *palazzo* style [4.11].

CORNUCOPIA A Horn of Plenty, or Goat's Horn, overflowing with corn, fruit, and flowers, often found in Classical decoration.

CORONA The flat, square part of a Classical cornice, more usually called the **drip** or **larmier**, situated between the **cymatium** above and the **bed-moulding** below, used to shed water from the building. It has a vertical face. In Latin usage corona seems to have implied the whole cornice, but now it means part of the projecting member (*see* **Orders**).

CORSA A **platband** or **square fascia**, with a height greater than its projection. A plain string-course.

CORTILE A small court surrounded by the apartments of a house, usually with arcades or colonnades, and of several storeys [4.13, 4.14, 4.16, 4. 20, 4.25, 4.49].

COTTAGE ORNÉ A rustic-style cottage of the **Picturesque** genre.

CREPIDOMA The stepped base of a Greek temple (usually with three steps), also called **crepis**, or **crepido**. These steps were usually too high to be used as a stair, so ramps or intermediate steps were introduced on main axes for use (*see* **Greek Orders**).

CRESCENT A series of buildings planned on the arc of a circle. An attribute of Artemis-Diana-Isis.

CREST A device fixed to the top of a helmet. At the base of the crest is a coronet or a wreath.

CRINKLE-CRANKLE A type of garden wall that on plan consists of alternate convex and concave curves in a continuous wavy line. If a tall wall (one or two bricks more than the height of a man) were built in a straight line without buttresses it would be unstable, but the undulating plan creates a stiffening and buttressed effect which makes the crinkle-crankle an economical and stable structure.

CROISÉE A French window (*see* **window**).

CROSSETTE A projection at the junctions of jambs and lintels, like consoles, on the flanks of the architrave, under the cornice. A projection, **lug**, **knee**, or **ear** in the architrave or casing around a door- or window-opening. The returns in the corners of doorcases or window frames. The term also signifies a ledged projection in the voussoirs of a built-up architrave or a flat 'arch', or a segmental arch, which rests within a corresponding recess in, or on, the adjoining voussoir, thus strengthening the construction [Figs. 9, 23, 24, 62].

CROWN OF AN ARCH The highest point, also called the **extrados** (*see* **arch**) [Fig. 9].

C-SCROLL and **S-SCROLL** Elements found in **Rococo** decorations, usually as parts of frames.

CULLOT A string of **husks** or **bell-flowers**, or the end of a **festoon** [Fig. 33].

CUNEUS A wedge-shaped section of the seating of a theatre bounded by stairs and passages. Also a **voussoir**.

CUPID Similar to a putto, but winged, and often armed with bow and arrows.

CUPOLA A drum or polygonal space on top of a dome, also called a **lantern**. A roof or vault over a circular, elliptical, or polygonal plan: a concave ceiling over such plans. A vaulted or domed roof of a building or part of a building, a diminutive domed form.

CURB ROOF A Mansard roof.

CURIA Meeting-house for councils, usually a rectangular hall with a niche or apse at one end opposite the door.

CUSHIONED A frieze that is convex in vertical section, seeming to cushion outwards or swell. Also called **pulvinated** (illustrated in several examples).

CYCLOPEAN Of masonry that is dressed to look as though the surface is naturally rough, and straight from the quarry, 'undressed' (but actually contrived to look so). It is also called **rock-faced** work (*see* **rustication** [Fig. 54]).

CYLINDRICAL VAULT A **wagon-head**, **barrel**, or **cradle-vault** without groins resting on parallel walls. It may also refer to segmental vaults or ceilings, that is with a cross-section showing less than half a circle (*see* **vault** [Fig. 69]).

CYMA A moulding which is hollow in its upper part, and cushioned or swelling out below, so called from its resemblance to a wave. Its section consists of a concave and convex line, like an elongated S. An ogee. A **cyma recta** is an S-shaped moulding at the top of a cornice, with the concave part uppermost, while a **cyma reversa** is similar, but reversed (i.e. with a convex upper part and concave lower part), and is also known as the **lesbian cymatium** (*see* **Orders moulding** [Fig. 44]).

CYMATIUM The top member of a group of Classical mouldings, usually the cornice. A moulding the section of which is a curve of contrary flexure (*see* **Orders**).

CYMBAL Often found with musical trophies, or in Bacchic decorations.

CYMBIA A **fillet**.

CYPHERING **Chamfering**. Cyphers consist of initials interwoven to form a design, often with reversed letters for symmetry.

DADO A solid block or cube forming the body of a pedestal or plinth in Classical Architecture, between the base and the cornice, also called a **die**. Rooms are often found decorated with a base, dado course, and cornice, resembling an elongated continuous pedestal all around the walls: in such a sense the cornice becomes the chair-rail, the plinth the skirting, and the dado the surface between the chair-rail and the skirting (*see* **balustrade** [Fig. 13]).

DAMASCENE To ornament metal with designs incised in the surface and filled with another metal, usually gold or silver.

DANCING STEP Steps in a curved stair, the narrow ends of which are almost as wide as the treads in a straight portion of a flight: they are also called **danced stairs** or **balanced winders.**

DAY Usually symbolized by Aurora, Eos, the cock, a flame.

DECASTYLE   A colonnade or portico of ten columns in a line.

DECLINATION   The angle which the planes of the wall and the soffites of the mutules of the Doric Order make with each other. All true Greek Doric mutules are inclined.

DECUMANUS   The main east-west street of a Roman military camp, fortress, or planned town.

DEMI-COLUMN   A column that is applied to a wall. An engaged column as distinct from a pilaster.

DENTILS   Ornaments consisting of small rectangular projections used in series in the bed mouldings of the **cornices** of the Ionic, Corinthian, and Composite Orders, and occasionally in the Roman Doric Order. Their width should be half their height, and the spaces between them should be two-thirds of their width. Dentilated is a term signifying cornices with dentils in the bed mouldings. A dentil is *denticulus* in Latin. It seems originally to have signified the cantilevered ends of beams supporting projecting upper storeys like jetties in mediaeval timber-framed work (*see* **Orders**).

DETACHED COLUMN   An **insulated column**, or one that is not engaged: a column that can be viewed from all angles.

DIASTYLE   One of the five species of **intercolumniation**: in this case the distance between columns is equal to three diameters of a shaft.

DIAZOMA   A passage separating tiers of seats in a theatre.

DIE   A cube, or the body of a pedestal between the plinth and the cornice, also called the dado [Fig. 13]. A die is also a term used instead of abacus.

DIGLYPH   A projecting face with two vertical channels or **glyphs** cut into it. It is found in late-Renaissance versions of the Doric Order in which the two half-glyphs of the Doric Order are omitted so that only two full glyphs are cut in the vertical block (otherwise known as **triglyph**).

DIMINISHED ARCH   A segmental arch, i.e. one less than a semicircle in elevation.

DIMINUTION   The term expressing the decrease of diameter in the upper part of a column: the continuing contraction of the diameter with height in order to give it the appearance of strength and elegance. A **diminishing rule** is a board cut with a concave edge to establish the profile of a column. From the eighteenth century the diminution was *de rigueur* from about one third of the height of the column, but in Greek Antique Architecture the diminution began from the bottom of the shaft immediately above the **apophyge**. It is also termed **contractura**.

DIOCLETIAN WINDOW   A semicircular window divided into three lights by two mullions, also known as a **thermal window** from its use in the Baths of Diocletian in Rome. It was revived by Palladio, and recurs in eighteenth-century Architecture [6.5].

DIPTERAL   An arrangement of two rows of columns on the flanks of a Classical building. A temple surrounded by two rows of columns, which meant that the porticoes at either end were at least octastyle [Figs. 4, 6].

DIRECTOIRE STYLE   A Neoclassical style prevalent in France from the end of the rule of Louis XVI to *c.* 1806, often including Egyptianizing elements.

DIRETTA   The **cyma recta**.

DISCHARGING ARCH   A relieving arch built into a wall over a lintel to relieve the latter from the weight above: it is usually a segmental arch (*see* **arch** [Fig. 9]).

DISPLUVIATE   An arrangement of the **cavum aedium** known as cavum aedium displuviatum, with compluvium and impluvium, but with the roof sloping outwards: it permitted a better natural illumination of the room.

DISTYLE   With a portico of two columns. As two columns are minimal as far as buildings are concerned, they are usually *in antis*, or set between the antae of the ends of walls [Fig. 65].

DITRIGLYPH   An interval between two columns admitting two **triglyphs** in the frieze above instead of the more usual single triglyph between the centre-lines of the columns of the Doric Order.

DODECASTYLE   A portico or colonnade with twelve columns in a line.

DOLPHIN   Often found in ornament with Nereids and Tritons. Dolphin-ornament occurs on well-heads, embankments, and fish-markets, among other places.

Fig. 25a *Sail dome*   **Fig. 25b** *Dome on pendentives on a square base*   **Fig. 25c** *Dome on a drum on pendentives, on a square base*

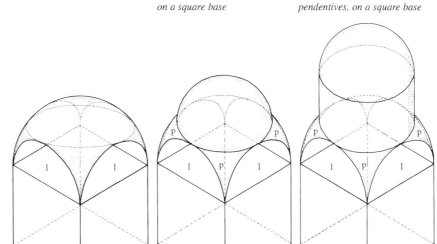

plan of sail dome   plan of dome on pendentives, on a square base   plan of dome on a drum on pendentives, on a square base

l = lunette
p = pendentive

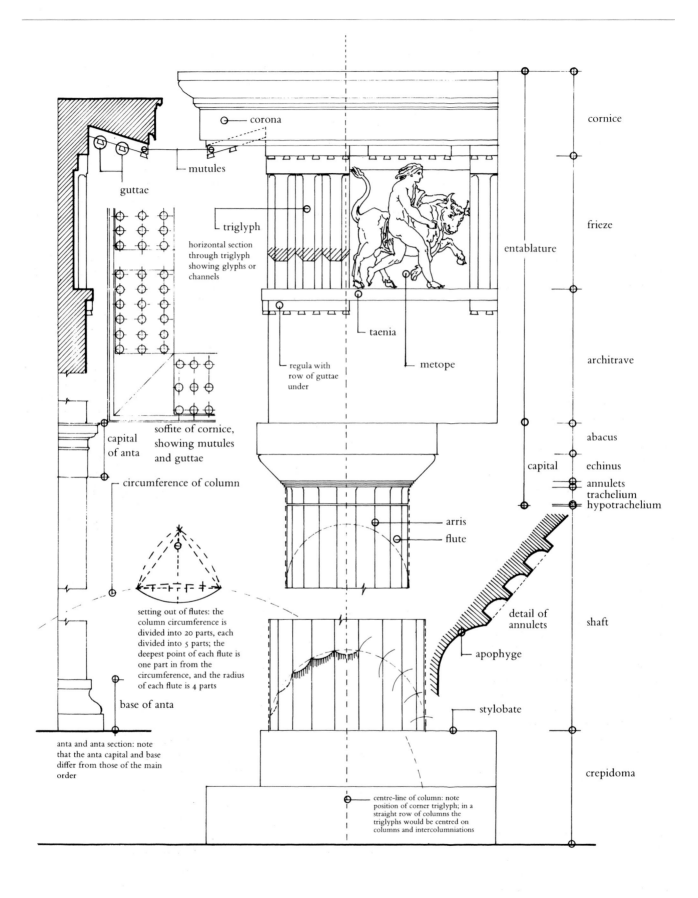

corona

mutules

guttae

triglyph

horizontal section
through triglyph
showing glyphs or
channels

taenia

metope

regula with
row of guttae
under

capital
of anta

soffite of cornice,
showing mutules
and guttae

circumference of column

setting out of flutes: the
column circumference is
divided into 20 parts, each
divided into 5 parts; the
deepest point of each flute is
one part in from the
circumference, and the radius
of each flute is 4 parts

base of anta

anta and anta section: note
that the anta capital and base
differ from those of the main
order

entablature

arris

flute

detail of
annulets

apophyge

stylobate

centre-line of column: note
position of corner triglyph; in a
straight row of columns the
triglyphs would be centred on
columns and intercolumniations

cornice

frieze

architrave

abacus

capital   echinus

annulets
trachelium
hypotrachelium

shaft

crepidoma

DOME The hemispherical or other concave vault over a circular, elliptical, or polygonal plan: it is semicircular, segmental, pointed, or bulb-shaped in section. Domes are often found over a square sub-structure, and if so the corners must be built up so that the dome, on its circular or polygonal plan, can sit comfortably: **pendentives** and **squinch arches** are used to accomplish this purpose (*see* **vault** [Figs. 25, 69, 70]).

DORIC DROPS *See* **guttae**.

DORIC ORDER The Doric Order exists in the Greek and Roman forms. In the Greek version [2.1–2.5, 2.7–2.13] it consists of a **stylobate** supporting a base-less column (usually fluted with sharp arrises between the flutes, but sometimes unfluted) with a pronounced **entasis**; a distinctive capital with annulets or horizontal fillets (from three to five in number) stopping the vertical lines of the arrises and flutes of the shaft, an **echinus** or cushion over them, and a plain square abacus; and an entablature (usually one quarter the height of the Order) with plain architrave or principal beam over which are the frieze and cornice: Greek Doric architraves may project slightly in front of the faces of the tops of columns below, but because of the pronounced entasis, do not project beyond the faces of columns at the bases. The frieze is separated from the cornice by a plain moulding called the **taenia** under which, at intervals under each triglyph, is a narrow band with six **guttae** called the **regula**. The Doric frieze is composed of alternate **metopes** (often ornamented with sculpture) and **triglyphs** (vertical elements with two V-shaped incised channels and two half-V channels at the edges producing three flat verticals and a flat band across the top). Above is the crowning cornice consisting of a **cyma recta** with **mutules** and guttae on the soffites of the corona under the cymatium. Greek Doric mutules are placed over triglyphs and metopes, slope downwards with the soffite, and project beneath it. They do not often occur under the raking cornices of pediments.

Fig. 26 *Greek Doric Order showing the various parts: the soffite with mutules and guttae, the anta details compared with the main Order, how to set out the flutes, etc. Note that the anta capital and base differ from those of the column*

The **Roman Doric Order** nearly always has a base, while the Greek version never has one. In the Roman version the **triglyphs** at the corners of the building are set on the centre-line of the columns, leaving a portion of metope on the corner, but in the Greek Doric Order the triglyphs join at the corner of the frieze, with the result that the corner columns are closer to their neighbours than elsewhere in the colonnade, so the corners of the Greek buildings appear to be more solidly proportioned. Roman Doric often has **bucrania** or **paterae** in the metopes, and moulded abaci, rosettes or other ornaments in the neck of the capital between the capital proper and the astragal, so the Order is quite distinct from the Greek version. Channels at the tops of the Greek triglyphs are rounded, but in the Roman versions they are rectangular. Roman Doric mutules,

usually set over triglyphs only, are very slightly inclined, and do not project beneath the soffite except in the so-called 'mutule' Order of Vignola [2.43], also used by Chambers. Roman Doric Orders often feature dentils, but in Greek Doric these never appear. The ornaments of the Roman Doric soffite between the mutules do not drop down lower than the soffite, and are usually shallowly cut with **thunderbolts**, **rosettes**, **lozenges**, and other patterns, while **guttae** are correctly conical, but are often carved as truncated pyramids. Greek Doric mutules occur over metopes as well as triglyphs, so the spaces between the mutules are usually too small for any ornamentation, except at the corners of buildings, where **anthemion** or other ornaments may sometimes be found on the soffites. Roman architraves do not project beyond the faces of the columns below [2.38–2.42].

DORMER A window inserted vertically in a sloping roof and with its own roof and sides. If the gable over it is low-pitched and is formed into a pediment it is called a

Fig. 27 *Doric Temple*

acroterion ornament

antefix

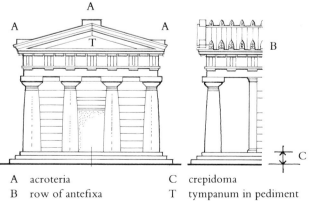

A acroteria
B row of antefixa
C crepidoma
T tympanum in pediment

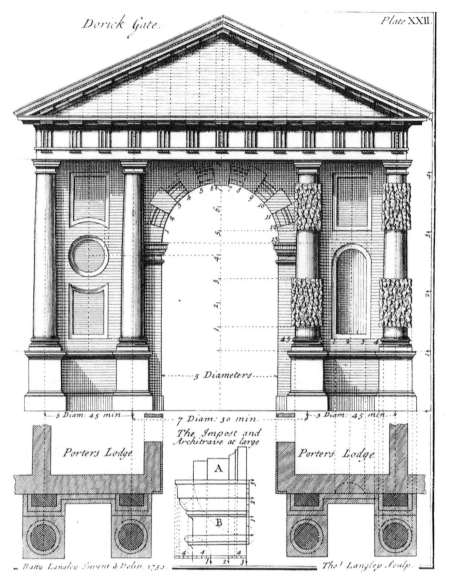

Fig. 28 *Doric gateway. Note the mutules in the raking cornice, and the frosted rustication. A variation on the triumphal arch and temple themes. Note that in Roman Doric the triglyphs are on the centre-lines of the end columns, and that there are two and five triglyphs over the intercolumniations. From Langley*

dormer-head. A dormer-window is placed vertically on the rafters and is *not* over the wall of the main façade below. If the windows over the main cornice are constructed perpendicularly over the naked or surface of the main façade below the entablature they are called **luthernes** or **lucarnes**.

DOVE   An attribute of Venus and symbol of love and constancy. The Holy Spirit.

DRESSINGS   The mouldings and ornaments around openings, or quoins. The term describes stone used in such positions.

DRIP   The projecting edge of a moulding, channelled or throated beneath so that water will be thrown off.

DROP   The conical shapes of **guttae** under triglyphs and the mutules of the Doric Order, also known as **droplets**, **campanulae**, or **lachrymae** (*see* **Doric Order**).

DRUM   A circular structure supporting a dome. The shaft-blocks of a column. Also the solid vase- or bell-shaped part of the Corinthian and Composite capital to which **foliage**, **stalks**, and **caulicoli**, etc. are attached.

DUCK FOOT, DUTCH FOOT   A three-toed foot on a cabriole leg.

DUTCH GABLE   A gable with curved sides or volutes, surmounted by a pediment [Fig. 35].

EAGLE   An attribute of power or victory.

EARS   (*See* **crossette**.) The trusses or consoles on the flanks of architraves under the cornice, also called **elbows**, **ancones**, or **prothyrides**. They are called ears because of their faint resemblance to those organs. Because of their positions on the flanks of architraves the term is also given to a type of architrave, the **supercilium** of which projects beyond the **antepagmenta**, forming 'ears', or 'lugs', or 'knees' [*see* Figs. 11, 23, 24, 52, 62].

EAVES   The lower edge of a pitched roof which overhangs the face of a wall. An **eaves cornice** is therefore a cornice in that position.

ECCLESIASTERION   A hall for the meeting of the sovereign assembly in a Greek city-state. A small theatre. Hence a place for the gathering of people for purposes of serious deliberation.

ECCLESIASTICAL HAT   A Cardinal's hat, often found in Baroque decorations.

ECHINUS   An ovolo moulding below the abacus of a Greek Doric capital, or any convex moulding in the form of a conic section or a quarter of a circle in Roman work. Continuous echinus mouldings are often ornamented with **egg-and-dart**, and it seems probable that the term echinus is only properly applied if this enrichment is present (*see* **Orders**).

ECLECTICISM   The use of wide ranges of motifs in design.

EGG-AND-DART   Also called **egg-and-anchor**, or **egg-and-tongue**, this is an enrichment found on ovolo or echinus mouldings, and consists of upright egg-like motifs with the tops truncated, between which are arrow-like elements, repeated alternately. Egg-and-dart is best confined to the late sharp arrow-head or spiked forms, which were narrower and spikier than the earlier tongue-like shapes, or leaves (*see* **Orders**, [2.20, 3.11]).

EGYPTIAN HALL   A large room with an internal peristyle with a smaller superimposed peristyle, having no connection with Egyptian Architecture [5.63].

EGYPTIAN STYLE   In Neoclassical Architecture or design the use of Egyptian motifs, and the simplification of form into stereometrically pure elements such as the pyramid and the obelisk.

ELBOW   Vertical linings of openings, such as panelled work, or the linings under shutters. Also see **Ears**, **prothyrides**, **ancones**, or **consoles**.

EMBOSSED   Raised design, or **relievo** work, chiselled or carved.

EMPIRE   A Neoclassical French style associated with Napoleonic times. Roman motifs were used to identify France with Imperial Rome, and Egyptian elements also were used.

EMPOLIA   The wooden blocks containing the dowels, or poloi, connecting the drums of Greek columns, and associated with the system of closely fitting each drum at the outer edge only (**anathyrosis**).

ENCARPUS   A festoon of fruit, flowers, and leaves used to decorate a frieze.

ENDIVE SCROLL   A type of marquetry pattern based on Moresque exemplars.

ENFILADE   A system of aligning the doors connecting rooms in large buildings so that long vistas through rooms are achieved: one room is therefore entered through another without any corridor.

ENGAGED   A column attached to a wall is engaged: it is also known as attached, inserted, or applied. An engaged column must not be confused with a **pilaster**. True engaged columns have between half and three-quarters of the shafts exposed. The geometry of the entasis makes the junction of the shaft and the wall extremely difficult to construct if more, or less, than half the shaft is to be exposed.

ENNEASTYLE   A portico or colonnade consisting of a line of nine columns.

ENRICHMENT   Any elaboration of mouldings in Classical Architecture: **egg-and-dart** on ovolo mouldings, **bead-and-reel** on astragals, and **anthemion** or palmette on cyma recta mouldings are examples of enrichment [2.20, 3.11].

ENTABLATURE   In Classical Architecture, the superstructure of the Order above the abacus, consisting of architrave, frieze, and cornice (*see* **Orders** [Figs. 29, 30]).

ENTAIL   Elaborate sculptured ornament.

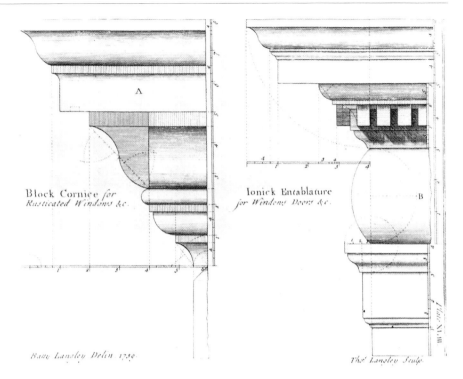

Fig. 29 *Entablatures. On the left is a block cornice, to be placed on chamfered rustication, while on the right is an Ionic entablature for windows, niches, or doorcases, with dentils and pulvinated frieze. From Langley*

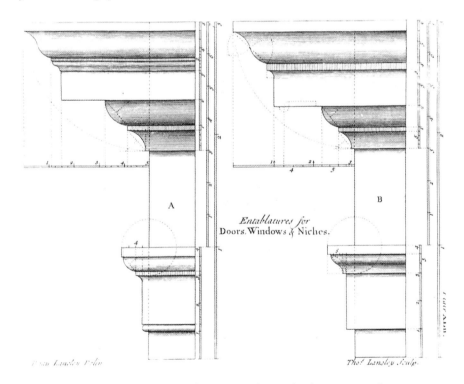

Fig. 30 *Tuscan and Doric entablature for doors, windows, and niches. From Langley*

ENTASIS In Classical Architecture columns are wider at the base than under the capital: the transition from the base to the top is not a straight line, but a curve, and the **diminution** usually begins from a point about a third of the height from the base. It was employed to prevent the columns from appearing concave.

ENTRESOL *See* **mezzanine**.

EPICRANITIS Crowning mouldings and enrichment along the outer walls of a cella resembling the capitals of the antae.

EPISTYLIUM The architrave of an entablature, also called **epistyle**.

EPITHEDES Upper mouldings of an entablature, or the **cymatium**.

ESCALLOP A scallop shell.

ESCAPE The part of the shaft of a column where it springs out of the base mouldings, also called the **apophyge**.

ESCUTCHEON A shield on which a coat of arms is fixed.

ESPAGNOLETTE Female mask with ruff around head and under the chin.

ESTÍPITE A pilaster ornament with panels containing geometrical patterns and cartouches, shaped like an inverted obelisk.

ESTOIL Heraldic star with six wavy-sided points.

EUSTYLE One of the five species of **intercolumniation** in which the distance between columns is equivalent of two-and-a-quarter diameters.

EUTHYNTERIA A levelling course of a Greek temple, connecting the buried foundation to the visible superstructure forming the **crepis** *or* **crepidoma**.

EXEDRA An apse or a large recess or semicircular niche, often containing stone seats. It *can* be rectangular on plan, but the term means an open recess in which persons may sit.

EXTRADOS The exterior curve of an arch measured to the top of the voussoirs or archivolt as opposed to the **intrados** or soffite (*see* **arch**).

EYE The centre of a part: the circle in the middle of an Ionic volute, an aperture at the summit of a dome, or a circular window in the centre of a pediment. A **bull's-eye** or *oeil-de-boeuf* window is a circular or elliptical opening (*see* **Ionic Order**).

Fig. 31 *Georgian fanlights in Armagh*

EYECATCHER A decorative feature (such as a folly or a temple) in a landscape as the terminating focus of a vista.

FAÇADE The exterior face or front of a building.

FACETTES The flat projections or fillets between the flutes of columns (*see* **Orders**).

FALSE ATTIC An attic storey without pilasters or balustrades.

FAME Winged female figure blowing a trumpet, often found in spandrels, as in triumphal arches.

FANLIGHT A window, often semicircular or segmental, over a door, and so called because of the radiating glazing-bars which suggested the shape of an open fan. The term has come to be applied to all glazed openings over doors, whether the glazing bars are in the shape of a fan or not [Fig. 31].

FASCES A bound bundle of rods enclosing an axe, a symbol of the authority of the law [Fig. 32].

FASCIA A broad band or face used in Classical Architecture, often in conjunction with other mouldings. **Architraves** are divided into two or three fasciae, each of which projects beyond the face of that below it. A broad fillet.

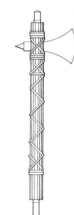

Fig. 32 *Fasces*

FASTIGIUM A pediment, the apex of a pediment, or a ridge. It can also mean an **acroterium** in the sense of blocks.

FAUCES A vestibule in a Roman house between the front door to the street and the atrium. If the door were to be set back from the line of the front wall the space outside the door is called **vestibulum** and the inside **prothyra**. Fauces implies a narrow space through which many pass to larger spaces.

FEATHERS Three or five upright feathers are common Neoclassical devices.

FENESTRATION The arrangement of windows in a façade.

FESTOON An ornament of carved wreaths, garlands of flowers or leaves, or both, suspended in swags on walls and friezes, and commonly found in Classical Architecture. The swags are represented as tied, so they are narrow at each extremity, and thickest at the centre of the hanging part [Fig. 33].

Fig. 33 *Festoon of husks or bellflowers*

FIELDED A raised central part of a panel.

FILLET A narrow band used between mouldings in order to separate and define them, found in cornices and bases. It is not always flat, but is often found cut into two or more narrow faces with sharp edges between. If it is a narrow flat band it is also called a **listel** or **annulet**. The small bands between the flutes of columns are also called fillets.

FINIAL In Classical Architecture surmounting any prominent terminal: it can be an obelisk, a thin pyramid, an acorn, a pinecone, a pineapple, a ball, or an urn [Fig. 2].

FLAT TILE Rain tile or **tegula**, meaning a common flat tile, the joints of which were covered with an **imbrex** *or* **covering tile**.

FLEUR-DE-LYS A stylized lily, related to anthemion ornament.

FLORENTINE ARCH An arch with intrados and extrados struck from different points [Fig. 10].

FLORIATED Carved in imitation of flowers or leaves.

FLUSH A flush bead moulding is a bead set in a channel so that its outermost part is flush with the surfaces on either side.

FLUTE (pl. **FLUTES, FLUTINGS**) The concave channels in the shafts of Classical columns or pilasters, cut perpendicularly, used in all Orders save Tuscan. There are 20 in the Greek Doric Order, segmental in section, meeting in sharp arrises, and 24 in the Ionic, Corinthian, and Composite Orders, deeper in section, and separated by fillets. Sometimes (except in the Doric Order) flutes are partially filled with a convex moulding or bead to one third of

the height of the shaft: this is called **cabling**. Flutes most usually terminate in hemispherical forms, but in the Greek Doric Order they terminate in the **annulets**. The horizontal fluting of the **torus** of an Ionic base is called **reeding** (*see* **Orders**).

FOLIATE MASK A humanoid face surrounded by leaves, sometimes with sprouting foliage coming from the mouth and nostrils.

FORNIX An arch or a vault, vaulted opening, archway, arched door, or an arch erected as a monument.

FORUM An open space in a town serving as a market-place and general place of rendezvous. It often was surrounded by

porticoes or colonnades. There are differences between the Greek **agora** and the Roman forum.

FOUNDATION The **fundamentum** or buried substructure of a building. The Greeks called it **euthynteria**, as a levelling course joining the foundation to the **crepidoma**.

FRENCH ORDER An Order with banded shafts, or one in which the cock and fleur-de-lys are introduced into the capital. An Order with spirals or leaves wound round the shafts and three columns arranged on a triangular plan.

FRENCH WINDOW A window or glazed door opening in two leaves to give access to a balcony or a garden.

Fig. 34 *How to set out flutes and fillets of columns and pilasters. From Langley*

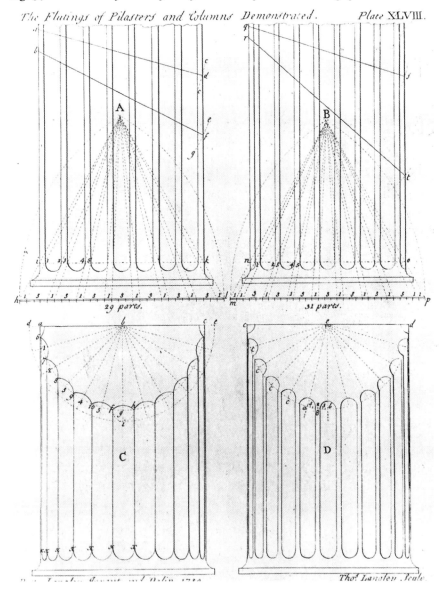

FRET, FRETTE, FRETWORK   Ornament consisting of fillets meeting at right angles arranged in bands of angular key-patterns. Also known as the **Greek key** or **angular guilloche** [Fig. 39].

FRIEZE   The middle division of an entablature lying between the cornice and the architrave. The Tuscan frieze is plain, but the Doric is subdivided along its length by **triglyphs** and **metopes**. Ionic, Corinthian, and Composite friezes are often embellished with continuous sculpture, but can be plain. Sometimes friezes can be **pulvinated**, **convex**, or **cushioned**, usually in the Ionic Order. The frieze of a capital is called the **hypotrachelium**, as in a species of Ionic. A **frieze panel** is the upper panel of a six-panelled door, while a **frieze rail** is the upper rail but one of a six-panelled door (*see* **Orders**).

FRIGIDARIUM   The room with cold-water basin in an ancient *Therma*.

FRONTISPIECE   The main façade. Also an entrance that is embellished with architectural motifs.

FRONTON   A pediment.

FROSTED   A type of rusticated work (*see* **rustication**).

FRUIT   Used in Horns of Plenty, baskets, and festoons.

FUSAROLE   A member with a semicircular section, or a bracelet-bead, found under the echinus of the Ionic and Composite Orders (*see* **Orders**).

FUST   The shaft of a column or the trunk of a pilaster. The ridge of a roof, and so also the top of a triangular pediment.

FYLFOT   The swastika.

GABLE, GAVEL   The end wall of a building, the top of which conforms to the slope of the roof which abuts against it. In modern usage the term is applied only to the upper part of such a wall above eaves level, and the entire wall is called a gable-end. A **Dutch gable** is one with curved or scrolled sides crowned by a pediment or an arch. In Classical Architecture the low triangular gable, framed by the low pitches of the roof, is called a **pediment** [Fig. 35].

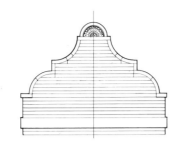

Fig. 35a *Shaped gable*

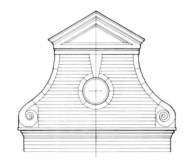

Fig. 35b *Dutch gable*

GADROON, GODROON   One of a set of convex mouldings joined at their extremities to form an enrichment: gadrooning is rather like the reverse of fluting, and is frequently found on the upper surface of convex mouldings, rather like fingers. Gadrooned means enriched with convex rods. It is also called lobes, (k)nulled decoration, or thumb mouldings [Fig. 36].

Fig. 36 *Gadroons*

GAINE   A herm.

GARLAND   Ornaments of flowers, fruits, and leaves, usually found in friezes or similar positions.

GAUGED ARCH   One with voussoirs radiating to a centre, with bricks finely rubbed, or stones finely cut [Fig. 9].

GAZEBO   Properly, a small apartment on a roof with a view, also called **belvedere**. A summer-house, or any ornamental structure commanding a view.

GEISON   A raked **cornice**, as on a pediment.

GEOMETRICAL STAIRCASE   One in which the flight of stone stairs is supported by the wall at only one end of the steps, each step resting on the next. There are no newels.

GEORGIAN   Architecture of the first four King Georges of England (1714–1830), but the term is usually applied to a very simple form of stripped Classical domestic Architecture featuring plain window-openings with sashes, doorcases that vary from the elaborate treatment with consoles, pediments, columns, and pilasters, to plain openings with fanlights. During the Georgian period **Rococo**, **Chinoiserie**, and **Gothick** influences occurred, often in interior decoration or in ornamental buildings.

GERMAN ORDER   Similar to the Britannic Order.

GIANT ORDER   An Order rising from the ground or from a plinth more than one storey, also known as a Colossal Order. A **Gigantic Order** is the Tuscan Order, so named by Scamozzi.

GIBBONWORK   Exquisite naturalistic carving in the manner of Grinling Gibbons (1648–1721).

GIBBS SURROUND   The architrave or surround of a door, window, or niche consisting of large blocks of stone interrupting the architrave, named after James Gibbs (1682–1754) [Figs. 6, 37, 52].

GIGANTIC ORDER   The Tuscan Order.

GIRANDOLE   A large branched candlestick.

GIRDLE   A circular band or fillet surrounding a part of a column.

GLACIS   A slope or declivity, originally falling from a fortress so that the slope could be raked by fire, but subsequently employed as a device in garden design.

GLYPH   A sunken channel, usually vertical. The term is used to denote the perpendicular channels cut in the projecting tablets of a Doric frieze which are called **triglyphs** from their having three vertical channels, or, more correctly two whole channels with a half-channel at each side of the tablet (*see* **Doric Order**).

GLYPTOTHECA   A building for the display of sculpture.

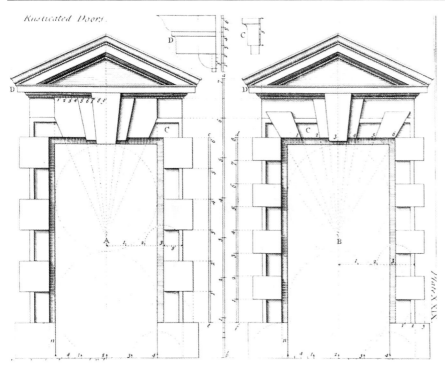

Fig. 37 *Rusticated doorways, treated as Gibbs surrounds, in which the plain ashlar blocks interrupt the architrave. From Langley*

GRADETTO (pl. **GRADETTI**)   An annulet.

GREEK CROSS   A cross with arms of equal length [Fig. 38].

GREEK KEY   A labyrinthine fret used in bands, often on string-courses and sometimes on friezes [Fig. 39].

GREEK ORDERS   The Doric, Ionic, and Corinthian, each of which is distinct from Roman versions.

GREEK REVIVAL   The phase of **Neoclassicism** that involved using archaeologically correct elements from Ancient Greek Architecture following the publication of a number of accurate surveys, notably Stuart and Revett's *The Antiquities of Athens*, which appeared from 1762. The adoption of Greek Architecture involved considerable ingenuity on the part of designers: towers and spires involving pile-ups of Greek motifs, and churches with galleries are but two obvious examples where the style had to be used in highly original ways [2.7–2.13, 2.21, 2.23–2.29, 2.31, 6.1–6.6, 6.12–6.13].

GNOMON   A rod or other object which serves to indicate the time by casting its shadow on a marked surface: the pin or triangular plate on a sundial. A column employed in order to observe the meridian altitude of the sun. A **gnomonic column** is a cylinder on which the hour of day is indicated by the shadow cast by the stylus (fixed or moveable).

GOLA   An **ogee**, or the cymatium.

GORGE   A cavetto moulding or throating. It is less recessed than a scotia, and is chiefly used in frames. The term is also used for the **cyma recta** or to denote the neck of a column.

GORGERIN   The small frieze at the top of a Roman Doric capital between the astragal at the top of the shaft and the annulets. It is also called the **neck**, or a **collarino**, while Vitruvius calls it the **hypotrachelium**.

GORGONEIA   Keystones carved with the heads of gorgons.

GRACES   Three female figures, supposedly called Aglaia, Thalia, and Euphrosyne, usually depicted holding each other's hands.

GRADATION   Rising by steps or degrees, as in a theatre. Also a barely discernible change of colour.

Fig. 38 *Commonest varieties of the Cross*

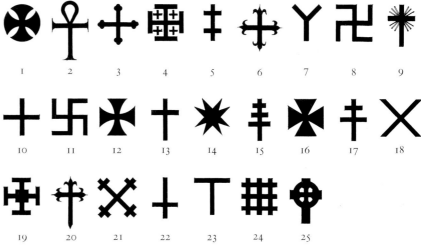

1. Alisée Patée or Patée cross
2. Ancient Egyptian Ankh
3. Bottonée or Clover-leaf cross
4. Crusader's or Jerusalem cross. Without the four small crosses it is a *Potent* cross
5. Double cross
6. Fleurée or Fleury cross. If the centre leaf of each arm is omitted it is a *Moline* cross
7. Forked cross
8. Fylfot or Swastika
9. Glory cross
10. Greek cross
11. Hakenkreuz or Potent Rebated cross
12. Iron Cross or Eisenkreuz of Prussia
13. Latin cross
14. Maltese cross
15. Papal cross
16. Patée Formée cross
17. Patriarchal cross
18. St Andrew's cross or *Saltire*
19. St Chad's cross
20. St James's cross
21. St Julian's cross
22. St Peter's cross
23. Tau cross or St Anthony's cross
24. Triparted cross
25. Wheel-head or Celtic cross

Note that Nos 8 and 11 are related to the Greek Key, Fret, or Labyrinth, and to the Potent Cross

Fig. 39 *Two forms of Greek Key or Labyrinthine Fret*

GRIFFIN　Animal with head, wings, and claws of an eagle, and body of a lion.

GRISAILLE　A decorative painting in grey tints to suggest bas-reliefs.

GROIN　The intersection of two simple vaults, crossing each other at the same height, and forming an arris, or sharp edge.

GROTESQUE　Light and fanciful Classical ornament consisting of foliage, figures, and animal forms, fantastically combined and interwoven [5.37]. The term seems to originate from the fact that much Antique ornament of this type was found in underground apartments, and such underground volumes are called grottoes. A Grotesque ornament, containing human and animal forms, is not the same as Arabesque [Fig. 8].

GROTTO　An artificial cave, usually decorated with shells, and often incorporating a water cascade and fountain. Grottoes were sometimes built in houses, and were fashionable in the

Fig. 40 *Elaborate shell-work grotto of the eighteenth century at Pommersfelden*

eighteenth century [Fig. 40]. More often, however, they were garden buildings, often adorned with '**rustick**' Architecture on the outside.

GROUND FLOOR　The storey of a building at ground level, often containing important rooms. The ground floor is not always the lowest floor, and can be set over a basement. The best rooms are often found on the first floor, or elevated, as a **piano-nobile** level.

GROUND TABLESTONES　The projecting course of stones above the surface of the ground, known as the **plinth**.

GROUPED COLUMNS　More than two columns grouped together on one pedestal. When only two columns are used they are called **coupled columns**.

GUILLOCHE　A Classical ornament in the form of two or more bands or strings twisting over each other so as to repeat the same figure in a continuous series, leaving circles in the centres [Fig. 41]. The term is also loosely applied to the fret or Greek key pattern, which is really an angular guilloche [Fig. 39]. Also called a **plait-band**.

Fig. 41 *Two forms of guilloche*

GULA　The cymatium.

GUTTAE　Ornaments like the **frustum** of a cone hanging from the soffites of the mutules and regulae under the band of the architrave of the Doric Order. Sometimes they are cylindrical, like dowels. There are generally 18 of them under the mutules, set in three rows, each row parallel to the front, and six under the regula. In the case of the 'Roman' Doric Order the number of guttae under the soffite of the cornice varies. They may represent timber pegs, and thus suggest a wooden prototype for the Order. They are sometimes called **lachrymae**, or tears, sometimes **campanulae**, meaning bells, and sometimes **drops**, **droplets**, **nails**, or **trunnels** (see **Doric Order** [Fig. 26]).

GYMNASIUM　A meeting-place for athletic practice, usually several porticoes and rooms around a rectangular open space: it often had a type of cloistered colonnade around it. It is also known as **palaestra**. It must not be confused with *stadium* (racecourse for humans) or *hippodrome* (racecourse for horses), which were long and narrow on plan with rounded end or ends: the hippodrome reached its greatest development in the Roman circus with its central *spina* enriched with trophies, obelisks, and monuments, and the raked seats for spectators.

GYNAECONITIS　The women's quarters in a Greek house or palace, usually applied to the quarters of slaves.

HA-HA　A trench, consisting of a vertical or slightly battered side contained by a retaining wall or revetment of stone or brick on the side nearest the house (or the point from which the landscape is viewed), and with the other side of the trench sloping and grassed. The ha-ha thus prevented cattle or other livestock from straying to the area contained within it, but, being invisible from the vantage point or house, did not interrupt the view with a fence, wall, or hedge.

HALF-ROUND　A semicircular moulding, either a bead or a torus.

HARMONIC DIVISION or **PROPORTION**　Relation of successive numbers in a series proportional to the lengths of twanged cords that sound harmonious. $1:2$ = octave, $1:2:4$ = 2 octaves, and these proportions produce agreeable architectural relationships. The reciprocals of a series of numbers in arithmetical progression are said to be in harmonic proportion.

HARMONY　An agreement, balance, or repose between all the parts of a building, having connections with symmetry.

HARPY　A monster with head and breasts of a woman and wings and claws of a bird, usually found in **Grotesque** ornament.

HAUNCHES OF THE ARCH　The parts between the crown and the springing (*see* **arch** [Fig. 9]).

HAWKSBEAK　A crowning moulding of the Greek Doric Order like a cyma recta with the upper concave curve concealed by a beak-like overhang (*see* **Doric Order**).

HECATOMPEDON A temple with a portico one hundred Attic feet wide, or one with a **naos** one hundred feet long. 101.341 English feet = 100 Attic feet. An Attic foot is derived from studies of the dimensions of the Parthenon.

HEIGHT OF AN ARCH The distance from the line of the springing to the highest point of the intrados (*see* **arch** [Fig. 9]).

HELIOSCENE An exterior louvered blind which protects the room from the sun yet permits a view out from that room.

HELIX (pl. **HELICES**) Little spiral ornaments or volutes, 16 in number, in the Corinthian capital, also called **urillae**, under the abacus. There are two at each angle of the abacus, and two in the centre of each face, branching from the **caulicoli** or stalks that rise between the acanthus leaves. Vitruvius called the inner spirals only helices, calling the outer spirals at the corners **volutae**, which is also his term for the volutes of the Ionic capital (*see* **Orders**).

HEM The spiral protruberant part of an Ionic capital (*see* **Orders**).

HEMICYCLE A semicircular recess, such as those in the forum of Trajan in Rome, too large to be termed **exedrae**.

HEMISPHAERIUM A dome.

HEMITRIGLYPH A half triglyph at each side of the tablet in the Doric frieze (*see* **Orders**).

HEPTASTYLE A colonnade or portico with seven columns in one line.

HERM A pedestal, square on plan, terminating in a head of Hermes or some other deity. The pedestal has the generalized proportions of the human body, and sometimes features feet at the base.

HERMAPHRODITE A figure combining male and female sexual characteristics.

HERMITAGE A small hut or dwelling in a secluded spot, usually built in a park or woodland as a resting-place or gazebo, and constructed in the 'rustick' style, often associated with a grotto, moss-hut, or cottage orné.

HEROUM A shrine dedicated to a deified dead person.

HEXASTYLE A portico of six columns in one line (*see* **temple**).

HIPPOCAMP A creature with the head and forelegs of a horse, and the tail of a fish.

HIPPODROME A racecourse for horses, as opposed to a **stadium**, which was a racecourse for men.

HISTORICISM An attempt to understand and use the styles of the past in a correct and archaeological manner.

HOOF FOOT, PIED DE BICHE, or CLOVEN FOOT Feet of goats or sheep used to terminate **cabriole** legs.

HORN The Ionic volute.

HUSK OR BELLFLOWER A stylized, bud-like ornament, usually found in a string, margent, or festoon [Fig. 33].

HYPAETHRAL An unroofed building, with columns.

HYPERTHYRUM The entablature or cornice over a door or window: a lintel. Vitruvius calls the frieze course between the lintel of a door or window and a cornice further up, the hyperthyrum (*see* **Doorcases, window surrounds**).

HYPOCAUST A subterranean space for heating by means of hot air.

HYPOGAEUM All parts of a building underground.

HYPOSTYLE A covered colonnade: a hall with many columns.

HYPOTRACHELIUM (or -**ON**) The lower part of the Tuscan, Roman Doric, and some Ionic capitals between the astragal at the top of the shaft and the fillet under the ovolo. The frieze of the capital, or the part of the shaft below the capital, or the neck. The trachelium (-on) in the Greek Doric Order is the part of the shaft between the horizontal groove or grooves circumscribing the column (known as the **hypotrachelium**) and the annulets under the echinus. Thus, the hypotrachelium has a slightly different meaning for each Order, but the term seems properly to apply to the lower part of the neck (*see* **Orders**).

ICE HOUSE A cone-shaped structure, partly underground, for the preservation of ice collected in the winter for use during warmer weather. Occasionally such houses had architectural treatments above the ground.

ICICLE A representation of water in

ornament. Frosted or congelated rustication, often found in fountains and grotto ornament [Fig. 54].

IMBREX A convex tile covering the joint between two adjacent concave tiles, or covering the joint between plain tiles.

IMPLUVIUM The cistern in the centre of a courtyard used to collect water from the compluvium or opening in the roof: the courtyard itself.

IMPOST The capital, moulding, bracket, entablature, or pier from which an arch springs: the impost is generally held to be the actual point from which the arch springs. An **impost block** is a slab or element placed between a capital and the springing of an arch (*see* **arch** [Fig. 9]).

INBAND A stone laid with its length built into the return of a wall or reveal, showing only its face. A **quoin** or a **jamb-stone**.

INLAID WORK When the surface of one material is cut away to a minimum depth in patterns, and metal, stone, cement, wood, ivory, or some other substance is inserted to fill the hollows, and finished to a flush surface, the result is called inlaid work. Boule or Buhl work and marquetry are examples. If metal is inlaid in metal it is called **damascening**.

INSERTED COLUMN A engaged column or a column set in a reveal, or let into a wall.

INSULATED Detached. An insulated column stands free from a wall: thus the columns of peripteral temples were said to be insulated.

INTAGLIO Sculpture where the design is hollowed out or incised. **Intaglios** also means the carved work of an Order, or carving on any part of an edifice.

INTARSIA A wooden mosaic made up of different woods.

INTAVOLATA A cymatium.

INTERAXIAL Interaxial measurements are those from centre to centre, say, of adjacent columns, as opposed to **intercolumnar** measurements.

INTERCOLUMNIATION The distance between columns measured from the lower parts of the shafts in multiples of the diameter of a column. Greek Doric intercolumniation was generally that of the monotriglyph (i.e. having one triglyph between two columns), but at the corners of Greek Doric buildings, on account of the triglyphs being placed at the angles, the extreme intercolumnation is less than that of the intermediate columns. The main types of intercolumniation as defined by Vitruvius are: **Pycnostyle** (1½D), **Systyle** (2D), **Eustyle** (2¼D), **Diastyle** (3D), and **Araeostyle** (3 + D), where D = the diameter. Eustyle is the most commonly used intercolumniation, although the Doric Order intercolumniation is controlled by the triglyph/metope relationship, as triglyphs are centred on columns in Roman Doric at all times. In Greek Doric, as described above, the angle triglyphs are not on the centre-lines of columns.

INTERDENTILS The spaces between dentils: in Roman work the dentils are set closer together than in Greek work.

INTERFENESTRATION The space between window-openings.

INTERMODILLION The space between modillions, often ornamented.

INTERPENSIVAE **Cantilevers** formed by the ends of joists.

INTERPILASTER The space between pilasters.

INTERSECTIO The gap between dentils. The space between dentils seems also to have been described as μετόπη (metope) by the Ancient Greeks, but metope is never used in this sense today. **Metopon** is used for a piece of wall between doors or windows, a Classical **trumeau** or mullion.

INTRADOS The interior and lower curve of an arch: the upper curve is called the extrados. The soffite of an arch or vault, or its under-surface (see **arch** [Fig. 9]).

INVERTED ARCH One with the intrados under the centre, i.e. an arch turned upside down, used in foundations.

IONIC ORDER The second of the Orders used by the Greeks, and the third used by the Romans. The distinguishing feature is the **capital**, which is ornamented with spiral projections known as **volutes**. The proportions of the column are more slender than those of the Doric Order, and the Order has a **base**. The shaft is generally **fluted**, with fillets between the flutes. Ionic entablatures do not have triglyphs or metopes, and the frieze can be plain or enriched. In some variations of

the Order there is no frieze, but the **architrave** is usually divided into three fasciae. **Abaci** are moulded, often enriched, and much smaller than the Doric abaci. Cornice mouldings are often elaborate, and include **dentils**. The **echinus**, **astragal**, and **fillet** are common to both Greek and Roman Ionic capitals, and the echinus is uniformly cut into eggs surrounded with angular-sectioned borders, and with tongues between the borders. Astragals are rows of bead-and-reel ornament. When columns are used in the flanks of the buildings as well as in the 'front', the capitals of each angular column are made to face both contiguous sides of the building, with the two

adjacent volutes at the corner bending in a concave curve towards the angle. Roman Ionic capitals often have the four sides identical, with the volutes projecting diagonally at all four corners under the abacus. The Order used at the Erechtheion in Athens has a frieze of **anthemion** motifs around the necks of the columns below the astragal of the capital proper, giving it an especially rich flavour, especially as the astragal below the neck is also enriched with beads [2.15, 2.25, 2.43–2.50]. The **Ammonite** Order is an English version of Ionic, found in some numbers in Kent and Sussex, and named after the whorled chambered fossil shells that are used instead of the volutes [Fig. 5].

Fig. 42 *Corinthian gateway. Note the keystones and voussoirs, the attic storey, and the way in which the voussoirs are treated over the flat arches. From Langley*

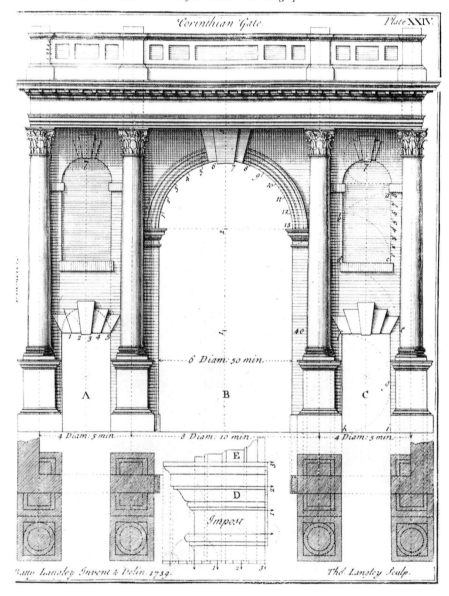

ISODOMUM   Masonry with courses of equal thickness.

ITALIANATE   A style based on the Architecture developed in Italy from the end of the fifteenth century, made fashionable by Barry at the Travellers' and Reform Clubs (London), and later by Prince Albert at Osborne House. It is essentially astylar, with aediculated openings, and a large **cornicione** capping the elevations [4.26, 6.28].

JAMB   Properly, the side of a window- or door-opening bearing the superincumbent weight of the wall, but more often simply to the vertical lining of the opening. The **antepagmentum** supports the lintel or **supercilium**.

KEY   A pattern, also called a fret or a Greek-key design [Fig. 39].

KEYSTONE   The highest and central stone or voussoir of an arch, sometimes called a **sagitta**. It is often carved with human heads, or in the form of an **ancon**, sometimes supporting a bust or other ornament. A keystone is wedge-shaped; it is equidistant from the springing extremities of the arch. In circular openings there are properly two keystones, one at the bottom and one at the top [Figs. 6, 9, 37, 42].

KIOSK   An open pavilion or summer-house of light construction, supported on columns and surrounded by a balustrade, often found in gardens.

KNEE   The projection of architrave mouldings at the ends of the lintel in the dressings of a Classical door- or window-opening [Fig. 11].

KNEELER   A block of stone at the top of a wall terminating the parapet, or coping, or gable. It is also called a **padstone**, a **kneestone**, and a **skew-stone**.

KNULLING   A very flat bead-and-reel moulding. Also a term for **gadrooning** or **lobing** [Fig. 36].

KNURL FOOT   A foot like an inward-turning scroll.

LABARUM   Roman Imperial standard surmounted by an eagle, usually associated with trophies in Neoclassical decoration.

LABYRINTH   A fret with many maze-like turnings, similar to a key pattern or Greek key [*see* Fig. 39.]

LACHRYMAE   Guttae (*see* **Doric Order**).

LACONICUM   A dry room for sweating in *Thermae*.

LACUNAR   Describes a ceiling or the under-surface of a cornice or entablature with sunken coffers but no platbands or spaces between the panels. When these platbands are present the soffite is termed **laquear**.

LAMP   A symbol of enlightenment and immortality, often found on urns or vases.

LANTERN   A turret, drum, or other structure raised above a roof or dome with windows around the sides to light the apartment below.

LAQUEAR   See **lacunar**.

LARMIER   The corona between the cymatium and the bed-moulding. A drip (*see* **Orders**).

LATER   Brick. **Later crudus** is a sun-dried brick, while **later coctus** or **testaceus** is baked. Burned bricks or tiles used as facings in Roman concretes are called **tegulae**.

LATTICE   Openwork, often associated with **Chinoiserie** [Fig. 19].

LATIN CROSS   One with three arms of equal length and the fourth much longer [Fig. 38].

LAUREL   Bay, often used in Classical decoration, as in bay-leaf garland [Fig. 16].

LEAF-AND-DART   A moulding similar to the egg-and-dart but with a leaf carved on the oval shape, or substituted for the egg (*see* **Orders**, [2.20, 3.11]).

LEAVES   Ornaments: carved and stylized versions of the leaves of the laurel, palm, bay, olive, acanthus, and other plants. Leaves of a door (*see* **Orders**).

LESBIAN CYMATIUM   What Vitruvius calls cymatium Lesbium seems to refer to the cyma reversa moulding, that is with a convex shape at the top, and a concave below, often enriched (*see* **Orders** and **moulding**).

LIMEN   A lintel or threshold.

LINTEL   A beam over an opening to support the wall above. A **limen superum** is specifically a lintel or **supercilium**, to distinguish it from a threshold.

LION MASK   Frequently found in Classical ornament, especially keystones, corbels, and bosses.

LIST or **LISTEL**   A fillet or an annulet.

LODGE   A small house at the gate of an estate (often paired with a similar structure to provide symmetry) or any small house in a park. A Masonic Lodge.

LOGGIA   A lodge, but more usually part of a building where one or more sides are open to the air, the opening being colonnaded or arcaded. It can be a separate building, but it is more often an open gallery or an arcaded or colonnaded large recess at ground-floor or *piano-nobile* level [4.66].

LORYMER   The corona.

LOTUS   A common Greek and Egyptian ornament, often mixed with the **palmette**. Lotus-flowers and lotus-buds can sometimes be found together (*see* **anthemion**).

LUCARNE   *See* **luthern**.

LUNETTE   A semicircular opening or blind recess.

LUTHERN   A window standing perpendicularly above the entablature and built on the naked, or same plane as the main façade below the entablature, to illuminate space within the roof. Lutherns can be semicircular, elliptical, segmental-headed, and of other kinds, and are associated with French Classical Architecture. They are not the same as **dormers**, which rise vertically from the rafters of a sloping roof, and do not rise perpendicularly on the naked of the façade below.

LYRE   Instrument frequently found in Classical decoration, often associated with Apollo.

LYSIS   A plinth above the cornice of the podium of a Classical building.

MAEANDER   The key pattern (*see* **Greek Key**).

MAENIANUM   A lattice, balcony, or projecting storey, or a tier of seats in theatres.

MANNERISM   A style of sixteenth-century Architecture characterized by the use of Classical motifs outside their normal context, or in a wilful or illogical manner. It was the precursor of Baroque, and is generally associated with Italian Architecture from the time of Michelangelo until the beginning of the seventeenth century. Dropped keystones or triglyphs, columns inserted into recesses and apparently carried on consoles, and distorted aedicules were features of the style. Subsequently the School of Fontainebleau and the Flemish Mannerists created a lavish style of decoration with **strapwork** and Grotesquerie much in evidence, with swags, herms, cartouches, etc. [4.47–4.49, 4.51]

MANSARD ROOF A roof with two inclined planes, named after François Mansart (1598–1666). Also called a **Curb Roof**.

MANTEL or **MANTLEPIECE** Properly, a decorative shelf in front of the **manteltree** (or mantletree) or horizontal beam over a fireplace. The mantelpiece is carried on the jambs of the chimneypiece. The term has become corrupted to mean the frame surrounding a fireplace.

MARBLE **Marmor**, or a crystalline limestone. It can be easily and accurately carved and can be burned to provide **quicklime**.

MARGENT A strip of leaf and flower forms hanging from a point [Fig. 43].

Fig. 43 *Margent*

MARIGOLD WINDOW A circular window with radiating glazing-bars or mullions, often found in gables or in pediments.

MARINE DECORATION This features Neptune, Amphitrite, hippocamp, dolphin, Nereid, Triton, and mermaid forms, with seaweed, shells, fish, corals, chains, anchors, and frosted rustication.

MARMORATUM OPUS Fine stuff of calcinated gypsum and crushed stones, including marble, which, when set, is rubbed down to a fine marble-like surface. An imitation marble.

MARQUETRY Inlaid work of thin plates of ivory, or different veneers of wood glued to a ground and forming a decorative pattern.

MASONRY The craft of cutting, jointing, and laying stones for building.

MASON'S MITRE When mouldings meet at an angle the joint does not (or ought not to) occur at the diagonal because the resulting acute angle of the masonry is brittle and fragile. The moulding is therefore carried through on the return face, and the joint occurs at right angles to the face. A Mason's Mitre does not, therefore, have a diagonal joint.

MAUSOLEUM A built, roofed, sepulchre with architectural pretensions containing sarcophagi, coffins, or cinerary urns, so called after the celebrated tomb of King Mausolus of Caria at Halicarnassus [6.8, 6.14–6.16].

MEDALLION A square, elliptical, circular, or oval tablet on which are figures, designs, or busts, usually carved in relief.

MEDUSA One of the Gorgons, often used as a decoration on a keystone.

MEGARON A hall, temple, inner sanctuary, underground cavern, or a main hall or significant apartment.

MEMORY, THE ART OF A system of mnemonic devices evolved in Antiquity and revived and developed in Renaissance times: it was sometimes called the **Phoenix**. It involved the study of a building; the student would visit the rooms in a specific order, memorizing that order and architectural details of each room. When memorizing a speech he would revisit the building in imagination, associating the images with arguments or words that would then become the trigger for the speech. The Art of Memory is fully discussed by Frances A. Yates in *The Art of Memory* (London, 1966).

MEROS The flat face between the channels in the Doric triglyph.

METATOME, METOCHE The space between dentils in Classical Architecture, or the space between the triglyphs of the Doric Order.

METOPA, METOPE, METOPSE The square space between two triglyphs of the frieze of the Doric Order, either plain or decorated with bucrania, trophies, or sculptured reliefs. Vitruvius also states that metope is an equivalent for intersectio, or the space between two dentils (*see* **Doric Order**).

METOPON The solid between doors or windows, or a pier, square on plan, like a mullion.

MEWS A terrace of stables or coach-houses with living-quarters above, associated with grander houses.

MEZZANINE A storey of medium height between two higher storeys. An entresol. It is only possible with sufficient floor-to-ceiling heights of the principal storeys.

MEZZO-RELIEVO The projection of sculptured ornaments by half their normal three-dimensional depth.

MIDDLE RAIL The middle rail of a door to which the lock or bolt is fixed, also known as the lock rail.

MINUTE The sixtieth part of the diameter of a column at the base of the shaft. It is therefore a proportional measure by which the sizes of parts of an Order are calculated.

MITRE The line formed by the meeting of two elements intersecting each other at an angle.

MODILLION A projecting ornament like a console or embellished bracket under the corona of the Corinthian and Composite Orders, and occasionally in the Roman Ionic Order. Modillions are placed with intervening coffers or other ornaments between them. They should be regularly placed, i.e. the centre of one should always stand over the centre-line of a column or pilaster. Corinthian modillions are usually more elaborate than those of the Ionic or Composite Orders. A mutule, which is confined to the Doric Order, is always spaced in relation to the triglyphs, and is very different in form compared with a modillion, although the origin is probably the same, and the architectural function, that of enriching the soffite of the corona, is identical (*see* **Order**).

MODINATURE The distribution, profiles, and arrangements of the mouldings of an Order, a building, or an architectural member.

MODULE Any measure which regulates proportion by means of its multiples or subdivisions. In Classical Architecture a module is the diameter measured at the base of the shaft, and each module is subdivided into 60 minutes. Some authorities suggest that a module is a half-diameter of 30 minutes, and that it is only used in the Doric Order. However, architectural proportion always depends on some repetition of measurement, and the term refers to any system of measurement that facilitates repetition of a standard unit.

MONEY PATTERN   *See* **Coin Moulding**.

MONOLITH   A shaft of a column, an obelisk, or any part that consists of a single stone.

MONOPODIA   An animal's leg topped by a head, often of a leopard, used as a support.

MONOPTERAL   A building in which there are no walls, only columns carrying a roof to define the volume. Properly, it is circular, but Soane described his own tomb as a 'monopteral' temple although it has four square shafts carrying the monolithic lid on a square plan. It appears to mean a sacred built enclosure with no cell, but with a peripteral arrangement of columns.

MONOSTYLE   A building of one style throughout, a column with a single shaft instead of a cluster, or with one column.

MONOTRIGLYPH   Intercolumniation where only one triglyph and two metopes are introduced between the centre-lines of columns in the frieze.

MONUMENT   Any edifice to commemorate a person or an event.

MOSAIC   Properly, ornamental work formed by inlaying small pieces (tesserae) of stone, glass, pottery, marble, etc., in a pattern which may be either geometrical or naturalistic. However, the term is also applied to a type of chequerboard pattern of black and white squares used in flooring and associated with Masonic Lodges.

MOULDED CAPITAL   A capital with mouldings, unlike a plain or block-capital.

MOULDING   Part of an Order or a building shaped in profile into various curved or angular forms. Any ornamental contour given to features of a building, whether projections or cavities, such as an architrave, an astragal, or a cornice. Regular mouldings [Fig. 44] in Classical Architecture are: the **fillet** or **list**; the **astragal** or **bead**; the **cyma recta** and **cyma reversa**; the **cavetto** or **hollow**; the **ovolo** or **quarter-round**; the **scotia** or **trochilus**; and the **torus** or **round**.

MOUTH   A cavetto.

MUNTIN   The central upright framing in a door. The outside uprights are called **stiles** or **styles**. Muntins butt into the horizontal rails.

MURAL   Belonging to a wall. A mural monument is fixed to a wall. A mural also means a painting on a wall.

MUTILATED   A cornice or a pediment that is broken or discontinued, also called **broken**. It is a device common in Baroque Architecture.

MUTULE   A block, like a bracket, under the corona of the Doric Order. It may have guttae or drops on the underside, and it will be centred over the triglyph. In the Tuscan Order after Inigo Jones [Fig. 68] the mutules are like simple cantilevered brackets, but in the Corinthian and Composite Orders they are termed **modillions**, and are like consoles on their sides. The term mutule, or **mutulus**, seems to imply a structural beam, although where it is used with the Doric Order it is more like a rafter, or the top member of a primitive truss. Vitruvius seems to imply that in Etruscan temples the **trabes compactiles**, architraves, or lintels that were carried on the widely spaced columns, supported a second set of beams at right angles to the architraves, and that these second beams were called mutuli, and were placed on the cell walls and on the centre-lines of each column of the porch, projecting in cantilevers forward of the line of the colonnade (*see* **Order**).

NAKED   The unornamented plain surface of a wall, column, or other part of a building: the main plane of a façade.

NAOS   The sanctuary of a Greek temple, equivalent of the cell or cella, or the part of a temple within the walls (*see* **temple**).

NARTHEX   Part of a church, screened off and situated near the west door. An ante-chamber or vestibule at the west of the church, acting as a variety of porch [4.43].

NAVE   The part of a church west of the choir. It is usually a central space with two or more aisles to the north and south, and is often separated from the choir by a screen [4.43].

NECK   The plain part of a Roman Doric or Tuscan column between the astragal at the top of the shaft and the fillet annulets on the capital. Some Greek Ionic columns have necks, usually enriched with anthemion ornament. It is also called the **collarino** or **hypotrachelium**. A neck-moulding separates the capital from the shaft proper (*see* **Order**).

NEOCLASSICISM   A movement in Architecture that had its beginnings in a rejection of Baroque and Rococo, and in a seeking to rediscover the Architecture of Classical Antiquity, considered a less corrupted source than the Architecture of the Italian Renaissance. An interest in the Architecture of Ancient Rome was encouraged by Piranesi's views of Rome, with their exaggerated scale and Sublime visual effects, but the noble simplicity and

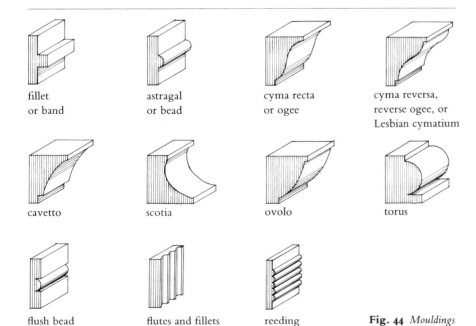

fillet
or band

astragal
or bead

cyma recta
or ogee

cyma reversa,
reverse ogee, or
Lesbian cymatium

cavetto

scotia

ovolo

torus

flush bead

flutes and fillets

reeding

Fig. 44 *Mouldings*

serene grandeur of Greek Architecture extolled by Winckelmann encouraged investigation of the buildings of Classical Antiquity on a new scale. Buildings were re-examined and described, so that many Renaissance sources were rejected in favour of the archaeologically proven correctness of the Antique. Neoclassicism, however, was rarely a mere copying of the works of Antiquity: although accuracy was prized in archaeologically correct motifs it was also concerned to return to first principles, basic forms, clear uncluttered geometry, and a rational approach to design, encouraged by the writings of Laugier and Lodoli. In this was an implicit faith in the superiority of primitive forms of stereometrical purity, which led designers such as Boullée, Ledoux, Ehrensvård, Gilly, Latrobe, and Soane to experiment with an Architecture from which enrichment was often eliminated.

Of all the Orders, Greek Doric was most appreciated for its severity and primitive qualities, first in the surviving remains of the Greek colonies in Sicily and at Paestum, then in the systematic investigations of Greek Architecture by Stuart and Revett which led to the publication of *The Antiquities of Athens* from 1762. The latter provided accurate measured drawings of the Architecture of Ancient Greece for designers, and had a profound effect on taste. Two years later the publication of the *Ruins of the Palace of the Emperor Diocletian at Spalatro*, based on the measurements and drawings by Robert Adam and Charles-Louis Clérisseau, gave further impetus to an understanding of the Antique, while in the 1730s and 1740s work began on the excavation of the cities of Herculaneum and Pompeii, buried since AD 79 as a result of the catastrophic eruptions of Vesuvius: the Architecture, artefacts, and decorative schemes uncovered during the excavations led taste and design further towards an evocation of the Antique. Winckelmann's championing of Greek Art and Architecture together with the work of Stuart and Revett prompted a Greek Revival that was one of the more remarkable aspects of Neoclassicism. Later, the publication of Denon's *Voyage dans la Basse et la Haute Égypte* in 1802, and of the monumental *Description de l'Égypte* by the Commission des Monuments d'Égypte from 1809 gave designers accurate illustrations of real Ancient Egyptian buildings, and were to the Egyptian Revival what the works of Stuart and Revett had been to the Greek Revival. Egyptian Architecture, with its primitive, massive elements, and its simple, pure forms, such as the obelisk, pylon, and pyramid, appealed to those Neoclassical Architects who sought a stereometrical purity in their designs, and a plain, tough, masculine expression of forms. Thus, certain Egyptian elements, such as the pyramid, obelisk, battered walls, and pylon-like shapes entered the vocabulary of Neoclassical design as though responding to the theories of Laugier and Lodoli.

Neoclassical Architecture tends to be severe, stark, serious, and even rather forbidding at times. It is very controlled, and purged of much enrichment, while the Orders, usually Greek and sometimes extremely primitive Greek (such as unfluted, simplified, stumpy Doric) are used to express structural ideas, and are rarely engaged or used as mere decoration. Forms are usually starkly defined, and volumes are expressed both inside and out [2.7–2.13, 2.21, 2.23–2.29, 3.3, 3.4, 5.35, 5.36, 5.66, 5.69, 6.1–6.13, 6.19–6.26].

NEWEL   The central column or solid or imaginary solid around which the steps of a circular staircase wind. Also the principal posts or colonnettes at the angles and foot of a stair balustrade.

NICHE   A recess in a wall for a statue, vase, or other ornament. Niches are often semicircular on plan, and are arched. Some niches contain a shell motif, and some are treated as an aedicule. Others are absolutely plain, without any frame [Fig. 48].

NOSING   The prominent edge of a moulding or drip, or the projecting rounded moulding on the edge of a step.

NULLING   **Gadrooning** or lobing [Fig. 36].

NYMPHAEUM   A grotto, or a structure containing pools, plants, rockwork, fountains, and statues.

OAK   Oak leaves often appear in wreaths or on pulvinated friezes, with acorns.

OBELISK   A tall tapering shaft, usually square on plan, with battered sides and a pyramidal top. Obelisks are usually placed on pedestals in Classical Architecture, and are an instance when Ancient Egyptian forms entered into the language of Classicism. Obelisks were often confused with **pyramids**, so much so that some early drawings show pyramidal forms with obelisks on top.

OCTASTYLE   A portico of eight columns in line (*see* **temple**).

OCULUS   A round window. A disc or button in the centre of a volute-spiral as in the Ionic capital. An opening at the top of a dome, as in the Roman Pantheon.

ODEUM, ODEON   A theatre for musical performances.

OECUS   An odd word, with many meanings, including 'house', 'temple', 'room'. It appears to have come to mean a large and important room in a private house.

OEIL-DE-BOEUF   A window of circular or elliptical form, often with four keystones.

OGEE   An S-shaped double curve, one convex and the other concave. The **cyma** moulding [Fig. 44].

OGIVAL   Ogee (as adjective).

OLIVE   Leaves often confused with bay or laurel.

OPAE   The beds of the roof beams in a Greek building, the spaces between which are called **metopes**.

OPAION   A lantern, or part of a roof pierced and raised for the admission of light.

OPEN WELL   Describes a stair which has a space or a well between the outer strings, unlike the dog-leg which has no space or very little space between the outer strings.

OPISTHODOMUS   The space at the rear of the cell of a temple. An open porch, like the **pronaos** (*see* **temple**).

OPUS ALBARIUM   A coating of **stucco** applied to bricks, coarse stone, and the like.

OPUS ALEXANDRINUM   Paving of marble cut in geometrical shapes, with mosaic in **guilloche** designs. It usually therefore embraces **opus sectile**.

OPUS CAEMENTICIUM   Concrete, or rubble.

OPUS INCERTUM   A wall made of rubble or concrete or both, faced with rubble.

OPUS LISTATUM   Walling of alternate courses of brick and stone.

OPUS QUADRATUM   Walling of squared stone, or ashlar.

OPUS RETICULATUM Walling of concrete with faces of squared stones set diagonally, hence the name from the similarity to a net.

OPUS SECTILE Ornamental paving of marble slabs cut and arranged in geometrical patterns.

OPUS STRUCTILE Concrete.

OPUS TECTORIUM Stucco.

ORANGERY A gallery or a building with south-facing windows for the growing of oranges. Orangeries can be ornamental buildings in gardens, or can be part of a grander composition, physically attached to a house.

ORATORY A small chapel or closet set apart for devotions. A religious establishment of the Order of S. Philip Neri, also known as the Oratorians.

ORCHESTRA The circular area in front of the stage. In Greek theatres it was where the chorus performed. In Roman theatres it was the part containing the seats for the senators and other dignitaries.

ORDER In Classical Architecture, an assembly of parts consisting of column, with base (usually) and capitals, and entablature, proportioned and embellished in consistency with one of the Five Orders. These are the **Tuscan**, **Doric** (Greek and Roman versions), **Ionic**, **Corinthian**, and **Composite**. The Greek Doric column has no base, and the Tuscan column is unfluted. The Ionic Order has an English variant in the **Ammonite** Order [Fig. 5], named from the fossil-like forms of the capital, replacing the standard volutes. A **Colossal Order** is one with columns or pilasters rising from the ground through several storeys. It is also called a **Giant Order**. A **Gigantic Order** is the Tuscan Order [2.1–2.7, 2.9–2.19, 2.21–2.28, 2.30–2.34, 2.36–2.69].

ORDONNANCE The arrangement of a design and the disposition of its various parts.

ORIEL A bay-window on a canted or bowed plan, cantilevered or corbelled out on an upper floor, and projecting in front of the naked of the wall below.

ORLE A fillet under the ovolo or quarter-round of a capital. When it is at the top or bottom of the shaft of a column it is called a **cincture**. The term also means the plinth or the base of a column or pedestal.

ORTHOSTATES Large facing slabs on the outer face of a temple wall, used as a variety of **dado** below the smaller blocks of the wall above.

ORTHOSTYLE Columns set in a straight line.

OUNDY A wavy moulding.

OVA Egg-shaped ornaments.

OVERSAILING Courses of brick or stone corbelled out above the one below.

OVOLO A convex moulding. Greek examples are flattened, like part of the profile of an egg, while Roman ovolos are more mechanical, usually quarter-rounds. The Greek section can be called an **echinus**. Ovolos are often ornamented with egg-and-dart (*see* **Greek Orders**; **Roman Orders** and **moulding**).

OVUM Ovolo.

PACE A dais. A step round a tomb.

PACKING Small stones between larger ones in rubble walls.

PAD A padstone is a stone set on or in a wall to carry a truss, joist, or some other load. It is also known as a **template**.

PALAESTRA A gymnasium. Although the original meaning is narrower, suggesting a wrestling-school, it is often used in the wider sense of gymnasium.

PALLADIAN A style of Architecture that evolved from the work of the sixteenth-century Architect Andrea Palladio (1508–1580), and was brought to Britain in publications, and by the works of Inigo Jones (1573–1652). A revival of the style in the eighteenth century occurred in the area around Venice, but achieved considerable success in Britain largely through the efforts of Lord Burlington (1694–1753) and Colen Campbell (1676–1729), who also revived interest in Inigo Jones's contributions. Under the aegis of the Palladians there evolved appropriate grammar and vocabulary that exercized a veritable tyranny of Taste during the reign of the first three Georges. Palladian ideas were exported to Prussia, Saxony, Russia, and the British Colonies in America [4.61–4.66, 5.57–5.71]. Palladian Architecture was the style favoured by the Whig Oligarchy, and is associated with Anglophiles during the *Aufklärung* in German-speaking lands. A **Palladian Window** is a Serliana or Venetian Window, and recurs in many Palladian designs (*see* [5.46] and **Serliana** or **Venetian Window**).

PALMETTE An ornament rather like a fan made up of narrow divisions or digitations, somewhat resembling a palm-leaf. It is found alternating with the lotus (*see* **anthemion**).

Fig. 45 *Panel mouldings*

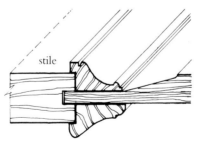

a Raised and fielded panel secured with two versions of bolection mouldings.

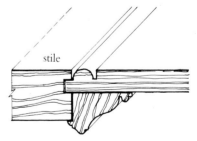

b Flush panel with beaded edge secured with bolection moulding

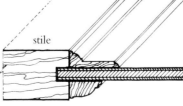

c Flush ply panel secured with two varieties of planted mouldings

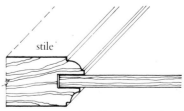

d Flush panel held in stile with solid or struck ovolo upper moulding and cavetto lower moulding

PAMPRE An ornament of vine-leaves and grapes, usually associated with twisted or barley-sugar columns, and often used as the spiral around columns, thus suggesting the twisted form [5.7].

PANCARPI Garlands and festoons of fruit, flowers, and leaves for ornament.

PANEL MOULDINGS Panels are usually held in place within a framework by means of moulded beads. These mouldings can be of various types, including **bead**, **flush**, or **bolection**, while panels can be carved, raised and fielded, or have other decorations [Fig. 45].

PANIER An upright **corbel** over a pilaster and under a truss.

PANTHEON DOME A very simple dome resembling that of the Pantheon in Rome, with a series of concentric rings outside and coffers inside, sometimes with an oculus in the centre.

PANTILE A tile with an S-shaped section used in roofing.

PARAPET A low wall to protect any place where there is a drop. It may be battlemented, plain, pierced, or ornamented. In Classical Architecture it may have an engaged balustrade, panels, dies, and other treatment.

PARCLOSE A screen separating chapels or tombs from the body of a church.

PARASKENION A wing running forward from each of the ends of the **skene** of a Greek theatre.

PARKER'S CEMENT Also called **Roman Cement**, this was a rendering made from powdered, burnt clay nodules mixed with sand and water. It set hard, and fast, and was much used for covering façades with a representation of ashlar.

PAROTIS A console, bracket, or ancon, from a Greek word associated with the ear [Figs. 23, 24, 62].

PARQUET Flooring of hardwood blocks laid in patterns on a base, and polished. Parquetry is inlaid work of thin veneers of hardwood, also called inlaid or plated parquet.

PARTERRE A flat part of a garden designed with formal beds of flowers set in patterns.

PARTING BEAD A slip in the centre of the pulley stile of a sash-window to separate the two sash-cords.

PASTAS A recess off the south-facing side of the peristyle in a Greek house.

PATERA A circular ornament, resembling a dish, worked in relief. When further embellished to become a stylized representative of a flower it is called a rosette. It is also known as phiala.

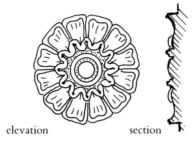

Fig. 46 *Patera in the form of a rosette*

elevation   section

PAVILION A turret, a small building, or a wing of a building. It may be an ornamental building such as a gazebo or a summer-house, or it may be a projecting element of a larger building, often square and independently roofed, used to terminate the wings, or to form an angle element. A **pavilion roof** is one hipped equally on all sides, like a pyramid.

PEDESTAL A substructure placed under some columns in Classical Architecture. It consists of a base or plinth, a dado or die, and a cornice. It may support a statue, a vase, an obelisk, or some other element. It is also found as a part of a balustrade.

PEDIMENT In Classical Architecture, a low-pitched gable crowning a portico or a façade, and often containing sculpture in

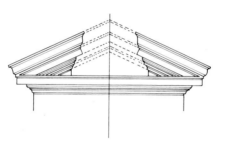

Fig. 47a *Triangular pediment (with pecked and solid lines); and open-topped or broken-apex triangular pediment (with solid lines only)*

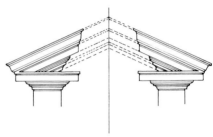

Fig. 47b *Open-bed or broken-base triangular pediment (with pecked and solid lines); and true broken or open triangular pediment (with solid lines only). NB The entablature at an angle is called the raking cornice*

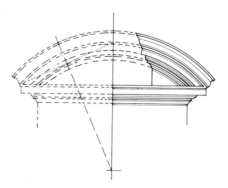

Fig. 47c *Segmental pediment (with pecked and solid lines), with (right) open-topped segmental pediment (with solid lines only). The centre of the segment is obtained by drawing a line from the apex of the corona-fillet of a corresponding triangular pediment to the extremities of the fillet, bisecting the line, and drawing a line at right angles to the first line through the point of bisection*

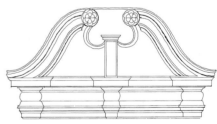

Fig. 47d *Scrolled pediment*

its tympanum. Greek pediments are generally flatter in pitch than Roman pediments. A pediment is formed with the top part of the entablature repeated on its gable. Pediments are found over niches, windows, doors, and other features. While **triangular pediments** are the most common, **segmental pediments** were introduced during the Roman Empire, and are associated with the cults of Isis and Artemis/Diana of Ephesus because of the shape of the crescent-moon and the bow-shape of the Huntress' weapon. Some Isiac temples built by the Romans had segmental pediments. An **open pediment** has sides that stop short of the apex, and is also called an open-topped or broken-apex pediment. If a pediment has a triangular or segmental top, but the bottom has a gap, it is called an **open-bed** or a **broken-base** pediment. A true **broken** pediment has an incomplete bottom cornice and no apex (or top if segmental). Pediments often occur in eighteenth-century doorcases where the horizontal cornice is interrupted by a fanlight, so they would be open-bed or broken-base pediments. A **scrolled pediment** is an open segmental pediment in which the segments terminate in scrolls or volutes.

PENDENTIVE   The portion of a domical vault which descends into the corner of an angular building where a dome is placed on a square base. It is really a variety of concave **spandrel**, forming the junction between the corner of the square compartment and the base of a circular dome or drum [Fig. 25].

PENTASTYLE   A portico of five columns in a line.

PERCH   A bracket or a corbel.

PERGOLA   A path flanked by columns carrying joists, the whole to carry climbing plants.

PERIBOLUS   An enclosing walk or colonnade around an area.

PERIDROME   The space between a row of columns and the wall of the cell or building behind.

PERIPTERAL   A building with a continuous row of columns around it. The periptery is the row of columns around the walls, and the peridrome is the space between the wall and the colonnade. Ancient writers used the term to denote columns round an inner court (*see* **temple**).

PERISTYLE   The range of columns surrounding a building or a court, also called the periptery. A **peristylium** is an inner court with columns surrounding it.

PERITHYRIDES   Ancones.

PERRON   External steps and the landing leading to the principal floor of a building, or the *piano nobile*. Common in Palladian Architecture [5.68].

PERSIENNES   Outer shutters with louvres.

PIANO NOBILE   The principal floor of a building, containing the main reception rooms. It is higher than other storeys and usually set over a basement. It is often approached by an external stair known as a **perron** [5.68].

PIAZZA   A square or rectangular open space surrounded by buildings. In the seventeenth and eighteenth centuries it came to mean any covered ways or arcaded ground floors with buildings over them, as in the Covent Garden Piazza (London) by Inigo Jones. 'Piazzas'

therefore came to mean colonnaded or arcaded walks, pentices, or even cloisters.

PICTURESQUE   From the Italian *pittoresco*, meaning 'in the manner of the painters', this was an eighteenth-century concept. It defined a building, a building in a landscape, or a landscape that resembled a composition by Poussin, Claude, or Salvator Rosa as 'Picturesque'. Asymmetrical composition, natural features (whether real or contrived), and buildings that seemed to belong to the setting were important ingredients of the Picturesque.

PIEDROIT   A pilaster with no base or capital, also known as a **lesene**, and often found in Neoclassical work.

PIER   Any isolated mass of construction, such as the solid between two windows or a support. Piers are much more massive than columns. An arch that springs from a pier is called a pier-arch. Piers are quite distinct from columns and pillars [Figs. 49, 50].

Fig. 48 *Classical piers, two with niches. That on the left sits on a plain plinth, is constructed with chamfered or V-jointed rustication, has a plain triangular pediment, and an apron under the sill. The central pier is surmounted by a sphinx and sits on a plain plinth. Rustication is chamfered or V-jointed, and is rock-faced. Note the Greek Key pattern and the swag. The base of the right-hand niche has raised panels of frosted rustication on the die of the pedestal, while the rest of the rustication is plain chamfered or V-jointed, except for the panel of rock-faced work above the arch. From Langley*

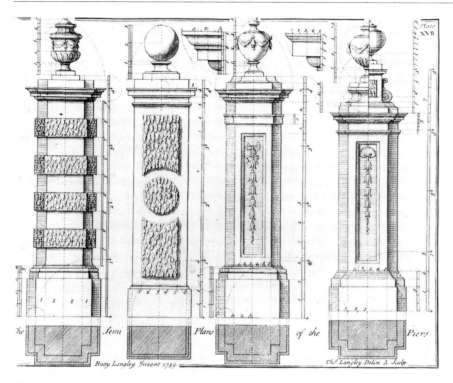

Fig. 49 *Gate-piers. That on the left is banded with frosted rustication. Its neighbour has raised panels of frosted rustication, and the other two have recessed panels with margents. The system of proportion is indicated. Note the urns and ball. From Langley*

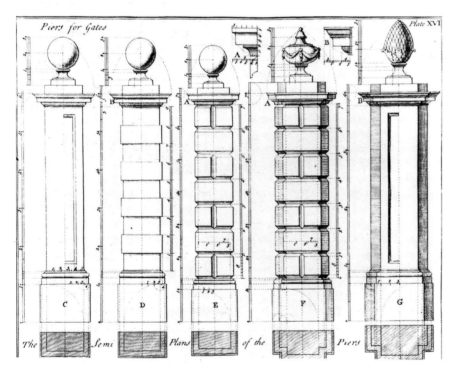

Fig. 50 *Classical gate-piers with proportional systems. C and G have panels in the die or dado; D plain, banded rustication; E and F chamfered or V-jointed rustication. Note the finials in the form of balls, urn, and a pinecone. From Langley*

PILA A freestanding masonry pier, square or rectangular on plan, with no moulding or decorations, and not conforming in any way to the Orders, otherwise known as a **pillar**.

PILASTER A rectangular projection attached to a wall, that is similar to the column of one of the Orders and carries an entablature. A **pilaster-strip** is one with no base or capital, also known as a **piedroit** or a **lesene**. While an **anta** is a species of pilaster, its details differ from those of the columns of the same Order: Ionic antae, for example, have plain capitals without volutes. Pilasters, on the other hand, conform exactly to the details of columns except that they are rectangular, projecting only slightly from the wall, and not curved on plan [Fig. 51].

PILLAR A vertical, isolated, freestanding upright element, which need not be circular on plan, and must not be confused with a column. Generally speaking, pillars do not conform to the Orders. In fact a pillar is really a pier, rectangular or square on plan, with no architectural or decorative pretensions, and known in Latin as *pila*.

PINEAPPLE A symbol of hospitality. Like the pinecone, acorn, and ball, a common form for a finial on a gate-pier [Figs. 2, 50].

PINECONE Used as a finial or a pendant, and frequently confused with the pineapple [Figs. 2, 50].

PINNACLE A summit or an apex. A terminating feature on buttresses, pedestals, dies, parapets, and other elements, usually pyramidal in form.

PLAFOND, PLATFOND A ceiling or a soffite.

PLAISANCE A summer-house or a pleasure pavilion.

PLAIT-BAND A guilloche ornament, so-called from its resemblance to plaits (*see* **guilloche**).

PLANCEER The soffite or under-surface of the **corona**.

PLANTED When a moulding is shaped on a separate piece of material and subsequently fixed in place it is said to be planted, as a bead may be planted.

PLATBAND A flat fascia, band, or string-course, with a projection less than its width. A lintel. A landing.

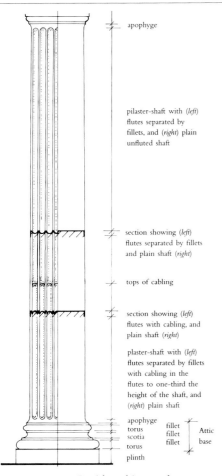

apophyge

pilaster-shaft with (*left*) flutes separated by fillets, and (*right*) plain unfluted shaft

section showing (*left*) flutes separated by fillets and plain shaft (*right*)

tops of cabling

section showing (*left*) flutes with cabling, and plain shaft (*right*)

plaster-shaft with (*left*) flutes separated by fillets with cabling in the flutes to one-third the height of the shaft, and (*right*) plain shaft

apophyge
torus
scotia
torus
plinth

fillet
fillet
fillet

Attic base

Fig. 51 *Pilasters with flutes, cabling, and Attic base*

PLATERESQUE Lavish architectural ornament that is quite distinct from the structure.

PLINTH The plain projecting base of a wall immediately above the ground, usually chamfered or moulded at the top. The square block below the base of a column or pilaster. A **plinth-block** is the plain rectangular block at the base of an architrave, frame, or chimney-piece, which acts as a stop for the plinth, skirting and architrave itself. The plinth or lowest member of the podium is called a **quadra**. Vitruvius also calls the abacus of the Greek Doric capital a **plinthus**.

POCKET The space in the **pulley-stile** of a sash-window.

PODIUM A continuous pedestal or basement, or a dwarf wall. A podium usually carries the colonnade, and is moulded at its top and base [2.60].

POLOS A cylindrical member on the heads of caryatides, or a dowel.

POLYSTYLE With many columns.

POLYTRIGLYPHAL Having more than one triglyph to a single intercolumniation.

POMMEL The ornament on top of a pinnacle, finial, etc. Any globular ornament.

POMPEIAN STYLE Derived from the decorations of Pompeii, the town engulfed by volcanic ash in AD79, and excavated in the eighteenth century.

PORCH An exterior adjunct over a doorway, forming a covered approach. If a porch has columns it is called a **portico**, perhaps more usually if it also has a pediment and resembles the front elevation of a temple.

POROS Limestone that is coarser than marble.

PORTICO A structure forming a porch in front of a building, and consisting of a roofed space open or partially enclosed at the sides, with columns, forming the entrance. A portico often has a pediment. If the portico projects beyond the face of the building it is called **prostyle**, but if it is recessed within the building so that the columns are in the same plane as the front wall but framed by the wall, it is called **in antis** (because the columns are between the antae of the walls). The number of columns at the front determines whether it is **tetrastyle**, **hexastyle**, **octastyle**, **decastyle**, or **dodecastyle**, meaning with four, six, eight, ten, or twelve columns in front respectively. A projecting portico with four columns is therefore **prostyle tetrastyle**, while a recessed portico with two columns would be **distyle in antis**. A portico must have a roof supported on at least one side by columns (*see* **temple**).

POSTICUM The **epinaos**, or rear porch, or the **opisthodomus**.

POYNTELL A pavement of small lozenge-shaped tiles or squares laid in a diagonal pattern.

PRAECINCTIO The great passage dividing the seats into two tiers in a Greek theatre.

PRISMATIC ORNAMENT Simple geometrical forms in relief, such as diamond-pointed rustication [Fig. 54].

PRODOMUS The portico standing before the cell or naos (*see* **temple**).

PROFILE The vertical section, especially of a moulding.

PRONAOS Both the portico and the vestibule flanked by walls behind the portico. It is therefore partly enclosed by walls and partly by columns (*see* **temple**).

PROPORTION The just magnitude of each part, and of each part to another; the relationship existing between parts or elements that should render the whole harmonious in terms of balance, symmetry, and repose.

PROPYLAEUM Any court or vestibule before a building, but more usually a formal entrance gateway to such court or enclosure.

PROSCENIUM The stage of a theatre, or the area between the curtain and the pit, including the arch and frame facing the audience. In a Greek theatre the **proskenion** was a stone structure, consisting of a row of columns standing in a low stylobate in front of the skene wall. Later, the roof of the proskenion seems to have been the platform on which the actors moved, but originally it seems only to have been a background.

PROSTAS A recessed space or vestibule in a Greek house, open on one side; the same as **pastas**.

PROSTYLE With columns standing before the front of the building in a line (*see* **temple**).

PROTHYRON The porch of a Greek house open to the street outside the front door.

PROW Representation of the bow of a ship as in the **Rostral Column** and in schemes of marine decoration [Fig. 22].

PRYTANEUM The headquarters of the administration of a Greek city, usually containing the perpetual fire.

PSEUDODIPTERAL Arranged to appear to be **dipteral** (i.e. with two rows of columns along the flanks) but where the inner rows are omitted although the portico would suggest otherwise (*see* **temple**).

PSEUDOPERIPTERAL   A disposition of columns around a Classical building in which the columns along the sides are engaged with the walls (*see* **temple**).

PTERA   The colonnade around the cell of a Greek temple (*see* **temple**).

PTEROMA   **Ambulatory** or space between the cell of a Greek temple and the columns of the peristyle (*see* **temple**).

PTERON   An external colonnade of Greek buildings, i.e. a **peripteral** colonnade (*see* **temple**).

PULLEY STILE   One of the vertical side-pieces of a window sash-frame in which the pulleys and counterweights are housed.

PULVINATA, PULVIN, or **PULVINUS**   A pillow or cushion, as in the side of the volutes of the Ionic Order. A **dosseret** above a capital (*see* **Orders**, [Fig. 52]).

PULVINATED   A convex-profiled moulding, especially a frieze, looking as though it is subjected to great pressure from above. It is often decorated with bound bay– or oak–leaves (*see* **Orders**, [Fig. 52].)

PUTTO (pl. **PUTTI**)   A small boy or chubby baby, often found in Classical and Baroque sculpture, especially funerary monuments. Putti are usually unwinged, and are found in attitudes of overt displays of grief, shedding copious tears, and clutching inverted torches. They have a curiously knowing air about them, are often given to obesity, and possess a sense of retarded physical development rendering them curiously unwholesome.

PYCNOSTYLE   One of the five species of intercolumniation defined by Vitruvius. The space in this case is one-and-a-half diameters of a shaft.

PYLON   The battered towers that flanked the entrance to an Egyptian temple. Pylon-like forms became used as the supports for suspension bridges, as the section for basements, dams, and retaining walls, and as chimney-pots during the Neoclassical period.

PYRAMID   A solid standing on a square base with steeply battered triangular sides meeting at an apex, used in Neoclassical Architecture. Thin pyramids are often confused with **obelisks**, and fat obelisks with pyramids, but the two forms are quite distinct although obelisks have small flattened pyramids or **pyramidions** on top of them [6.8].

PYRAMIDION   A small pyramid. The top of an obelisk.

QUADRA   A square border or frame. The fillets of the Ionic base on the top and bottom of the scotia. The plinth or lowest member of a podium.

QUADRANGLE   A figure with four angles and four sides. A square or rectangular court with buildings all round it.

QUADRATUM, OPUS QUADRATUM   Ashlar.

QUADRATURA   *Trompe l'oeil* architectural designs painted on walls and ceilings.

QUADRIFORES   Folding doors consisting of four hinged panels, ie folding into four leaves.

QUADRIGA   A sculptured group consisting of a chariot, driver, and four horses, found on triumphal arches, monuments, etc.

QUARTER ROUND   A moulding, the section of which is the quadrant of a circle. An **ovolo** or **echinus**.

QUASI-RETICULATE   A type of facing of Roman concrete formed of small regular facing-blocks creating a vaguely net-like appearance.

QUIRK   A piece removed from the corner of a room, or a re-entrant angle. An acute-angled channel by which the convex parts of Greek mouldings are separated from the fillets. Any V-shaped incision between mouldings.

QUOIN   An external angle of a building. Dressed stones in this position, usually laid so that the faces are either long or short, or headers and stretchers, and often with chamfered edges. If they project beyond the face of the wall (as they frequently do) they are termed **rustic quoins** (*see* **rustication**).

RAFFLE LEAF   A leaf in ornamental foliage with indentations at its edges, like an acanthus. It is usually freely flowing and asymmetrical.

RAIL   A horizontal piece of timber between panels in a door or in wainscoting.

RAINWATER HEAD   A box-shaped structure of cast iron or lead into which rainwater is poured from behind a parapet in order to convey it to a pipe.

Fig. 52 *Ionic rusticated doorways. Note the pulvinated frieze on the left, and the ears on the right. From Langley*

RAKE The slope of a roof. A **raking cornice** is that on the slope of a pediment.

RAMS Heads or skulls of rams or goats appear in Classical ornament, associated with altars and festoons. They are called **aegicranes**.

RAMP A slope to join two levels. Part of a handrail of a stair that rises more steeply at a landing or where there are winders.

RANDOM TOOLING Stone dressing by advancing a wide chisel over the face at one eighth of an inch per stroke, to leave a series of regular indentations.

REED, REEDING A moulding consisting of three or more beads side by side, like reeds laid parallel. Some elaborate Ionic bases have many horizontal flutes and mouldings called **reeding** (*see* **moulding**).

REGENCY Properly the period 1811–20, but includes the styles prevalent in England from around 1795 to 1830.

REGLET A flat narrow moulding.

REGULA A band below the **taenia** and above the **guttae** in a Doric entablature (*see* **Doric Order**).

REIGNIER WORK Ornamental inlaid patterns in the manner of **Buhl** work.

RELIEVING ARCH An arch built over a lintel to take the weight off the lintel. Also called a **discharging arch** [Fig. 9]. A **relieving triangle** is a triangular space contrived over lintels formed by corbelled convergence of the blocks of the wall.

RELIEVO, RELIEF The projection of any sculpture or ornament from its background. **Alto-relievo** stands out pronouncedly from the ground; **mezzo-relievo** projects only half the forms; **basso-relievo** projects less than half.

RENAISSANCE Meaning, literally, rebirth, the Renaissance suggests a rediscovery of the Architecture of Ancient Rome. In common usage the term implies Architecture based on Italian prototypes from the early fifteenth century until it was superseded by Mannerist and Baroque styles. It is generally held to begin with the work of Brunelleschi in Florence.

RENDERING The plastering or facing, with stucco, pebbledash, or similar, of an outside wall.

REPLUM A panel in a framed door.

REREDOS A screen or a wall behind an altar, usually much ornamented, forming part of the retable.

RESPOND Anta, corbel, or element where an arcade or colonnade engages with a wall.

RESSAULT Projecting part of an entablature, with two returns, over a pilaster, column, or other support [4.60, 4.61].

RESSAUNT An ogee (*see* **moulding**).

RETABLE Carved structure behind an altar, including the reredos, or the shalf behind the altar, or the frame around reredos panels.

RETAINING WALL A wall built to hold up a bank of earth, also called a **revetment**, which is usually battered.

RETICULATED Like a net, as in rustication or in lozenge-shaped patterns.

RETICULATUM **Opus Reticulatum** was concrete faced with square-based pyramidal blocks set with the points inwards and the squares diagonally.

RETURN The continuation of a moulding or projection in an opposite or different direction, with a terminating feature. The part that returns, usually at a right-angle, from the front of a building.

REVEAL The jamb or side of an opening between a window- or door-frame and the outer face of the wall. If it is angled it is called a **splayed reveal** or simply a **splay**.

REVETMENT A retaining wall, or the finish or facing fixed to a wall of some other material.

RHONE A half-round gutter.

RIBBON Used with **bucrania**, **laurel** and **oak wreaths**, and **festoons**. Ribbon mouldings can occur between rosettes, or can be twined around a continuous thread.

RINCEAU A continuous wave of foliate ornament, often a vine, on a band.

ROCAILLE Rockwork of pebbles, shells, and other stones, used in the building of grottoes, follies, and other decorative conceits. Ornament like marine flora.

ROCKWORK Constructions of real and imitation rocks, associated with grottoes and garden buildings.

ROCOCO A light, frothy, elegant, and playful late phase of Baroque, more than **rocaille**, but with much of the shell-like, coral, or marine forms associated with grottoes and the like. Much Rococo ornament is asymmetrical, with S- and C-shaped curves, resembling artistically draped seaweed. Chinoiserie, Gothick, Indian, and other elements and motifs fuse in this remarkable eighteenth-century art form, which is more surface decoration than architectural style, although its stylistic flavour is quite distinct [5.25].

ROD OF ASCLEPIUS Neoclassical motif, like the **caduceus**, minus wings.

ROLL MOULDING A **bowtell** or **common round** of semicircular or greater than semicircular profile.

ROMAN CEMENT **Parker's** or **brown cement**, a common early nineteenth-century rendering.

ROMAN ORDER The Composite Order (*see* **Orders**).

ROPE MOULDING A moulding like a cable or twined rope.

ROSE, ROSETTE A rose-shaped **patera** ornament used to decorate strings, architraves, etc.

ROSTRAL COLUMN *See* **Columna Rostrata**.

ROSTRUM A beak like the prow of a ship, and formed in **rostral columns**. An elevated platform or dais.

ROTUNDA A circular building or a room, usually with a dome or a domed ceiling over it. Rotundas may have peristyles inside or out, or both.

ROUNDEL A **bead** or **astragal**. A circle or a circular panel.

RUDENTURE Cabling [Fig. 51].

RUNDBOGENSTIL Round-arched style, largely derived from the Italian Early Christian, Romanesque, and Proto-Renaissance styles, used by important Neoclassical Architects such as Schinkel, von Klenze, and Gärtner in the first half of the nineteenth century.

RUNNING DOG A repetitive Classical ornament in a frieze, also called a **Vitruvian scroll**, with a wave-like scroll or volute form endlessly repeated (*see* **Vitruvian scroll**).

RURAL ARCHITECTURE **Picturesque** cottage Architecture often deliberately asymmetrical and derived from vernacular traditions, with materials such as thatch, rough tree-trunks as columns, and a contrived attempt to appear 'rustick'.

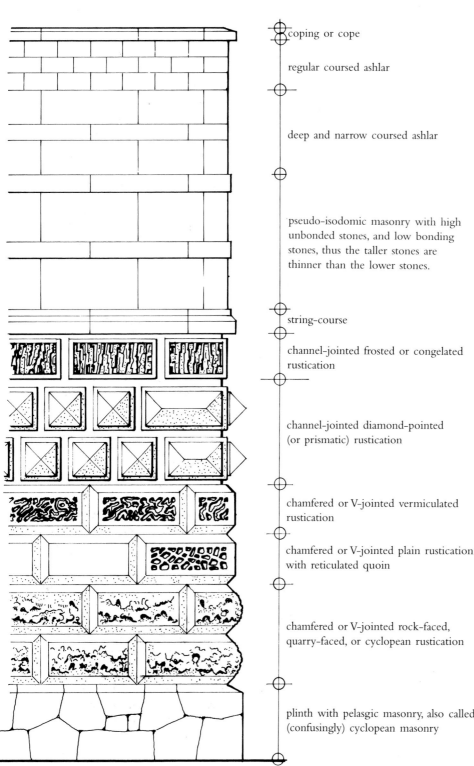

coping or cope

regular coursed ashlar

deep and narrow coursed ashlar

pseudo-isodomic masonry with high unbonded stones, and low bonding stones, thus the taller stones are thinner than the lower stones.

string-course

channel-jointed frosted or congelated rustication

channel-jointed diamond-pointed (or prismatic) rustication

chamfered or V-jointed vermiculated rustication

chamfered or V-jointed plain rustication with reticulated quoin

chamfered or V-jointed rock-faced, quarry-faced, or cyclopean rustication

plinth with pelasgic masonry, also called (confusingly) cyclopean masonry

Fig. 54 *Rustication*

RUSTIC-WORK, RUSTICATION Ashlar masonry, the joints of which are worked with grooves or channels to emphasize the blocks. Grooves may be moulded or plain. **Banded rustication** has only the horizontal joints grooved or emphasized. **Chamfered rustication** has V-shaped joints. **Cyclopean rustication** consists of big rough-faced blocks designed to appear as though straight from the quarry, but, of course, dressed with precise joints: cyclopean work is also called rock-faced rustication. **Diamond-pointed** or **pyramidal rustication** has square blocks with projecting faces terminating in points, so they resemble pyramids, while quoins will be longer and rectangular, rather than square, and so will resemble hipped roofs on their sides rather than pyramids laid on edge. **Frosted rustication** has carving that simulates icicles or stalactites, giving a grotto-like effect. **Smooth-faced rustication** has blocks with chamfered edges emphasizing the joints, but smooth flat faces framed by the V-shaped joints. **Vermiculated rustication** has irregular grooves, channels, and holes all over the surface, as though a section had been cut through worm-holes and worm-tracks, hence the name. **Rustic quoins** are stones at the corners of buildings, or reveals that project beyond the naked of the wall proper. A **rusticated column** has blocks of stone, square on plan, set at intervals up the height of the shaft and alternating with the drum-like blocks of the shaft: in a rusticated column the square blocks (rectangular on their faces) may be dressed, usually in the vermiculated manner, or may be plain-faced.

SACELLUM A small roofless enclosure, or a chapel within a church, like a screened chantry-chapel.

SACRARIUM A sacred apartment: the cell or **adytum** of a temple. The part of the chancel enclosed by altar-rails.

SACRISTY A room attached to a church or within a church where sacred vessels, vestments, and other items used in liturgies are kept.

SADDLE The board on a floor in a doorway between jambs. A **saddle stone** is the apex stone of a pediment of a gable, or a splayed coping. A **saddle-back** roof is a common pitched roof with gable ends, on a tower. **Saddle-bars** are iron or other

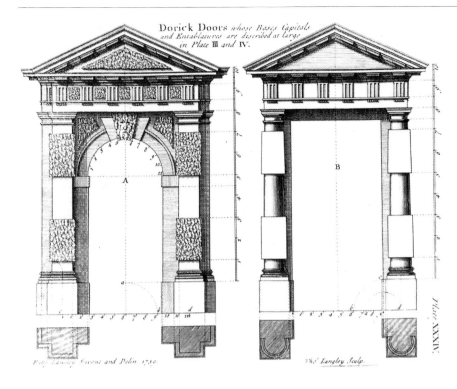

Fig. 55 *Doric rusticated doorways. From Langley*

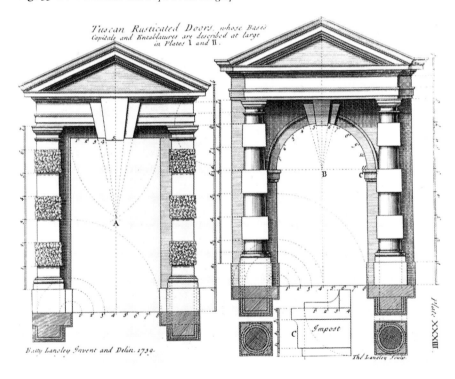

Fig. 56 *Tuscan rusticated doorways. From Langley*

metal bars, set into the mullions and jambs of a window, to which the lead cames are tied.

SAGITTA An unusual name for a keystone.

SALAMANDER A beast resembling a newt, lizard, and dragon.

SALIENT A projection of any part of a building, but more usually applied to the projections of fortifications or garden architecture.

SALON, SALOON A large, spacious, tall apartment in the centre of a Classical building, often vaulted or domed, usually one-and-a-half or two storeys high, and illuminated by an oculus, clearstorey, or lantern-light.

SANCTUARY The presbytery or eastern part of the choir of a church, where the High Altar stands.

SARCOPHAGUS A stone coffin, usually ornamented, and often heroic in scale. It may be elaborately ornamented, with a pitched roof, and may have **acroteria** at the corners. The name is derived from the Greek, meaning 'flesh-eater' [4.1, Fig. 60].

SASH, SASH-WINDOW A type of frame for holding the glass in a window, and capable of being raised or lowered in vertical grooves. Sashes are single- (with one moveable sash) or double- (with two moveable sashes) hung, and their weights are counterbalanced by lead or iron weights in the lining. The frame in which sashes are fitted is called a **sash-frame**, and the ropes or chains on which sashes are suspended from pulleys are called **sash-lines**, **sash-cords**, or **sash-chains**. Very heavy sashes in first-class quality work are usually suspended from chains rather than cords. Sashes became fashionable in England in the latter part of the seventeenth century. Yorkshire sliding-sashes are moved horizontally.

SATYR A creature with goat-like legs and hoofs, a human male torso and face, and horns. It represents fecundity, lust, and unbridled nature.

SAVES, SAVERS, SAVING-STONES Stones built over a lintel to distribute the loads. They are often in the form of a **relieving-arch** [Fig. 9].

SAXA QUADRATA Blocks of dressed squared stone for **ashlar** work.

SCABELLUM A high pedestal to carry a bust, urn, statue, or other ornament.

SCAENA, SKENE The structure which faced the audience in a Classical theatre, set behind the orchestra.

SCAGLIOLA A type of plaster or stucco, with colouring matter introduced so that the finished, polished material resembles marble. Although scagliola was used in interior decorative schemes in Classical times, it was widely used and perfected in the seventeenth and eighteenth centuries.

SCALE PATTERN Imbrication or petal diaper, in which the ornament is like overlapping scales.

SCALE STEPS Steps with parallel nosings and equal goings.

SCALLOP An ornament resembling the shell of a scallop, often found at the heads of niches.

SCALPTURATUM Inlaid work, the pattern being chiselled out and filled with coloured marble.

SCAMILLI Plain blocks which, unlike pedestals, have no mouldings, and are smaller in size. **Scamilli Impares** refer to the horizontal lines of a Classical building, which incline almost imperceptibly from the ends to the centre in order to correct the optical illusion of the centre sinking.

SCANDULAE Shingles.

SCANTLING The length, breadth, and thickness of a stone.

SCAPE, SCAPUS The shaft of a column, or the **apophyge** of a shaft (the curved portion where the shaft expands to meet the fillet above the base, or under the astragal of a capital of a Classical column).

SCAPPLING, SCAPLING, SCABBLING A way of tooling the face of a stone with a small pick known as a **scappling hammer**. The face is worked to a flat, but not smooth, surface.

SCARCEMENT A plain band or a flat set-off in a wall, used as a shelf on which the ends of joists or trusses are carried.

SCARP The bank below the ramparts of a fortress down which fire may be directed. It was also adapted for use in garden design. It is also called an **escarp**, a term also applied to the inner side of a ditch. A batter of a bank.

SCENE An alley or portico set in rural surroundings where theatrical performances could be given.

SCHEME, SKENE A segmental arch. Also the structure facing the audience in a Greek theatre.

SCONCE An earthwork or a fortress. A screen or palisade. An arch formed across the internal corners of a room, or a **squinch**.

SCONCHEON, SCONTION, SCUNTION, SCUNCHEON The return of a pilaster from the face to the naked of the wall.

The side of an aperture from the back of a jamb to the face of a wall.

SCOOP PATTERN A series of short vertical flutes with curved closed ends, often used in ornamental friezes.

SCOTIA A concave moulding, usually found at the base of a column or a pilaster between the fillets of the **torus** mouldings, or under the nosing of a stair.

SCOUCHON, SKOUCHIN The same as a squinch.

SCRATCH WORK A type of decorative plasterwork consisting of a ground of coloured plaster, which is covered with a white coat. The latter is then scratched to reveal the colour below. Also known as **sgraffito**.

SCROLL A convoluted or spiral ornament. A volute of an Ionic, Corinthian, or Composite capital, or any moulding in the form of a volute or scroll. Scrolling foliage often appears as ornament in Classical Architecture.

SCUTCHEON As **sconcheon**. Also a plate on a door, from the centre of which the handle projects. A plate around a keyhole.

SEGMENT A part cut off from the whole. Part of a circle, or a semicircle.

SERLIANA A **Venetian Window**: any central opening with a semicircular arch over it flanked by two rectangular openings. The rectangular openings have pilasters or engaged columns on either side of them, and have entablatures over. The central arched opening is always wider than the rectangular openings, and its archivolt springs from the top of the cornices on either side. It is named after Sebastiano Serlio (1475–1554) who first illustrated the form in his *Architettura* of 1537–51 [Figs. 57, 58].

SERPENT This is found in Classical Architecture associated with the Messenger (SS John, Hermes, Harpocrates, etc). It is associated with healing and with wisdom, and with the **caduceus** or **wand** of the Messenger. When serpents are found in circular form, their tails in their mouths, they denote immortality or eternity.

SEVERANS Strings or cornices.

SEVERY A web or cell. *See* **vault**.

SGRAFFITO *See* **scratch work**.

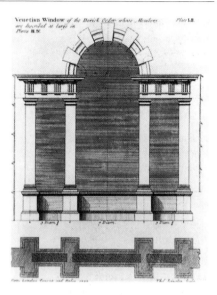

Fig. 57 *Venetian Window, or Serliana, with Doric entablature and voussoirs interrupting the archivolt. From Langley*

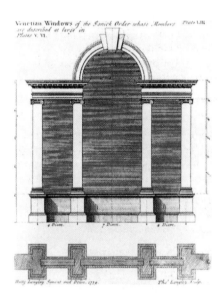

Fig. 58 *Venetian Window, or Serliana, using the Ionic Order with pulvinated frieze. From Langley*

SHAFT The body of a column between the capital and the base.

SHANKS Spaces between the channels of Doric triglyphs.

SHINGLES Wooden tiles, also known as **scandulae**. Loose stones used for gravel, or as concrete aggregate.

SHOULDERED A lintel or flat arch carried on shaped corbels over the jambs.

SILL, CILL, SOLE, SULE The horizontal member forming the bottom of a window, door, or other opening, designed to throw water away.

SIMA The top moulding of a pediment, placed above the raking cornice. Not to be confused with **cyma**.

SINGERIE A style of decoration like **Grotesque** [5.37], but with figures of monkeys imitating humans.

SINGLE HUNG A sash-window in which only one sash moves.

SKENE The structure facing the audience of a Greek theatre.

SKEW The coping of a gable, also called a **skew-table**. A **kneeler**, or block of stone set at the top of a wall to terminate the eaves of a parapet or a coping. A **skew-back** is the portion of an abutment that supports an arch. A **skew-put** is the lowest stone of a gable.

SKIRTING The board placed around the base of an internal wall at the junction of the floor and the wall. It is frequently moulded or chamfered at the top, and corresponds to a plinth.

SKYLIGHT A window in a ceiling or roof.

SLATE A type of stone capable of being split or cut into thin regular slabs and used for roofing or for cladding. **Slatehanging** describes a slate-clad wall.

SLEEPER WALL A wall placed between two structural elements, such as piers, in order to prevent movement.

SNAKE A wavy line moulding (*see* **serpent**).

SOCLE, ZOCLE A plain block or low pedestal without mouldings.

SOFFIT, SOFFITE, SOFFITA A ceiling. The lower surface of any arch or vault, or the underside of the corona of a cornice. The underside of any part of a building, including arches.

SOLAR A loft, garret, or upper chamber. A sunny room on a roof.

SOLARIUM An upper chamber. A sun terrace. A **loggia**. A sun-dial.

SOLOMONIC COLUMN A twisted, spiral, or barley-sugar column, so-called from its supposed use in the Temple of Solomon. Also called **Salomónica**. It is much used in Masonic iconography [4.20, 4.46, 5.7].

SOPRAPORTA Sculpture over a doorway contained within a frame so that the door and sopraporta form one composition. Attic storey over a doorway cornice.

SOUNDING BOARD, SOUND BOARD The canopy or **tester** over a pulpit.

SOUSE A corbel.

SPANDREL, SPLANDREL The approximately triangular space between an arched opening and the rectangle formed by the outer mouldings over it, drawn from the apex in a horizontal line, and from the springing of the arch in vertical and horizontal lines. The surface between two arches in an arcade. Also called **hans** or **haunch**.

SPAN OF AN ARCH The distance between the points of springing, or imposts (*see* **arch**).

SPAN ROOF A roof with two inclined sides.

SPEAR OR LANCE Used in groups for trophies, panoplies, and military decorations, but more usually for the tops of metal railings, gates, and balconies.

SPERONI **Anterides** or **buttresses**, usually interpreted as a species of pilaster.

SPHINX A recumbent lion, sometimes winged, with a human head.

SPIRA The circular column-base of an Ionic or Corinthian Order.

SPRINGER, SPRINGING The impost, or point at which an arch unites with its support. The bottom voussoir of the arch on the impost is called the springer. A springer can also be the bottom stone of a gable. A **springing course** is a horizontal course of stones from which an arch springs (*see* **arch**).

SPUR STONE A stone placed at the corner of a building or on either side of an entrance to prevent damage by carts or other wheeled vehicles.

SQUARED Rubble where the stones are roughly squared.

SQUINCH A small arch or beam spanning across an angle of a square or rectangular plan, to support the alternate sides of octagonal spires or the base of a dome. Squinches can also be corbelled pieces built out, course by course, across a corner to carry a structure above (*see* **dome**).

STADIUM A racecourse for men.

STAFF BEAD A corner or angle-bead.

STAGE A floor or storey, especially of towers.

STAIR, STAIRCASE The part of a building with steps to provide access from one level to another. Parts of a staircase are as follows: **apron** is the board covering the trimmer joist of a landing; **balusters** are vertical supports for the handrail and barriers for the open sides; a **balustrade** is the handrail, string, balusters, and newel – **banister** is a vulgar term for a baluster, while banisters is an equally vulgar term for a balustrade. **Bearers** support steps; **blocks** are fixed to the upper edges of bearers to give additional support to the treads: blocks are also the small triangular pieces glued to the angles between treads and risers on the underside; **brackets** are the same as blocks. **Cappings** are the cover mouldings planted on the upper edges of strings; **easing** is a curved portion connecting two strings. A **flight** is a continuous set of steps from one landing to another. The **going** or **run of a step** is the distance measured horizontally between two risers: the **going of a flight** is therefore the horizontal distance between the face of the bottom riser and that of the topmost riser. **Headroom** is the distance measured vertically from the line of the nosings to the lower edge of the apron or to the soffite of a flight above. A **landing** is a platform between flights, or the floor at the top of a stair; a **quarter-space** landing is one on which a quarter-turn has to be made between the end of one flight and the beginning of the next; if a landing extends for the combined widths of both flights and a complete half-turn has to be made, it is known as a **half-space** landing. The **line of the nosings** is a line drawn to touch the projecting edges or nosings of the treads. **Newels** are vertical members placed at the ends of the flights to support the strings, handrails, trimmers, and bearers; the top of a newel is called a **cap** and the lower end the **drop**. **Nosing** is the front edge of a tread projecting beyond the face of the riser. The **pitch or slope** is the angle between the line of nosings and the floor or landing. The **riser** is the vertical part or front member of a step. A **rise of a step** is the vertical distance between the tops of two consecutive treads; the **rise of a flight** is the total height from floor to floor, or landing to landing, or floor to landing. A **scotia** is the concave moulding under the nosing. The **soffite** is the under-surface of the stair or flight. A **spandrel** is a triangular surface between outer string and floor. **Strings** or **stringers** are inclined timbers supporting the steps. **Treads** are horizontal members forming the upper surfaces of steps. The **well** is the space between the outer strings of the several flights of a stair: a **closed-string** stair has strings of continuous raking members supporting identical balusters; an **open**, or **cut-string** stair, has strings cut to the profiles of the treads that support balusters of unequal length: in the latter case, two balusters per tread are usual in early eighteenth-century work, increasing to three by the middle of the century, and accompanied, in the better class of work, by elaborately carved **tread-ends**. Different types of stair include: the **dog-leg** (two flights parallel to each other with a landing between them and no well between the outer strings); **flying stairs** (steps cantilevered from the stair-well without any newel); **geometrical stairs** (no newels, and usually circular or elliptical on plan, with stone strings with one end built into the wall and resting on the step below); **newel**, **turngrece**, **vice**, **winding**, **turnpike**, **cockle**, or **spiral** stairs (steps wind round a central pier or column called a newel, and thus the narrow ends of the steps are supported by the newel); **open-well** stair (space or well between outer strings, thus differing from dog-leg); **straight-flight**; and **turning** (including **quarter-turn**, **half-turn**, **three-quarter turn**, and **bifurcated** (where stairs divide into two branches)). A stair that starts with one flight and returns in two is called a **double-return stair**.

STALACTITES   Corbelled squinches carved to resemble stalactites, or stucco-work resembling stone, often found in grottoes. Also called **Muqarna**.

STALK   An ornament in the Corinthian capital from which volutes and helices spring (*see* **Orders**).

STANCHIONS   Mullions.

STARLING   A pointed cutwater on a bridge pier to divide the thrust of water.

STAR MOULDING   A decoration resembling a band of stars.

STEEPLE   The tower and spire of a church, taken together, and properly containing bells.

STEREOBATA, STEREOBATE   *See* **stylobate**.

STILE   The upright pieces of a frame into which the ends of horizontal rails are fixed with mortices and tenons as in a panelled door.

STILLICIDIUM   Drips or eaves of a Doric building.

STILTED ARCH   An arch where the springing begins above the impost, i.e. with straight sides before the curve begins.

STOA   A colonnade or a long portico.

STOP   Anything against which a moulding stops, such as a block of stone or wood at the bases of architraves, stopping both architraves and skirtings (or plinths).

STOREY   The vertical division of a building. The space between two floors, between two entablatures, or between any other horizontal division. Storeys are divided into basement, ground, first, second, third, etc, then attic, meaning above the main cornice. An attic storey may have a subsidiary entablature, less important than the main entablature. **Entresols** and **mezzanines** are intermediate storeys. The vertical divisions of towers must not be described as storeys; they are called **stages** (e.g. belfry-stage). The storey containing the principal rooms of a house is called the **piano nobile**.

STRAIGHT ARCH   A lintel of voussoirs based on the principle of wedges of an arch, but with a flat or slightly cambered intrados (or soffite), usually made of brick rubbers or finely dressed stone. It is also called a **skewback** arch (from the steeply raked abutments from which the arch springs).

STRAPWORK   Decoration, usually of wood, plaster, or masonry, consisting of interlaced bands like fretwork or leather straps, much used in early Renaissance Architecture of the Elizabethan or Jacobean periods [Fig. 59].

STRETCHER   A stone or brick laid with its longer face in the surface of the wall. A stretching, or stretcher course, is a course of stretchers.

STRIAE   Grooves, channels, or flutes.

STRIATED   Chamfered, channelled, or fluted.

STRIGES   Flutes of a column or pilaster flanked by lists, fillets, or striae.

Fig. 59 *Strapwork*

STRIGILLATION   Curving flutes, often found on sarcophagi [Fig. 60].

STRING   Sloping timbers carrying the ends of treads and risers of a stair. A string or string-course is also any horizontal band (whether moulded or plain) on a building.

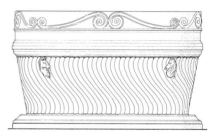

Fig. 60 *Strigillation*

STRIX   A flute in a column or pilaster.

STRUCTURA CAEMENTICIA   Concrete.

STUCCO   Plasterwork, or calcareous cement render, plain or modelled. Properly, stucco is calcium carbonate mixed with marble dust, glue, and hair, providing a fine finish. It can be made to resemble ashlar, by means of inscribing lines in it, and it can be coloured, as in **Parker's Roman Cement**, and other finishes. It is known as **opus albarium** or **opus tectorium**.

STYLOBATE, STEREOBATA, STEREOBATE   A continuous base or substructure, consisting of the topmost step of a structure of three steps called the **crepidoma**, on which a colonnade or a building with a peristyle is placed. In Classical Architecture it has come to mean any continuous base or substructure or a solid mass of masonry on which a colonnade or wall is erected, but, properly, it should be distinguished from a podium, which is like a continuous pedestal with plinth and cornice, while a stylobate is the top step of a crepidoma. Vitruvius defined stereobatae as the walls under the columns above the ground; he was clearly thinking of the walls of temple-podia.

SUBSCUS   A peg or dowel.

SUMMER STONE   The lowest stone of a gable stopping at the eaves. The first stone of the tabling or coping is supported on the summer stone, which is also called a **skew-corbel**.

Fig. 61 *Sunburst*

SUN   A face or disc surrounded by rays, and also called a **sunburst** [Fig. 61].

SUPER-ALTAR   A shelf over the altar, or to the east of it.

SUPERCILIUM   The lintel of an aperture. Fillet over a cyma.

SUPERIMPOSED   When the Orders are used to define the storeys of a Classical façade and set one above the other, they have a hierarchical order: Doric is used at the bottom (being tough, primitive and masculine), with Ionic above, and Corinthian above that. In taller buildings Tuscan is used first, then Roman Doric, then Ionic, then Corinthian, and finally Composite [2.66, 2.67, 4.52].

SURBASE   The upper mouldings or cornice of a pedestal or dado.

SURBASED   An arch, vault, or dome of a height less than half its span. A segmental arch.

SURMOUNTED   An arch, vault, or dome rising higher than half its span. **A stilted arch**. A way of stating that something is placed over part of a building: e.g. the composition is surmounted by a sculpture of cornucopiae and putti.

SWAG   A festoon resembling a cloth, or a string of flowers, or fruit, suspended from two supports [Figs. 62, 63].

SWAN-NECK   A double-carved member, or an ogee. The form of a handrail when it rises to join the newel-post. The type of elegant handle found on Georgian furniture.

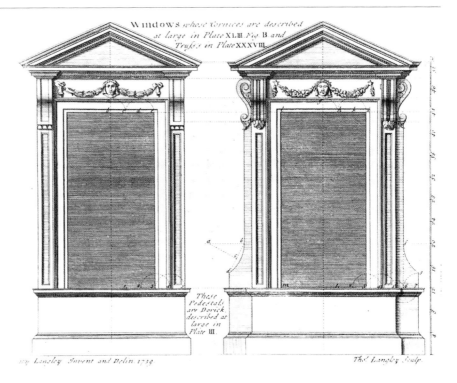

Fig. 62 *Window surrounds with triangular pediments and swags (the swag on the left is composed of husks, or bellflowers). Note the crossettes. From Langley*

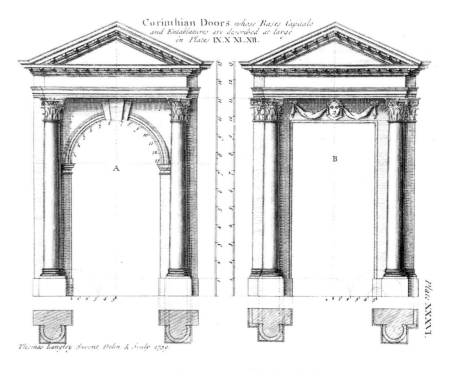

Fig. 63 *Corinthian doorways. Note the swag on the right. From Langley*

SYMBOL   An attribute or a sign accompanying a statue or picture to denote identity, sometimes substituted for the figure. Some common symbols or attributes associated with Christianity are as follows:

Almond Tree in Flowerpot	Blessed Virgin Mary (BVM)
Arrow	Martyrdom, especially SS. Sebastian and Edmund

Asperge — Purity
Book — Evangelist or Doctor of the Church
Chalice — SS. John the Evangelist, Benedict, Thomas Aquinas
Cross — Missionary, especially S. John the Baptist
Crown, Sceptre (or both) — Royal rank, Sainthood
Dove — Holy Spirit, Purity
Fountain — BVM
Garden — BVM
Lamp — Virginity
Lily — BVM
Lily among Thorns — BVM and Confessors
Palm — Victory, Martyrdom
Rose — BVM
Skull — S. Jerome
Sword — Martyrdom, especially Saints decapitated
Wheel — Patriarchs, S. Catherine.

Readers are referred to Bond, Francis, *Dedications and Patron Saints of English Churches. Ecclesiastical Symbolism. Saints and their Emblems.* Oxford, 1914.

SYMMETRY Uniformity or balance of one part of a building and another. Equal disposition of parts and masses on either side of a centre line, as a mirror-image.

SYSTYLE One of the five series of intercolumniation in which the columns are two diameters apart.

TABERNACLE The receptacle for the Sacraments placed over the altar, or any niche or canopy, especially a freestanding canopy. A **ciborium** or **baldacchino**.

TABLE The same as a string-course.

TABLE-TOMB A flat rectangular stone carried on two or more upright stones over a grave, so that the finished object looks like a table.

TABLET A wall-slab or mural monument.

TABLING Coping.

TABLINUM A room with one side open to a courtyard, colonnade, or portico. It is also called the **tabulinum**.

TAENIA, TENIA The fillet or band at the top of a Doric architrave separating it from the frieze (*see* **Doric Order**).

TAMBOUR The core of a Corinthian or Composite capital on which the acanthus leaves, etc, are placed. The wall or drum carrying a dome.

TARRAS Strong cement.

TARSIA Inlays of different woods.

TAS-DE-CHARGE The lowest course of an arch or vault, tied into the wall.

TASSEL A very common ornament in Classical decoration, flags, standards, and trophies. The tassel also occurs as a variety of spear-head in railings.

TEBAM A rostrum or dais.

TECTORIUM OPUS A type of plastering or stucco.

TEGULA A roof-tile, or facing-brick for walls.

TELAMONES, TELAMONI (sing. **TELAMON**) Supports in the guise of sculpted male figures, used instead of columns to carry entablatures.

TEMENOS The sacred precinct of a Classical temple.

TEMPLATE A block set under a truss or a joist, also called a **pad**, or a **padstone**. It provides a fixing, and distributes the weight.

TEMPLE A building dedicated to pagan deities. Classical temples were usually rectangular, and consisted of an enclosed part called the **cell** or naos, a **portico**, and a **sanctuary**. Often the columns were carried all the way round in what is known as a **peristyle** or **peripteral** arrangement of columns. *See* **colonnade**. [See Figs. 64, 65].

TENDRIL The tendril form of plants is combined with the **anthemion** and **palmette** in scrolling foliage [Fig. 7].

TENIA *See* **taenia**.

TEPIDARIUM A warm room between the cold and hot rooms of Roman *Thermae*, with facilities for bathing in warm water.

TERAM A scroll at the end of a step.

TERM A pedestal resembling an inverted obelisk (i.e. tapering towards the base) supporting a bust, or merging with a bust. It is sometimes called a **terminal** (pl. termini) [Fig. 66].

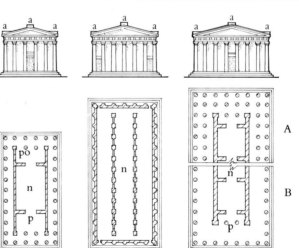

a   acroterium
n   naos
p   pronaos
po posticum or epinaos, sometimes protected with a grille to serve as the opisthodomus

Peripteral Hexastyle arrangement, with a row of columns all round, and six columns at each end

Pseudo-peripteral Septostyle (or Heptastyle) arrangement (i.e. with all columns engaged with the temple walls, and with seven engaged columns at each end, which results in the need for entrances off-centre)

A   Half-plan, Dipteral Octastyle arrangement (with a double range of columns at the sides, and with eight at each end)
B   Half-plan, Pseudo-Dipteral Octastyle arrangement (with a wider space between the walls of the cell and the peristyle, and with eight columns at each end. The wide space would suggest that a row of columns ought to be behind the first row. Another arrangement is if the second row is engaged with the cell walls as in some Roman examples)

Fig. 64 *Temple plans*

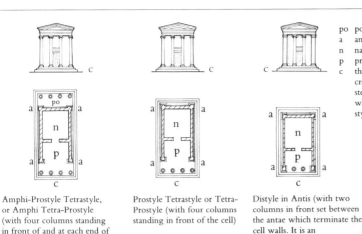

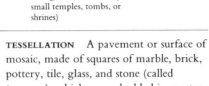

po posticum or epinaos
a   anta
n   naos
p   pronaos
c   three-step
    crepidoma, the top
    step or platform of
    which is the
    stylobate

Amphi-Prostyle Tetrastyle, or Amphi Tetra-Prostyle (with four columns standing in front of and at each end of the cell)

Prostyle Tetrastyle or Tetra-Prostyle (with four columns standing in front of the cell)

Distyle in Antis (with two columns in front set between the antae which terminate the cell walls. It is an arrangement found only in small temples, tombs, or shrines)

Fig. 65 *Column arrangement in temples*

Fig. 66 *Two terms from the palace of Sanssouci, Potsdam*

TERRACE   A raised space or platform adjoining a building. A row of houses joined together as a unified design.

TERRACOTTA   Baked clay, unglazed, and often cast in moulds of some elaboration, used for ornament, or for facing buildings, or for parts of buildings.

TERRAZZO   Floor or dado finish made of marble chips set in mortar which, when dry, is ground down and polished, providing a hard, decorative, and easily cleaned surface.

TESSELLATION   A pavement or surface of mosaic, made of squares of marble, brick, pottery, tile, glass, and stone (called **tesserae**), which are embedded in mortar.

TESSERA   A small square of glass, pottery, tile, brick, etc, used to make up the pattern of a mosaic. Also called **tessella**.

TESTA   A brick or a tile, or a shard of an object made of burnt clay.

TESTER   A canopy over a pulpit, tomb, or bed.

TESTUDO   A vault over a hall, or any grand arched or vaulted roof. A **testudinate** roof is one which completely covers a house, with four sides converging to a point or a ridge and points.

TETRASTYLE   Having four columns in one line. A **tetrastyle atrium** is one with the columns arranged around it to support the roof (*see* **temple**).

THATCH   A roof covering of straw, rushes, or reeds, much favoured for the **cottage orné** or for 'rustick' buildings.

THEATRE   A semicircular tiered structure with seats, and a stage on which plays were performed. An **amphitheatre** consists of two of these joined together, producing a circular or elliptical structure.

THERMAE   Roman public baths, often of great magnificence, and containing many amenities apart from baths. The complex planning and the ruins in Rome and elsewhere were sources for much Renaissance and later Classical Architecture [3.7]. Small baths were called **balneae**.

THERMAL WINDOW   A semicircular opening subdivided by means of two mullions, known also as a **Diocletian Window** from its use in the *Thermae* of Diocletian. It was used often in Renaissance Architecture, notably by Palladio and his followers [6.5].

THOLOS   A circular building, often domed, its dome, its pseudo-dome, or a cupola.

THROUGH STONE   A stone or bond-stone in a wall that reaches through its thickness, or a **parpen**, **parpent**, or **parpend**. A table-tomb.

THUNDERBOLT   A zigzag or forked-arrow form rather like a tightly-bound cigar-shaped missile, often gripped in the talons of an eagle, and widely used in Classical Architecture: it is usually winged, with forked arrows protruding from it representing lightning [2.40].

THYRSUS   A staff with a pinecone at the end, entwined with ribbons, grapevines, and ivy leaves, found in schemes of Bacchic decoration.

TILE   A thick piece of baked clay used for flooring, wall-covering, or roof-covering. Flat tiles are called **plain tiles**, and curved are termed **pan-tiles**. Walls clad with tiles are called **tile-hung**. Tiles may be glazed or unglazed.

TOMB-CHEST   A monument shaped like a chest or an altar, also called an **altar-tomb**. A **table-tomb** is a flat slab carried on two, four, or six columns. Tomb-chests may be plain or can have effigies on top, either as sculptured figures or as incised designs, and may have standing figures, called **weepers**, around the sides [4.1].

TOP RAIL   The upper frame of a dado (or wainscot) or door.

TORCH, INVERTED   This symbol, usually placed on funerary monuments, and often held by a putto, represents death (the extinguishing of the flame). Upright torches are often associated with candelabra, and occur as decorative motifs in Neoclassical Architecture.

TORUS   A large convex moulding at the base of a column or at the top of a plinth.

TOWER   A tall building, circular, square, or polygonal on plan, used for defence, as a landmark, for the hanging of bells, or the display of a clock. The storeys of a tower are called **stages**.

TRABEATION   An entablature, a beam, or a combination of beams in a structure. A trabeated building is constructed with

beams and lintels rather than arches. A
columnar and trabeated structure is
one with posts or columns and beams.
The opposite type of structure (with
arches) is termed **arcuated**.

TRABES COMPACTILES   The main beams
of architraves over the columns of
Etruscan temples.

TRACERY   The intersection of mullions
and transoms of windows, screens, panels,
or vaults. While most tracery is found in
the various styles of Gothic Architecture,
early Renaissance variants featuring
Classical mouldings, semicircular arches,
and capitals, do exist.

TRACHELION, TRACHELIUM   The neck of
a Doric column between the shaft ring
and the hypotrachelion (*see* **Doric Order**).

TRAIL   A running enrichment of
mouldings, a term usually applied to
Gothic work.

TRANSENNA   A screen of lattice-work,
often of marble.

TRANSEPT   The transverse portion of a
cruciform church; the arms on either side
of the crossing, usually between the nave
and the chancel.

TRANSITION   A term used to denote the
passing from one style to another.

TRANSOM   A horizontal bar dividing a
window into two or more lights in
height.

TRANSVERSE ARCH   An arch dividing one
compartment of a vaulted ceiling from
another.

TRAVERSE   A screen, with curtains to
give privacy, as in an *enfilade* system of
rooms, or a gallery or loft acting as a
corridor or passage.

TRAVERTINE   A calcareous building stone
much used in Ancient Rome.

TREAD   A horizontal part of a step of a
stair.

TRELLIS   A frame of thin bars of wood
used as a screen or on which plants may
climb. The structure is cross-barred or
lattice-work. **Treillage** is trellis-work
constructed with false perspectives to
suggest niches, arches, or even greater
length than is really the case.

TRIBUNE   An apse in a basilican structure.
A raised platform, dais, rostrum, pulpit, or
bishop's throne. A gallery in a church.

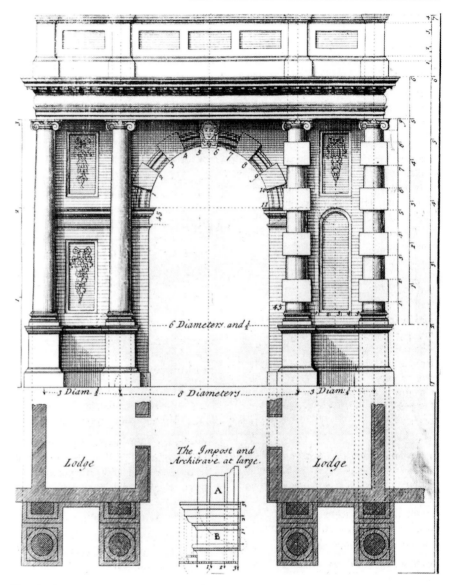

Fig. 67 *Ionic gateway. An interpretation of the triumphal arch theme. Note the pulvinated frieze
and the attic storey. From Langley*

TRICLINIUM   A room where Romans
feasted and received guests. A
dining-room.

TRIFORIUM   Upper aisle with its own
arcade forming an important part of the
elevation of a nave interior above the
nave-arcade and below the clearstorey.

TRIGLYPH   The vertical block in a Doric
frieze comprising two glyphs and two
half-glyphs (hence the 'three' glyphs),
separating the **metopes**. In late-
Renaissance versions the two half-glyphs
are often omitted, so the block becomes a
diglyph. Triglyph blocks occur over the
centre-lines of columns and spaces
between columns. In the Greek Doric

Order the triglyphs at the corners of the
building join, so they are not over the
centre-lines of the columns at the corners,
and the spaces between columns at the
corners of a building are smaller: in
Roman Doric the triglyphs are over the
centre-line of the column at the corner, so
that there is part of a metope at the angle
of the frieze separating the triglyphs (*see*
Doric Order).

TRILITHON   Two vertical stones
supporting one horizontal stone like a
lintel, so three stones are involved.

TRIPOD   A table or bowl with three legs,
usually placed on high, above the
crowning corning on a pedestal. The legs
often terminate in the feet of animals.

TRIPTERAL   With a treble pteron or external colonnade.

TRISTYLE   A colonnade or porch with three columns in the same line.

TRITON   A male figure, fish from the waist down, usually found in decorations with a marine theme.

TRIUMPHAL ARCH   An arch erected to celebrate a person or event, usually a military victory, and often surmounted by a **quadriga**. There are two main types: those with a single arch over an axis (Titus, Rome, first century AD), and those with a large central arch flanked by two smaller arches (Septimius Severus, Rome, third century AD). In both types a rich Order was applied to the arcuated form, and over the entablature the attic storey was inscribed with the dedication. The form was revived in Renaissance times, not only for festive Architecture, but in a variation, for building façades or parts of façades. Later triumphal arches, such as the Arc de Triomphe in Paris (1806–35) by Chalgrin, and the great Thiepval Arch by Lutyens of the 1920s, exploit more than one axis [Fig. 67, 2.68, 3.3–3.5, 4.9, 4.32–4.33, 7.1].

TRIUMPHAL COLUMN   A large, single column on a pedestal, erected as a public monument. The most celebrated example is that of Trajan (second century AD) with its spiral bands of sculpture, and its massive base that contained the tomb-chamber of the Emperor [5.19].

TROCHILUS   A **scotia**, or concave moulding.

TROMPE L'OEIL   Decoration to imitate three-dimensional form, or to suggest a texture or a finish.

TROPHY   A sculptured arrangement of armour and arms, occasionally incorporating wreaths, garlands, and festoons.

TRUNNELS   Guttae.

TRUSS   A combination of timbers to form a frame, placed at intervals, and carrying the purlins. The term also means a projection from the face of a wall, or a large **corbel**, **modillion**, or **console**.

TUCK POINTING   Lines to mark the joints in brick-work, made with ridges of lime-putty, after joints have been raked out and replaced with mortar coloured to match the brickwork. It gives an ultra-refined appearance to a façade.

TUFA   A Roman building-stone, formed of volcanic material.

TURNGRECE   A winding stair.

TURNPIKE STAIR   A circular, spiral, or winding stair with a solid central post on which the narrow ends of the steps are carried.

TURRET   A small tower, usually slender in form, or a large pinnacle.

TUSCAN ORDER   The simplest of the five Orders of Classical Architecture. The shaft of the column is never fluted, and the capital has a square **abacus**. The base consists of a square **plinth** and a large **torus**, and the **entablature** is quite plain. In a primitive version of the Order the frieze and cornice are omitted, and a wide overhanging eaves carried on long mutules is placed directly above the architrave (*see* **Orders**). The Tuscan **cavaedium** had an inward tilt in all four directions so that rain drained through the **compluvium** [Fig. 68, 2.33–2.36].

TUSSES   Projecting stones left in a wall to which another building is to be joined, also called **toothing stones**, or **tusking**.

TYMPANUM   The face of a pediment between the level fillet of the corona and the raked cornice of the sloping sides. The space between a lintel and an arch over the lintel. **Tympana** are frequently embellished with sculpture in relief.

TYPE   A **tester** or **sound-board** over a pulpit. The capping of a cupola roof or a turret. An exemplar.

UNDERCROFT   A vaulted space or a crypt under a church or chapel or other space.

UNDULATE BAND   Ornament in a strip, in a continuous scroll of waves, the stem of which is a repeat series of S- or ogee forms.

URILLAE   The volutes under the abacus of a Corinthian capital, also called **helices**.

URN   A lidded vase (often draped) for ashes or cremated remains. Urns are also used as decorative motifs on top of the dies of balustrades, or on walls, or in niches, or as garden ornaments.

VAGINA   The lower part of a **term** or **terminal** pedestal with which the bust merges [Fig. 66].

VALANCE   Hung drapery or simulated drapery round a tester, etc. [5.7]. The wooden vertical boards resembling such hangings at the edges of canopies.

VALLEY   The internal meeting of two slopes of a roof.

VAMURE   The walk on top of a wall behind a parapet.

VANE   A metal banner or other motif fixed to the top of a tower or cupola to show the direction of the wind, also called a **weathercock**.

VASE   An ornamental unlidded vessel, distinct from an urn. The bell of a Corinthian capital. Vases occur in a huge variety of forms in Classical Architecture.

VAULT   An arched structure over a room or an apartment, constructed of stone or brick, and occasionally of wood or plaster in imitation of stone or brick. The simplest vault is the **cylindrical**, **tunnel**, **barrel**, or **wagon** vault that springs from opposite parallel walls: it is a continuous

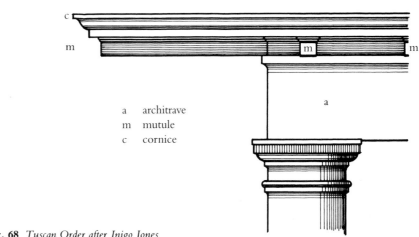

a   architrave
m   mutule
c   cornice

Fig. 68 *Tuscan Order after Inigo Jones*

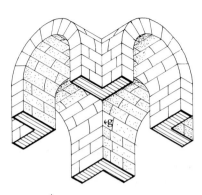

g   groin

quadripartite groin vault, or two
intersecting barrel vaults

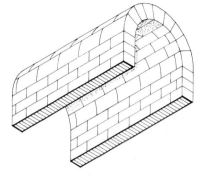

barrel vault

Fig. 69 *Vaults*

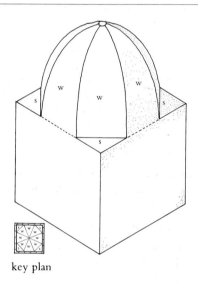

key plan

w   web
s   squinch

Fig. 70 *Square plan with domical vault on
octagonal base. The webs, severies, or cells,
forming the domical vault, meet at groins.
The corners of the square are bridged by
arches, called squinches, to accommodate the
octagonal form*

arch of semicircular or segmental section
that requires thick walls to support it. It
presents a uniform concave surface
throughout its length [Fig. 69]. If a **tunnel
vault** is divided into bays by means of
arches carried on piers then the arches are
called **transverse**, and are at right angles
to the walls. Two identical barrel vaults
intersecting at right angles form **groins**
(sharp arrises) at the junctions between the
concave surfaces, and result in a **groin** or

cross vault [Fig. 69]. A **domical vault**
has a square or a polygonal base, and the
curved vaults (called **severies**, **webs**, or
cells) rise directly from the walls, the
curved surfaces meeting at groins. A
domical vault is not a true dome [Fig. 70].
A dome is a vault with a segmental,
semicircular, bulbous, or pointed section
rising from a circular base. A **sail dome**
or vault is constructed on a square base
with the diagonal of the square being the
diameter of the sail dome: thus the dome
form actually begins in the corners of the
compartment to be covered, rising as on
pendentives, but the curve continuing
smoothly. The term 'sail' derives from the
resemblance to a sail, with the corners
fixed, billowing in a strong wind. Sail
domes are also called **handkerchief
vaults** [Fig. 25]. A dome on a square base
involves the construction of members
between the square plan and the circular
plan of the dome proper: these members
can be **squinches** (or arches) at 45
degrees, between the sides of the square,
or **pendentives**, which are triangular
elements on curved planes [Fig. 25]. In the
cases of pendentives and squinches the
diameter of the dome is the same as the
dimension of one side of the square, but
the diameters of the pendentives are the
same as the diagonal of the square base.
Domes of segmental section (called
calotte from their resemblance to clerical
skull-caps) placed directly on the circle
formed by the pendentives or squinches
are called **saucer domes**. A drum placed
between the circle formed by the
pendentives and squinches over which a
saucer dome or a dome of different section
is placed enables windows, peristyles, and

other architectural treatment and
elaboration to be included. A squinch can
be formed of several layers of arches, each
with a greater diameter than that behind
it, so that the corners of a square
compartment are filled with diagonals: the
resulting octagonal form can carry either a
domical vault with groins, or, by
corbelling out over the angles of the
octagon (or 'fudging' these corners) a
circular base for the dome over can be
erected. It should be noted that a dome on
pendentives or squinches rises from a
distinct circular or polygonal base, but
that a sail dome does not possess that
distinct circular base, because the concave
surfaces beginning in each corner of the
square compartment merge smoothly
with the dome proper, as the diagonal
dimension of the square compartment is
the same as the diameter of the form of
the sail vault or dome. A **melon,
parachute, pumpkin,** or **umbrella
dome** also sits on a circular base, but its
form is broken into **webs** that are
segmental on plan and rise up to a point in
a curve with groins between each
segmental web, so it is like an umbrella
with the fabric billowing convexly from
each rib rather than concavely, as is the
case with a real umbrella, hence the name
parachute dome. A **rampant** vault is a
tunnel vault with abutments at varying
heights. Another term for a vault is a
voussure.

A vault is, strictly speaking, so
contrived that the stones or other
materials of which it is composed support
and keep each other in place. When vaults
are more than a semicircle in section they
are called **surmounted vaults**, and when
less than a semicircle (i.e. segmental) in
section, they are termed **surbased**. A
vault is also a burial chamber, from the
form, but the term can also be applied to a
burial chamber roofed with a flat slab.

VELARIUM   The awning over an
amphitheatre.

VELLAR CUPOLA   A dome over
staircases or salons (saloons), that is, over
any compartment that is more than one
storey high. A **sail dome** [25a].

VENETIAN ARCH   A form of arched
opening, either blind or open, consisting
of a semicircular-headed arch, in the
centre of which are two semicircular-
headed openings separated by a
colonnette. Above the colonnette is a
roundel or foiled opening [Fig. 71].

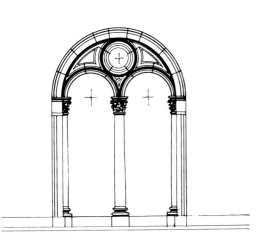

Fig. 71 *Venetian arch*

VENETIAN DOOR, VENETIAN WINDOW An arched central opening flanked by narrower flat-topped openings: over the flanking openings is an entablature from which the central arch springs. The entablatures are carried on columns or pilasters that sit on the sill, usually designed with full base, pedestal, or other Classical devices. The central arch has an archivolt and keystone. It is also called a **Serliana** or **Palladian Window** because it was first illustrated in Sebastiano Serlio's (1475–1554) *L'Architettura* of 1537–51 and was much used by Andrea Palladio. It was also used in Palladian architecture during the eighteenth century in England (*see* also **Wyatt window** and [Figs. 57, 58]).

VERANDA(H) An open gallery with a roof or canopy supported on light supports, also called a **stoep**. It is usually placed before the windows of the principal rooms to shelter them from the sun. It may be closed to form a conservatory. Verandahs were popular during the nineteenth century, from the Regency period onwards.

VERGE The junction between a pitched roof and a gable wall. When the roof-covering is flush with the wall the verge is finished with broken tiles, mortar, tumbled brickwork, or other details. If the verge is finished with mortar to make the junction watertight, it is called a **parged verge**. If the roof is extended over the wall and finished with a barge-board, the board is also called a **verge-board**.

VERMICULATION When a surface of stonework is dressed with irregular shallow channels resembling worm-tracks it is called vermiculated rustication (*see* **rustication**).

VERSURAE Projecting side-walls connecting the straight walls of the **cavea** with the **scaena** of a theatre.

VESICA PISCIS A figure of two segmental curves meeting in points, like an ellipse, but pointed at each end. It is formed by the interpenetration of two equal circles, the centre of each of which is on the centre line of each segment. It is also known as the **aureole**, **glory**, **almond**, or **mandala** (mandorla).

VESTIBULE An apartment serving as a space between rooms, usually for communication, as a waiting-room, or as an ante-chamber. Also an entrance-lobby or hall.

VESTRY, REVESTRY A room adjacent to the chancel of a church, sometimes called a **sacristy**, in which sacred vessels and vestments are kept.

VIADUCT A long bridge carrying a road, or railway, usually on a series of arches.

VIAE Spaces between mutules.

VICE, VIS, VYSE A spiral staircase wound around a column or a pier.

VILLA A country house or a farmstead in Classical times. In the Renaissance period the term meant a country house, as the Villa Capra near Vicenza. During the nineteenth century it meant a detached house on the outskirts of a town.

VITRUVIAN OPENING An opening, such as a doorway or a window, with battered sides, like an Egyptian pylon. It is found in Neoclassical Architecture, usually that with Greek and Egyptian influences. It is so called because it was described by Vitruvius [3.10].

VITRUVIAN SCROLL A continuous band of ornament like a series of stylized waves, found in Classical Architecture. It is also called a **Running Dog**, and is found in friezes, dados, etc [Fig. 72].

Fig. 72 *Vitruvian scroll*

VIVO The shaft of a column.

VOLUTE A spiral scroll forming the distinguishing feature of the Ionic capital. It is found in the Composite capital and, in a smaller form, in the Corinthian. It is also called a **helix** (*see* **Composite**, **Corinthian**, **Helix**, **Ionic**, and **Orders**).

VOMITORIUM The main exit from an amphitheatre.

VOUSSOIR A wedge-shaped stone or brick, forming part of an arch, also known as **cuneus** (*see* **arch**).

VOUSSURE A vault (*see* **vault**).

VOUTAIN The jointing of the web of a stone vault.

VYSE A spiral staircase around a central column or pier.

WAGON CEILING, WAGON VAULT A ceiling or vault over a rectangular space consisting of a simple half-cylinder carried on parallel walls. A wagon roof, or cradle roof, is formed of closely spaced rafters with arched braces that look like the covering of a wagon. Such roofs can be plastered or panelled.

WAINSCOT Timber lining to walls, or timber panelling. Also panelling of box-pews.

WALL ARCADE A blind arcade.

WATER TABLE A horizontal offset in a wall with a chamfered top, also known as an off-set.

WEATHERCOCK A vane.

WEATHERING An inclination given to horizontal surfaces to throw off water.

WEATHER MOULDING A projecting moulding with a weathered top.

WEATHER TILING or **SLATING** Walls clad in tiles or slates.

WEB A bay of a vault, between groins. It is also called a cell or a severy (*see* **vault**).

WEEPER A figure between the columns or pilasters or in the niches of an altar-tomb or sarcophagus [4.1].

WEIGHTS OF A SASH Two weights on either side of a sash by which the moveable parts are suspended on cords or chains over pulleys or wheels.

WELCH GROIN A groin formed by the intersection of two cylindrical vaults, one of which is of lesser height than another.

WELL   The space left beyond the ends of the steps or strings of a staircase.

WHEEL WINDOW   A circular window with radiating spokes like a wheel.

WICKET   A small door set within a large one.

WINDERS   Steps radiating from a centre.

WINDING STAIR   *See* **stair**.

WINDOW   An aperture in a wall to admit light. If the aperture is subdivided, each part is known as a **light**. Classical windows are usually vertical rectangular openings, sometimes surrounded by moulded architraves, and sometimes crowned with an entablature with or without a pediment. If the opening has columns or pilasters on either side supporting an entablature, pediment, gable, lintel, or plaque, it is said to be **aediculated**.

Window-frames in Classical Architecture are of two basic types: the **casement** and the **sash**. In the seventeenth century the frame was often cruciform, with quarries of glass in lead cames supported by saddle-bars, and the opening lights (often of iron) were hinged at the sides, opening in or out. In 1685 the frames of the Palladian Banqueting House in Whitehall were replaced by wooden sash-windows, one frame of which slid vertically in grooves in front of the other. The sashes were suspended on cords over pulleys and counterbalanced by means of weights held in the surrounding frames within the jambs. If only one sash could be moved, it was **single-hung**, and if both, the window was **double-hung**. This type of sash-window rapidly gained in popularity, and replaced the casement types in all the better-class work. Crown glass was generally used, but the sashes had to be subdivided by means of glazing-bars, which were generally thick and somewhat clumsy. During the eighteenth century the glazing bars became finer, with elegant mouldings, and the panes became bigger. In the first decades of the nineteenth century, the wider proportions of

windows fashionable with the Neoclassical styles produced the need to have narrow bands of glazing around the larger panes of glass: these are called **margin-panes** and were often coloured. From around 1830 larger panes of glass became available at cheap rates, and it became fashionable to remove glazing-bars: this altered the vertical emphasis of windows, and the proportional relationship of the window openings to the façade. The repeal of taxes in England on glass in 1845 and on windows in 1851 gave windows greater prominence in elevations from those dates.

Other types of window associated with Classical Architecture include bay- and bow-windows, canted, segmental or semicircular on plan, and found in eighteenth- and nineteenth-century domestic architecture. The term bay is usually applied to the canted form on plan, while bow suggests the segmental or semicircular type: both bays and bows rise from the ground. A bow may also be a projection of the window-frame only, rather than part of the structure. **French** or *croisée* windows are casements carried down to the floor level and opening like doors to gardens, verandahs, or terraces: they are so called from their use in the 1660s at Versailles. **Dormer** windows are set on the slope of a roof and are independently roofed themselves: they are named from the fact that they usually illuminated sleeping-quarters. A dormer should not be confused with a **lucarne** or **luthern** (*see* **dormer**). A Palladian window is also called a Venetian Window or a Serliana (*see* **Venetian door** or **window** and **Serliana**): it became a commonly used feature in English Palladian Architecture. The **Diocletian** or **Thermal Window**, named after its use in the Baths of Diocletian, was also used by Palladio, and was employed in Palladian Architecture in England: it is a semicircular window divided into three lights by means of two mullions.

WINGS   Side portions of a principal façade, subordinate to the central front:

small buildings flanking a main block. The wing of a moulding is the **fillet**.

WITHE   The partition between two flues of a chimney-stack.

WREATHED COLUMN   A column festooned with spirals of vines or other plants, including ivy: also a barley-sugar, spiral, or Solomonic column (*see* **baldacchino**).

WREATHED STRING   The circular portion of a stair string.

WYATT WINDOW   A **Venetian Window** or **Serliana** with a horizontal central head instead of an arched opening.

XENODOCHIUM   A room, building, or apartment for the reception of strangers.

XYSTUS   A spacious portico, usually attached to a gymnasium, in which athletes could exercise during inclement weather. An ambulatory. A long covered or open colonnade around a garden or court. A walk flanked by columns, trellises, or trees. An hypaethral walk.

YARD   A paved area, generally at the rear of a house. An enclosed utilitarian area, surrounded by walls or outbuildings.

YORKSHIRE LIGHT   A mullioned window containing two sashes, one fixed and the other sliding horizontally.

ZIGGURAT   Properly, a series of platforms, or a temple-tower, consisting of stages, each smaller in area than the one below. It is a form found in Ancient Mesopotamia, but the name has been applied to stepped pyramidal forms, as often found in Classical designs.

ZOCLE, ZOCCO, ZOCCOLO   A plain block or low pedestal with no mouldings. The same as **socle**.

ZOPHORUS, ZOOPHORUS   A frieze decorated with reliefs featuring animals.

ZOTHECA   A small room, usually off a larger space. An alcove.

SELECT BIBLIOGRAPHY

ADAM, ROBERT, *Classical Architecture: a Complete Handbook* (Viking, London, 1990).

ALBERTI, LEON BATTISTA, *De Re Aedificatoria*, Florence, 1486. See the version entitled *On the Art of Building in Ten Books*, translated by Joseph Rykwert, Neil Leach, and Robert Tavernor (The MIT Press, Cambridge, Mass., and London, 1988).

See also his *L'Architettura*, edited by Giovanni Orlandi with an Introduction by Paolo Portoghesi (Il Polifilo, Milan, 1966).

ALDRICH, HENRY, *The Elements of Civil Architecture, according to Vitruvius and Other Ancients, and the most approved Practice of Modern Authors, especially Palladio* (Prince and Cooke, Oxford, and Payne *et al.*, London, 1789).

AVILER, AUGUSTIN CHARLES D', *Cours d'Architecture qui comprend les ordres de Vignole, avec des commentaires, les figures & descriptions de ses plus beaux bâtimens & de ceux de Michel-Ange . . .*, etc. (Langlois, Paris, 1694).

BARON, HANS, *The Crisis of the Early Italian Renaissance* (Princeton University Press, Princeton, NJ, 1966).

BLONDEL, FRANÇOIS, *Cours d'Architecture, enseigné dans l'Académie Royale d'Architecture . . .* (Mortier, Paris, 1698).

BLUM, HANS, *Quinque Columnarum exacta descriptio atque deliniatio cum symmetrica earum distributione . . .* (Froschouerum, Zürich, 1550). See also *The Booke of Five Collumnes of Architecture . . . Gathered . . . by H. Bloome out of Antiquities* (Stafford, London, 1608).

BOLGAR, R. R., *The Classical Heritage and Its Beneficiaries* (Cambridge University Press, Cambridge, 1973).

BURCKHARDT, JACOB, *The Architecture of the Italian Renaissance* (Secker & Warburg, London, 1985).

See also Burckhardt's, *The Civilization of the Renaissance in Italy* (Phaidon, Vienna, and Allen & Unwin, London, 1928).

CAMPBELL, COLEN, *Virtruvius Britannicus or the British Architect*, Vols 1, 2, and 3, with an Introduction by John Harris. (First published in three volumes, London 1715–25. Reissued in one volume [Vol. 1 of the three-volume facsimile edition], Benjamin Blom, New York, 1967).

See also Badeslade *et al.*, *Vitruvius Britannicus or the British Architect*, the hitherto unpublished Vol. 4 by J. Badeslade and J. Rocque, and Vols 5 and 6 by John Woolfe and James Gandon. (First published 1767–71. Reissued in one volume [Vol. 2 of the three-volume facsimile edition], Benjamin Blom, New York, 1967).

See also Richardson, George, *The New Vitruvius Britannicus . . .* (First published in two volumes, 1802–8. Reissued in one volume [Vol. 3 of the three-volume facsimile edition], Benjamin Blom, New York, 1970).

See also Breman, Paul and Addis, Denise, *Guide to Vitruvius Britannicus . . .* (Vol. 4 to *Vitruvius Britannicus*), (Benjamin Blom, New York, 1972).

CHAMBERS, SIR WILLIAM, *A Treatise on Civil Architecture, in which the Principles of that Art are laid down; and illustrated by a Great Number of Plates, accurately designed, and elegantly engraved by the best hands* (Haberkorn, London, 1759).

See also *A Treatise on the Decorative Part of Civil Architecture, by Sir William Chambers . . . , with Illustrations, Notes, and An Examination of Grecian Architecture, by Joseph Gwilt . . .* (Priestley & Weale, London, 1825).

See also a fourth edition with an essay by John B. Papworth and nine new plates (J. Taylor, London, 1826). Chambers's great book is of considerable importance in refining and classifying the Classical Language of Architecture.

CHITHAM, ROBERT, *The Classical Orders of Architecture* (The Architectural Press, London, 1985).

CORDEMOY, J.-L. DE, *Nouveau Traité de Toute L'Architecture, ou L'Art de bastir; utile aux entrepreneurs et aux ouvriers . . . Avec un Dictionnaire des Termes d'Architecture . . .*, etc. (Coignard, Paris, 1714).

CURL, JAMES STEVENS, *Dictionary of Architecture* (Oxford University Press, Oxford, 2000).

DIETTERL(E)IN, WENDEL, *Architectura Von Ausztheilung. Symmetria und Proportion der Fünff Seulen, und aller darausz folgender Kunst Arbeit, von Fenstern, Caminen, Thürgerichten, Portalen, Bronnen und Epitaphien. Wie dieselbige ausz jedweder Art der Fünff Seulen, grund, aufzureissen, zuzurichten, und ins Werck zubringen seyen, allen solcher Kunst Liebhabenden, zu einem beständigen, und ring ergreiffenden underricht, erfunden, in zwey-hundert Stuck gebracht, Geetzt, und an tag gegeben*, in five books (Caymor, Nürnberg, 1598). Another edition was published in Nürnberg by Pauluss Fürst in 1655, again in five books with a portrait. A French version was published in 1861.

DINSMOOR, WILLIAM BELL, *The Architecture of Ancient Greece* (B.T. Batsford, London, 1950 edition).

DURAND, JEAN-NICHOLAS-LOUIS, *Essai sur l'Histoire Générale de l'Architecture . . . pour servir de texte explicatif au recueil et parallèle des édifices de tout genre, anciens et modernes, remarquables par leur beauté, leur grandeur, ou leur singularité . . .* (Soyer, Paris, 1809).

See also Durand's, *Précis des Leçons d'Architecture données a l'École Polytechnique* (Durand, Paris, 1817–21).

FRÉART DE CHAMBRAY, ROLAND, *Parallèle de l'Architecture Antique et de la Moderne, avec un recueil des dix principaux autheurs qui ont écrit des cinq ordres; sçavoir Palladio et Scamozzi, Serlio et Vignola, D. Barbaro et Cataneo, L. B. Alberti et Viola Bullant et De Lorme, comparez entre aux . . . , etc.* (Martin, Paris, 1650). This appeared in a translation by John Evelyn as *A Parallel of the Ancient Architecture with the Modern* (Roycroft & Place, London, 1664).

FYFE, THEODORE, *Hellenistic Architecture: An Introductory Study* (Cambridge University Press, Cambridge, 1936).

GADOL, JOAN, *Leon Battista Alberti, Universal Man of the Early Renaissance* (University of Chicago Press, Chicago, 1969).

GERSON, H., and TER KUILE, E. H., *Art and Architecture in Belgium 1600 to 1800* (Penguin, Harmondsworth, 1960).

GIBBS, JAMES, *A Book of Architecture, Containing Designs of Buildings and Ornaments* (s.n., London, 1728).

See also Gibbs's, *Rules for Drawing the Several Parts of Architecture, in a More Exact and Easy Manner than has been heretofore practised, by which all fractions, in dividing the principal members and their parts, are avoided* (Bowyer, London, 1732).

GRAFTON, ANTHONY, *Joseph Scaliger: A Study in the History of Classical Scholarship* (Oxford University Press, Oxford, 1983).

GWILT, JOSEPH, *An Encyclopaedia of Architecture*, revised by Wyatt Papworth (Longmans Green, London, 1903).

HERSEY, GEORGE, *The Lost Meaning of Classical Architecture*, (MIT Press, Cambridge, Mass., and London, 1988).

KALNEIN, WEND GRAF, and LEVEY, MICHAEL, *Art and Architecture of the Eighteenth Century in France* (Penguin, Harmondsworth, 1972).

LANGLEY, BATTY, *The City and Country Builder's and Workman's Treasury of Designs: Or the Art of Drawing and Working the Ornamental Parts of Architecture* (S. Harding, London, 1745).

LAUGIER, ABBÉ MARC-ANTOINE, *Essai sur l'Architecture* (Duchesne, Paris, 1753). Another edition, augmented with a dictionary of terms and plates to explain the terms, was published in Paris in 1755. See also the version tr. by W. & A. Hermann (Hennessey, Los Angeles, 1977).

LAWRENCE, A. W., *Greek Architecture* (Penguin, Harmondsworth, 1962).

MARTIN, THOMAS, *The Circle of the Mechanical Arts: Containing Practical Treatises on the Various Manual Arts, Trades, & Manufactures* (Bumpus, Sherwood, Neely, and Jones, London, 1820).

MIDDLETON, ROBIN and WATKIN, DAVID, *Neoclassical and 19th Century Architecture* (Electa, Milan, and Faber & Faber, London, 1987).

MURRAY, PETER, *Renaissance Architecture* (Electa, Milans and Faber & Faber, London, 1986).

NICHOLSON, PETER, *An Architectural and Engineering Dictionary* (John Weale, London, 1835). Another edition, called *Encyclopedia of Architecture* (Caxton Press, London, 1852).

NORMAND, CHARLES, *Nouveau Parallèle des Ordres d'Architecture des Grecs, des Romains et des Autres Modernes* (Normand Ainé and Carilian, Goevry and Dalmont, Paris, 1852).

ONIANS, JOHN, *Bearers of Meaning. The Classical Orders in Antiquity, the Middle Ages, and the Renaissance* (Cambridge University Press, Cambridge, 1988).

ORME, PHILIBERT DEL', *Architecture* (Morel, Paris, 1567).

PALLADIO, ANDREA, *I Quattro Libri dell'Architettura* (de'Francheschi, Venice, 1570).

See also *The Architecture of A. Palladio in four books . . . to which are added several notes and observations made by Inigo Jones . . .* (Leoni, London, 1715).

PERRAULT, CLAUDE, *Ordonnances des Cinq Espèces de Colonnes* (Coignard, Paris, 1676). This was translated by John James and published as *A Treatise of the Five Orders of Columns* (printed by Motte and sold by Sturt, London, 1708).

PORPHYRIOS, DEMETRI, *Classical Architecture* (McGraw Hill, London, 1992).

ROBERTSON, D. S., *A Handbook of Greek & Roman Architecture* (Cambridge University Press, Cambridge, 1945).

SALMON, WILLIAM, *Palladio Londinensis* (Ward & Wicksteed, London, 1734).

SCAMOZZI, VINCENZO, *L'Idea della Architettura Universale* (Scamozzi, Venice, 1615).

See also his *The Mirror of Architecture . . . Reviewed and Inlarged . . . By Joachim Schuym . . . Translated out of the Dutch . . .* (Fisher, London, 1687).

SERLIO, SEBASTIANO, *Architettura di S. Serlio Bolognese, in sei libri divisa . . .* (Hertz, Venice, 1663).

See also his *The Booke of Architecture* (E. Stafford, London, 1611).

SHUTE, JOHN, *The First and Chief Groundes of Architecture* (Thomas Marshe, London, 1563).

SPIERS, R. PHENÉ, *The Orders of Architecture, Greek, Roman, and Italian Selected from Normand's Parallel and Other Authorities* (Batsford, London, 1893).

STRATTON, ARTHUR, *Elements of Form & Design in Classic Architecture Shown in Exterior & Interior Motives Collated from Fine Buildings of All Time on One Hundred Plates* (B.T. Batsford, London, 1925).

SUMMERSON, JOHN, *The Classical Language of Architecture* (Thames & Hudson, London, 1980).

TAVERNOR, ROBERT, *Palladio and Palladianism* (Thames & Hudson, London, 1991).

VIGNOLA, GIACOMO BAROZZI DA, *Regola delli Cinque Ordini d'Architettura* (Porro, Venice, 1596).

See also *The Five Orders of Architecture according to Vignola*, arranged by Pierre Esquié and edited by Arthur Stratton (Tiranti, London, 1926).

VITRUVIUS POLLIO, MARCUS, *Architettura*, edited Ferri (Palombi, Rome, 1960).

See also the edition published in Venice in 1567 with plates by Palladio.

See also the Frank Granger translation (Heinemann, London, and Harvard University Press, Cambridge, Mass., 1944–56); the Morris Hicky Morgan translation, with illustrations prepared under the direction of Herbert Langford Warren (Dover Publications Inc., New York, 1960); and the Ingrid D. Rowland translation, with commentary and illustrations by Thomas Noble Howe (Cambridge University Press, Cambridge, 1999).

VRIES, PAULUS VREDEMAN DE, *L'Architecture . . . avec quelques belles ordonnances d'Architecture, mises en perspective per J. Vredman Frison* (and P. V. de V.), (Jean Janson, Amsterdam, 1651). Many versions were published following the first

Antwerp edition of 1577 entitled *Architectura . . .* , etc.

See also Vries's, *Les cinq rangs de l'Architecture, a sçavoir, Tuscane, Dorique, Ionique, Corinthique, et Composée, - avec L'instruction fondamentale faicte par H.H.* (Henrik Hondius the Younger). *Avec . . . quelques belles ordonnances d'architecture, mises en perspective, inventées par J. Vredeman Frison et son fils* (Jean Janson, Amsterdam, 1617).

WARE, ISAAC, *The Complete Body of Architecture. Adorned with Plans and Elevations, from Original Designs* (Osborne and Shipton, Hodges, Davis, Ward, & Baldwin, London, 1756). One of the greatest works of the whole Palladian style.

WIEBENSON, DORA, *Sources of Greek Revival Architecture* (Zwemmer, London, 1969).

WITTKOWER, RUDOLF, *Architectural Principles in the Age of Humanism* (Tiranti, London, 1952).

See also the revised edition (Academy Editions, London, 1988).

See also his *Palladio and English Palladianism* (Thames & Hudson, London, 1974).

WOOD, JOHN, *Dissertation upon the Orders of Columns* (Bettenham & Leake, London, 1750).

WREN SOCEITY, *Publications*, Vols I–XX, (Oxford University Press, Oxford, 1924–43).

INDEX

THIS INDEX COVERS CHAPTERS I TO VII

Page numbers in **bold** refer to illustrations

Aalto, Alvar (1898–1976) 169
abacus
    Greek Orders 22, 24, 33
    Roman Orders 34, 37, 43
acanthus leaves
    Greek Orders, Corinthian 33, **34**
    Greek/Roman comparisons 48
    Hellenistic influences 57
    Roman Architecture **63**, 64
    Roman Orders 38, **47**, 49
Adam Brothers 140
Adam, Robert (1728–1729) 147, 151, **157**
Adam, Robert (b. 1948) 170n
AEG office block, Berlin 167
Akroyd, John (1556–1613) 96
Albert Dock, Liverpool **154**
Albert, Prince Consort (1819–1861) 163,
    164
Alberti, Leon Battista (1404–1472) 16, 68, 70,
    71–2, 73, **74**, **84–6**, 86, 98
Aldrich, Henry (1648–1710) 144
Alessi, Galeazzo (1512–1572) 94
American Classical design 151
antae, definition 66–7
Antiochus Epiphanes, King of Syria 57
apophyges, Roman Orders 34, 37
Archer, Thomas (c.1668–1743) 131
arches
    Arc de Triomphe du Carrousel **60**
    Arc de Triomphe de l'Étoile, Paris **59**, 159
    Constantine 59, **60**
    development 58–62
    Grand Palais, Paris **60**
    palazzi 68–79
    Roman triumphal 53, 67, **71**, **84–5**, 86
    Septimius Severus 58–9
    Thiepval memorial **170**
    Titus, Rome **49**, **52–3**, 58
architraves
    entablature components 16
    Greek Orders, Doric 24
    Greek/Roman comparison **63**
    Roman Orders 27, 34, **47**, **50**
arcuated construction **51**, 53, 58, 59, 62
Army and Navy Club, London 163
arrises 22, 37
art galleries, National Gallery, Berlin **161**

Asam, C. D. (1686–1739) and E. Q. (1692–1750)
    117
Asplund, Erik Gunnar (1885–1940) 168, 169
Asprucci, Mario (1764–1804) 159
Atkinson, R. F. (1871–1923) 167
Aufrere, Sophia **157**
axes 13–14, **61**, 62
Aylesford, 4th Earl (1751–1812) 151

Bacon, Henry (1866–1924) 167
banks
    Bank of Pennsylvania 151
    Belfast (Northern) Bank **80**, 166
Barelli, Agostino (1627–1679) 114, 116, 133
Baroque style 106–22
    definition 106
    ellipses/Western façades 106–19
    England 123–32
    French examples 119–22
    Neoclassicism disfavour 146–7, 151
    precedents 59, 64
    revival 166–7, 169
    transition (Vignola) 97–8
Barrière de la Villette, Paris **154**
Barry, Charles (1795–1860) 163
Bartolommeo, Michelozzo *see* Michelozzi
bases
    Asiatic 24, **29**
    Attic 24, **28**, 38, **40**, 43, 49
    Greek Orders 24, 28, 33, **34**
    Order component 16
    Roman Orders 43, 49
        Corinthian 43
        Doric **38**
        Ionic 38, **41**
        Tuscan 34, **35**
Basevi, George (1794–1845) 159
basilica
    churches 61
    Giant Order **91**, 92
    Vicenza **99**, 100
baths *see* Thermae
Befreiungshalle, Bavaria **159**
Behrens, Peter (1868–1940) 167, 170
Belcher, John (1841–1913) 166, 167
Belfast (Northern) Bank **80**, 163
Belle Isle, Windermere, Westmorland **158–9**
Belsay Hall, Northumberland 155, **156**
Bentley, John (c.1573–1613) 96

Bentsen, Ivar (1876–1943) 168, 169
Bernini, Gianlorenzo (1598–1680) 106–7,
    109–10, 112, **114**, 116
Biblioteca Marciana, Venice 82–3, **84**
Bicknell, J. (b. 1945) 170n
Blenheim Palace, Oxfordshire 127, **128**
Blomfield, Reginald (1856–1942) 170
Blouet, G.-A. (1795–1853) **59**
Bond, J. L. (1764–1837) **33**
Bonomi, Joseph (1739–1808) 151, 155
Borromini, Francesco (1599–1667) 106, 108–10,
    112
Boullée, Étienne-Louis (1728–99) 155
Boyle, Richard (3rd Earl of Burlington)
    (1694–1753) 104, 135–6
Bramante, Donato (c.1444–1514) 17, 146
    Basilica of S. Peter, Rome 90, 92
    House of Raphael 74
    Tempietto 86, 88–90, 92
Brewer, C. C. (1871–1918) 167
Bridgewater House, London 163
Brodrick, Cuthbert (1822–1905) 166–7
Brompton Oratory, London 163
Brosse, Salomon de (c.1571–1626) **120–1**, 122
Brumwell Thomas, Sir Alfred (1868–1948)
    166–7, **166**
Brunelleschi, F. (1377–1446) 68, **70–1**
Brydon, J. McK. (1840–1901) **165**, 166
Burlington, 3rd Earl of *see* Boyle
Burlington House, London 135
Burnet, John James (1857–1938) 166
    British Museum, extension 167, 170
    Kodak House, Kingsway **167**
Burnham, D. H. (1846–1912) **167**
Burton, Decimus (1800–1881), Neoclassicism 151
Byzantine Architecture, influences 62

Cairness House, Aberdeenshire 154
Campania 58
Campbell, Colen (1676–1729) 135–8
capitals
    Aeolic **25**, 56
    diagonal 28, 38, 49
    Greek Orders
        Corinthian 33–4
        Doric **20**
        Ionic 24–8
    Order component 16
    ornament **151**

Roman Orders
    Composite 49, **50**
    Corinthian 43–8
    Doric 36–8
    Ionic 38, 41, **43**
Capitol, Washington, USA **151**, 167
Carlton Club, London 163, **164**
caryatides **28**, **150**
Castle Howard, Yorkshire **127**, **129**
    Temple of the Four Winds **128**
    The Mausoleum 129, **130**
Caux, Isaac de (*fl.* 1612–1655) 123
Cayart, J.-L. (1645–1702) **134**
Chalgrin, J.-F.-T. (1739–1811) 59, 122, 159
Chambers, Sir William (1723–1796) 17, 140,
    144
Charlemont, Earl of (1728–1799) 147
China, Classical Architecture 168
churches and chapels etc.
    Abbey-church, Neresheim **118**, 119
    Anglican chapel, General Cemetery of All
        Souls, Kensal Green, London **21**
    Ayot St Lawrence, Herts. 48
    basilican 61
    Benedictine Abbey-church, Weltenburg **117**
    centralized/circular plans 86–92
    Christ Church, London 127, **128**, 129
    Domkirke **23**
    Dreifaltigkeitskirche, Salzburg **114**, 116
    Florence Cathedral 86
    Gendarmenplatz, Berlin 133, **134**
    Hagia Sophia, Constantinople 90
    Il Gesù, Rome **97–8**, 112
    Il Redentore, Venice 98, **99**, **103**, 104
    Karlskirche, Vienna **115–16**, 117
    Madeleine, Paris 159, **160–1**
    Medici Chapel, Florence **92**, 93
    Panthéon, Paris **122–3**, 147
    Pazzi Chapel, Florence 68, **70–1**, 86
    S. Agnese in Agone, Rome 109, **110**, 112
    S. Alphege, Greenwich 127
    S. Ambrogio, Milan 146
    S. Andrea al Quirinale, Rome 106, **107**, **109**
    S. Andrea, Mantua **84–5**, **86**, 98
    S. Andrea, Via Flaminia, Rome **94**, **97**, 98
    S. Anna dei Palafrenieri, Rome 97, **98**
    S. Anne, Limehouse 127
    S. Biagio, Montepulciano 90
    S. Carlo alle Quattro Fontane, Rome 106,
        108, 109
    S. Croce, Florence, Pazzi Chapel 68, **70–1**, 86
    S. Francesco, Rimini 70, **71**
    S. Geneviève (Panthéon), Paris **122–3**, 147
    S. George-in-the-East, Limehouse 127
    S. George, Bloomsbury, London 127, **128**
    S. Gervais, Paris 120, **121**, 122
    S. Giorgio Maggiore, Venice 98, **99**, **102**,
        103–4
    S. James, Great Packington, Warwicks. 151,
        152
    S. John, Westminster **131**
    S. Kajetan, Munich **114**, 116
    S. Lawrence, Jewry, London **125**
    S. Lorenzo, Florence 68, 86, **92–3**
        library vestibule **93**
        Old Sacristy 86
    S. Louis des Invalides **120**, 122
    S. Maria degli Angeli, Florence 86, **87**
    S. Maria del Calcinaio, Cortona 86
    S. Maria della Pace, Rome 88, **111**, 112
    S. Maria della Salute, Venice **112–13**, 116
    S. Maria delle Carceri, Prato 86

S. Maria delle Grazie, Milan 88
S. Maria Maggiore, Rome **62**
S. Maria Novella, Florence 84, **85**, 86, 98
S. Maria presso S. Satiro, Milan **88**
S. Maria, Via Lata, Rome **112**
S. Martin-in-the-Fields, London **44**, **130**, 132
S. Mary-le-Strand, London 132
S. Miniato al Monte, Florence 67, 68, **69**
S. Pancras, London 148, **149–50**
S. Paul, Covent Garden, London **135**
S. Paul's Cathedral, London 120, 122, 125
S. Peter's Basilica, Rome 125
    Baldacchino (canopy) **109**
    Constantinian (begun *c.*333) **90**
    Piazza (elliptical) 107, **114**, 116
    reconstruction (from 1450s) 90, **91**, 92
S. Pietro in Montorio, Rome (*Tempietto*) 86,
    88, **89**, **90**, 92
S. Satiro Chapel, Milan 88
S. Spirito, Florence 68, **69**, 86
S. Sulpice, Paris **122**
S. Susanna, Rome **111**, 112
S. Vincent de Paul, Paris **31**
SS. Vincenzo ed Anastasio, Rome **111**, 112
Salzburg Cathedral 116
Sorbonne, Paris 122
Tempio Malatestiano, Rimini 70, **71**, 86
Theatinerkirche of S. Kajetan, Munich **114**,
    116
Val-de-Grâce, Paris **120**, 122, 125
Vierzehnheiligen, Franconia **117–18**, 119
Wallfahrtskirche 'Die Wies' **118**
Wallfahrtskirche Steinhausen **118**, 119
circular structures 61, 63, 86–92
Clarendon Building, Oxford **131**, 132
Classical Architecture
    American design 151
    definitions 12–14
    England 123–32
    Graeco-Roman roots 56–64
    Schools/regional variations 56–8
Classical Revival 170
clubs, London 163, **164**
Cockerell, C. R. (1788–1863) 28, **29**
    Neoclassicism 151, 159
Cockerell, S. P., (1753–1827) 151
colonnades 63
Colosseum, Rome **51**, 53
columnar construction 51, 56, 62
columns 66–7
    circular 56
    definition 66
    engaged 51–3, 57, 58, 146
    Greek Architecture 57, 62
    Greek Orders
        Corinthian 33
        Doric 17–18
        Ionic 24
    Hellenistic influences 57
    Neoclassicism 146–7
    Order component 16
    polygonal 56
    Roman Orders
        Composite 16, 28, 49–50
        Corinthian 43, 46
        Doric 36–7
        Ionic 41, 43
        Tuscan **35–6**
    Solomonic **109**, **115**
    square 56
    superimposed 53
    wooden 17–18, 56

Composite Order 16, 28, 49–50
Concert Hall, Stockholm 168
concrete, development 58, 59, 62
consoles, Greek/Roman comparison 64
Cooley, Thomas (*c.*1740–1784) **143**, 144
Cordemoy, J.-L. de (1631–1713) 146–7
Corinthian Orders
    evolution 57
    Greek 16, 33–4
    Hellenistic 57
    Renaissance 57
    Roman 43–8
cornices
    entablature component 16
    Greek Orders, Doric **19**, 24
    Roman Orders 34, 43, **47**, **50**
cornicione, Renaissance **72**, 73, **79**
cortile, palazzi **73**, **74–7**, **79**
Cortile della Mostra (Cavallerizza) 77, 80
Cortile of Palazzo Marino, Milan **94**
Cortona, Pietro da (1596–1669) 111–12
country houses
    Burghley House, near Stamford 123
    Burley-on-the-Hill, Rutland 135
    Casino, Marino, near Dublin 140
    Castle Ward, Co. Down 140, **141**
    Chatsworth House, Derbyshire 127
    Chiswick House, London **136**
    Holkham Hall, Norfolk 137, **138–9**, 140
    Houghton Hall, Norfolk 137, **138**
    Kedleston Hall, Derbyshire **140–1**
    Kirby Hall, Northants 123, **124**
    Schloss Wörlitz 140
    The Vyne, Hampshire 123
    Wanstead House 135
    Wilton House, Wiltshire 123
Country Life offices, Tavistock Street, Covent
    Garden, London 167
Crete, Egyptian/Asiatic influences 56
Cronaca, Simone del Pollaiuolo (1457–1508)
    72–3
Cubitt, Thomas (1788–1855) 163, **164**
Cuvilliés, J.-F.-V.-J. (1695–1768) 114, 116

Dalton, Richard (*c.*1715–1791) 147
Dance, George (1741–1825) **155**
Danish, Pavilion, Paris International Exposition
    168
Deglane, H. (1855–1921) 60
Delphi 17–18, 57
dentils, Greek/Roman comparison 64
Desgodetz, Antoine (1653–1728) 147
Dilettanti Society 147
Dobson, John (1787–1865) 155, **156**
domes 129, 132
    centralized/circular plans 86–92
    development 58, 59, 62
    Karlskirche, Vienna **115–16**, 117
Doric Orders
    columns 66
    Egyptian influences 56
    Greek 16, 17–24
    Hellenistic modifications 57
    Roman 36–8
Dormer, Henry (d. 1727) 135

Eastern Europe, Classical Architecture preference
    168, 169
echinus
    Greek Orders 22–4
    Roman Orders 34, 37
Egyptian influences 56, 154–5, 169

Ehrensvård, Carl August (1745–1800),
        Neoclassicism 151, **153**, 154
Eleusis, Greek Orders, Ionic **28**
Elis, wooden columns 18
ellipses 98, 106–19
Elmes, H. L. (1814–1847) 159, **162–3**
England
        Classical Architecture 123–32
        Palladianism 123–4, 129–30, 135–44
Enlightenment 147
entablatures
        columns 6
        curved 59
        Greek Orders
                Corinthian 34
                Doric 24
                Ionic 31
        Hellenistic influences 57
        Order component 16
        Roman Architecture 58
        Roman Orders
                Composite **50**
                Corinthian 43, **44**, 47
                Doric 36–8
                Ionic **41**
                Tuscan 34
        wooden 58
entasis, Greek Orders, Doric 22
Ephesus, Temple of Artemis 24, 57
Epidaurus, Corinthian designs 57
Erdmannsdorff, F. W. von (1736–1800) 140
Erechtheion **26–8**, 31, 57, **63**
Erlach, J. B. Fischer von (1656–1723) 114–16,
        132–3
Etrurian School 57–8

Feichtmayr, F. X. (1705–1764) 118–19
Feichtmayr, J. M. (1709–1772) 119
fillets
        Greek Orders, Ionic 24, **25**
        Roman Orders, Tuscan 34
Fischer von Erlach. See Erlach
Fisker, K. (1893–1965) 168
Florence, Renaissance 68–73
fluting
        Greek Orders
                Corinthian 33
                Doric 18, 22, **23**
                Ionic 24, **28**
        Roman Orders
                Composite 49
                Doric **36**, 37
                Ionic **41**
Fontaine, P.-F.-L. (1762–1853) **60**
fora, Nerva, Rome 43, **44–5**
Foreign Office, London 163
Francesco di Giorgio (1439–1501/2) 86
Frederick the Great, King (1712–1786) 133–4
friezes 16
        Greek Orders
                Doric 18, 24
                Ionic 31
        Roman Orders
                Composite **50**
                Corinthian 43, **44**, 47
                Ionic 41
                Tuscan 34
        wooden origins 18

Gandon, James (1743–1823) 143, 144
Garrett, Daniel (d. 1753) 130
Gärtner, Friedrich von (1792–1847) **159**

gates
        Menin Gate, Ieper 170
        Porta Palio, Verona **77**, 80
        Porta Pia, Rome 93, **95**
        Schools Quadrangle, Oxford **96**
Gell, Sir William (1777–1836) 155, **156**
geometry, Classical Architecture 12, 13–14
Germany
        Classical Architecture 168, 169
        palaces 132–4
        Palladianism examples 140
Giant Order **91**, 92
        Kirby Hall, Northants. 123, **124**
        Palladio application **100**
Gibbs, James (1682–1754) 129–30, 132
        Classical Orders description 17
        S.-Martin-in-the-Fields, London **44**
Gibson, John (1817–1892) 159, **162**
Gilly, Friedrich (1772–1800)
        Classical Architecture examples 13
        Eben Mausoleum **23**
        Neoclassicism 151, 155
Giorgio, Francesco di. See Franceso di Giorgio
Glyptothek, Munich 29–30
Goethe, J. W. von (1749–1832) 147
Gontard, Karl von (1731–1791) **134**
Gothic Architecture, Classical derivations 13
Grange Park, Hampshire 155
Greek Architecture
        rediscovery 147–8
        revival 148–55
        roots/influences 56–7
Greek Orders 17–34
        columns 66
        Corinthian 16, 33–4, 57
        Doric, capitals 19, 20, 57
        Ionic 16, 24–32, 57
        Neoclassicism revival 148–55
Greenwich Hospital **126**, 127
Greenwich Palace, King Charles II block 123,
        125
Gwilt, Joseph (1784–1863) 17

Halbig, Johann von (1814–1882) **159**
Hall of Fame, Munich 22
Hallerstein, Karl Freiherr Haller von (1774–1817)
        20–1
Hamilton, Thomas (1784–1858), Neoclassicism
        151, 155, 166
Hammerwood Lodge, East Grinstead 151
Hansen, C. F. (1756–1845) **23**
Hansom, J. A. (1803–1882) 159, **161**
Hardouin-Mansart, Jules (1646–1708) 120, 122
Harrison, Thomas (1744–1829) 151
Hartley, Jesse (1780–1860) **154**
Haus der Kunst, Munich **31**, 168
Hawksmoor, Nicholas (1661–1736) 127–32
Heliopolis, Baalbek 59
Hellenic Architecture 57, 62
Hellenistic Architecture
        Altes Museum, Berlin 30
        columns 66
        definition 57
        Ionic capitals 28
        Italy 58
        Lion Tomb, Cnidos **19**
        mixing Orders 53
Herculaneum 146, 151
High Renaissance 92
Hildebrandt, J. L. von (1668–1745) 132
Hitler, Adolf (1889–1945) 169
Hittorff, J.-I. (1792–1867) **31**

Hoffmann, Josef (1870–1956) 168
Holl, Elias (1573–1646) 94
hospitals
        Foundlings' Hospital, Florence **68**
        Greenwich **126**, 127
hypotrachelion, Greek Doric 22–4

Ictinus (*fl.* fifth century BC) 33
Inwood, H. W. (1794–1843) 148, **149–50**
Inwood, W. (*c.*1771–1843) 148, **149–50**
Ionic Orders
        Egyptian influences 56
        Greek 16, 24–32
        Hellenistic modifications 57
        Roman 38–43
Italy
        Greek architectural influences 57–8
        Medieval Architecture 67

Jones, Inigo (1573–1652) 94
        Palladianism 123–4, 135, 136
        The Queen's House **104**, 123, **126**
        Tuscan Order **36**

Kent, William (*c.*1685–1748) 136–9, 140
Klenze, Leo von (1784–1864) **20–2**
        Befreiungshalle, Bavaria **159**
        Egyptian influences 56
        Glyptothek, Munich **29–30**
        Neoclassicism 151, 168
Knight, Richard Payne (1750–1824) 147
Knobelsdorff, G. W., Freiherr von (1699–1753)
        133–4, 140
Kodak House, Kingsway, London **167**
Kreis, Wilhelm (1873–1955) 56, 168, 169, 170
Küchel, J. J. M. (1703–1769) 118–19

La Zecca (The Mint), Venice 83
Langley, Batty (1696–1751), Roman Orders,
        Ionic **41**, and sundry illustrations
language, Classical Architecture 13
Lanyon, Sir Charles (1813–1889) 80, 163
Latium School 57–8
Latrobe, Benjamin Henry (1764–1820),
        Neoclassical designs 151, 155
Laugier, Abbé Marc-Antoine (1713–1769) 51,
        146–7
Laurana, Luciano (*c.*1420–1479) 74, **75**
Le Brun, Charles (1619–1690) 119–20
Le Roy, Julien-David (1724–1803) 147
Le Vau, Louis (1612–1670) 119–20
Ledoux, Claude-Nicolas (1736–1806)
        Classical Architecture examples 13
        Neoclassicism 151, **154**, 155
Lemaire, P.-H. (1798–1880) **31**
Lemercier, Jacques (*c.*1585–1654) 120, 122
Lepère, J.-B. (1761–1844) **31**
Lewerentz, Sigurd (1885–1975) 168, 169
libraries
        Biblioteca Marciana, Venice 82–3, **84**
        Radcliffe Library, Oxford 129, **130**
        Trinity College, Cambridge 125, **126**
        University Library, Cambridge 159
Lion Tomb, Cnidos 19, 57
Lombardo, Pietro (*c.*1435–1515) 81
London Bridge Railway Terminus 163
Longhena, Baldassare (1598–1682) 82, 112–13,
        116
Longhi, Martino (1602–1660) 111–12
Loos, Adolf (1870–1933) 170
Louvet, A.-L. (1860–1936) **60**
Louvre, The, Paris **119**, 120

Lumley, John (1654–1721) 135
Lutyens, Sir Edwin (1869–1944)
    Country Life Offices, Tavistock Street, Convent Garden 167
    Heathcote, nr Ilkley, Yorks. 167
    Thiepval memorial, Somme **170**

Maderno, Carlo (c.1556–1629) **91**, 92, 111–12
Maiano, Benedetto da (1442–1497) 73
Mannerism
    disfavour 146, 151
    Fontainebleau centre 94
    Italy **92–3**, 104
    motifs 77–80
Mansart, François (1598–1666) 120, 122
Mansart, J. H. See Hardouin-Mansart.
Marcus Aurelius, Emperor (AD 161–180) **95**
Marcus Vitruvius Pollio see Vitruvius
mausolea
    Eben, Kreuzberg, Berlin **23**
    Hadrian 59
    Halicarnassus **25**
    James King Esq **153**
    Lenin, Moscow 168, 169
    Pelham, Brocklesby Park, Lincs. **157**
    Santa Costanza, Rome **61**
Medieval Architecture, Italy 67
memorials
    Ashton, nr Lancaster 167
    Chairman Mao, Beijing 168
    Lincoln Memorial, Washington 167
    Thiepval, Somme **170**
Menin Gate, Ieper 170
Mereworth Castle, Kent 136, **137**
Métezeau, J.-C. (1581–1652) 120, **121**, 122
metopes, Greek Orders, Doric 24
Michelangelo Buonarotti (1475–1564) 92–3, 95
    Basilica of S. Peter, Rome 90, **91**, 92
    Palazzo Farnese, Rome 79, 80
    Palazzo Medici windows, Florence 72
Michelozzi, Michelozzo (1396–1472) 72–3
Modern Movement 169–70
modillions, Roman Orders 43–8, **49**
modules 14
Monck, Sir Charles (1779–1867) 155, **156**
monuments
    Lysicrates, Athens 28, **33–4**, 57
    Nereid, Xanthos 57
    Septimius Severus 59
    Thrasyllus **21**
Moray Place, Glasgow **32**
mouldings
    Greek Orders, Doric 24
    Roman Architecture **63**, 64
    Roman Orders
        Composite 49, **50**
        Corinthian 43
        Doric 37
        Ionic **41**
        Tuscan 34
Municipal Chambers, Glasgow **165**
museums
    Altes, Berlin **30**
    Ashmolean, Oxford **29**, 159
    British, London 167
    Fitzwilliam, Cambridge 159
    National Museum of Wales 167
mutules, Roman Orders 34, 37

National Gallery, Berlin **161**
Neoclassicism 146–68
    after 155–68

Greek Architecture
    rediscovery 147–8
    revival 148–55, 170
    and Rome 146–55
    stripped 155, 167–8, 169, 170
Neue Wache, Berlin **22**
Neumann, J. B. (1687–1753) 117–19
New Scotland Yard 166
Newgate Gaol, London **155**
Nollekens, Joseph (1737–1823), statue **157**
Nottingham, 2nd Earl (1647–1730) 135

obelisks, Egyptian, Rome **91**
Olympieion, Athens **43**, 57
Olympia, wooden columns 18
Opera House, Berlin 133, **134**, **140**
Oppenord, G.-M. (1672–1742) 122
Orders
    application 51–4
    definition 16
    engaged 51, 146
    Greek 17–34
        Corinthian 16, 33–4
        Doric 16, 17–24
        Ionic 16, 24–32
        timber origins 17, 146
    mixing of styles 53, 58, 61
    Neoclassicism, revival 146–7
    Roman 34–50
        Composite 16, 28, 49–50
        Corinthian 43–8
        Doric 20, 36–8
        Ionic 38–43
        Tuscan 16, 34–5
    superimposed 53
        Palazzo Capitolino, Rome **95**
        Palazzo Farnese, Rome 80
        Roman Architecture 58, 63
        Venetian palazzi **82–3**
    trabeated 51, 53
Orme, Philibert de l' (c.1510–1570) 123, 124
ornament
    acanthus 28, 33, **34**, **47**, 64
        Roman Orders, Ionic 38
    American designs **151**
    anthemion 18, **22**, **23**, **26**, 28
    bay-leaf 64
        bead-and-reel 24, **28**, 37, **63**
    dolphin 64
    egg-and-dart **45**, 56, **63**, 64
        Erechtheion capital, Athens **28**
        Ionic capital 24
        Roman Doric 37
    Greek Architecture **28**, 56, 64
    honeysuckle 24, 64
    leaf-and-tongue **28**, **63**
    lotus 34, 64
    palmette 48, 56, **63**
        Greek Orders
            Corinthian **34**
            Ionic 24, **26**, **28**
        Roman Architecture **63–4**
        Roman Orders
            Corinthian **44**, **46**
            Doric **37**
            Ionic 41
            scroll 64
Osborne House, Isle of Wight 163, **164**
Outram, J. (b. 1934) 170n

Paestum
    capitals **20**, 23

Composite Order 49
    entasis 22
    Neoclassicism influence 147, 151
Paine, James (1717–1789) 140
palaces
    Blenheim, Oxfordshire 127, **128**
    Cortile della Mostra **77**
    design comment 119–20, 122
    Diocletian, Palace of, at Spalato (Split) 54, 59, 61, 147–8
    German 132–4
    Grand Palais, Paris **60**
    Greenwich 123, **125**
    Hampton Court, England 122
    House of Raphael 74, 77, 80
    Louvre, The, Paris **119**, 120
    Neues Palais, Potsdam 133
    Osborne House, Isle of Wight 163, **164**
    Palazzo Capitolino, Rome 93, **95**
    Palazzo Chiericati façade 100
    Palazzo Corner della Ca'Grande, Venice 81, **82**
    Palazzo Corner-Spinelli, Venice 81, 82
    Palazzo della Cancellaria, Rome **74**
    Palazzo Ducale, Urbino 74, **75**, **77**
    Palazzo Farnese, Rome **79**, 80
    Palazzo Marino, Milan **94**
    Palazzo Massimi, Rome **78**, 80
    Palazzo Medici, Florence **72–3**, 74
    Palazzo Pésaro, Venice 82, **83**
    Palazzo Porto-Breganza (Casa del Diavolo), Vicenza **100**
    Palazzo Rezzonico, Venice 82
    Palazzo Riccardi see Palazzo Medici
    Palazzo Rucellai, Florence 70, **72**
    Palazzo Strozzi, Florence 72–3
    Palazzo del Tè, Mantua **75–6**, 77
    Palazzo Thiene, Vicenza 136
    Palazzo Valmarano, Vicenza 100
    Palazzo Véndramin-Calergi, Venice **81**, 82
    Palazzo Venezia, Rome 74
    Palazzo Vidoni Caffarelli 77
    Sanssouci, Potsdam **133–4**
    Schloss Nymphenburg, Munich **132**, 133
    Schönbrunn Palace, Vienna 132–3
    Upper Belvedere, Vienna 132
    Zwinger, Dresden **133**
Palais de Chaillot, Paris 169
Palais de Justice, Brussels 166
palazzi
    see also palaces
    Northern Bank, Belfast **80**
    Renaissance period 72–80
    Venetian 81–3
palazzo style, post-Neoclassicism 163
Palladianism 104, 106–22, 123, 135–44
    Assembly Rooms, York **137**
    Banqueting House, Whitehall 123, **124**
    Chiswick House, near London **136**
    England 123–4, 129–30
    Four Courts, Dublin **141**, 144
    Germany 140
    Horse Guards, Whitehall 140
    Palladian motif 144
    Parliament House (Bank of Ireland), Dublin 140, **141**
    Wanstead House 135
Palladio, Andrea (1508–1580) 17, 98–104, 136
    see also Palladianism
palmette pattern 48, 56, **63**
    Greek Architecture 24, **26**, **28**, **34**, 56
    Roman Architecture **63–4**

Paris, Rue de la Bourse/Rue des Colonnes, Greek Orders, Doric **23**
Parnell, Charles Octavius (1807–1865) 163
Pausanias, describing Doric columns, wooden 18
Pearce, Sir E. L. (c.1699–1733) 140, 142
Peckwater Quadrangle, Christchurch, Oxford 144
pedestals
  Order component 16
  Roman Orders
    Composite **50**
    Corinthian **47**
    Doric **38**
    Ionic **41**
    Tuscan **35**
Percier, Charles (1764–1838) **60**
Permoser, Balthasar (1651–1732) 133
Perrault, Claude (1613–1688) 17, 119–20
Perret, Auguste (1874–1954) 13, 167–8
Peruzzi, Baldassare (1481–1536) 17, 78, 80
Petersen, J. C. C. (1874–1923) 168, 169
Petra, Khazna **53**
piers 66–7
pilasters 66–7
Piranesi, Giovanni Battista (1720–1778) 146, 147
plans
  centralized 86–92
  circular 61, 63, 86–92
  development 61–2, 63
Plaw, John (c.1745–1820) **158–9**
Playfair, James (1755–1794) 154
Playfair, William Henry (1790–1857) 151, 166
podia
  Neoclassicism 159, **160–2**
  Roman Architecture 58
Poelaert, Joseph (1817–1879) 166
polygonal structures 61, 63
Pompeii 146, 151
Pöppelmann, M. D. (1662–1736) 133
Porphyrios, D. (b. 1949) 170n
Porta, Giacomo della (c.1533–1602) 94
Porta Palio, Verona **77**, 80
Post-Modernism 170
Primitive Hut 51, 53, 146, 151
proportions, Classical Architecture 13–14

Queen's House, The Greenwich **104**, 123, **126**
Quincy, A.-C. Quatremère de (1755–1849) 147

Radcliffe Library, Oxford 129, **130**
Rafn A. (1890–1953) 169
Rainaldi, Carlo (1611–1691) 109–10, 112
Raphael (Raffaello Sanzio) (1483–1520) 17, 77, 90
Record Office, Rome 53
Reform Club, London 163
regulae, Greek Orders, Doric 24
Renaissance period 65–104
  centralized/circular plans 86–92
  columns/pilasters/antae 65–8
  foundations 16–17
  key buildings, early part 68–73
  palazzi 72–80
  Roman influences 59, 63
  Tuscan Order **35**
  Venetian *palazzi* 81–4
Republican School 57–8
Revett, Nicholas (1720–1804) 147, 148
rhythm, Classical Architecture 14
Roberts, Henry (1803–1876) 163
Rococo style 106–22

definition 106
disfavour 151
French examples 119–22
  Vierzehnheiligen, Franconia 119
Roman Architecture
  Neoclassicism influence 146, 159–63, 168
  ornament **63–4**
  roots/influences 57–62
  Schools/regional variations 57–8
Roman Orders 17, 34–50
  columns 66
  Composite 28, 49–50
  Corinthian 43–8
  Doric 36–8
  Greek influences 57
  Ionic 38–43
  Tuscan 34–6
Romanesque Architecture 13
Romano, Giulio (c.1499–1546) 75–6, 77
Rome, *Tempietto* at S. Pietro in Montorio 86, 88, **89**, 90, 92
Rousseau, J.-J. (1712–1778) 147
Royal Crescent, Bath **143**
Royal Guard House, Berlin 22
Ruhmeshalle (Hall of Fame), Munich **22**
Ruskin, John (1819–1900) 12
Rustic Orders, sixteenth century 83

S. Andrews House, Edinburgh 170
S. Georges Hall, Liverpool 159, **162–3**
Sandys, Francis (fl. 1788–1814) 159
Sangallo, Antonio da, the Elder (c.1455–1534) 90
Sangallo, Antonio da, the Younger (1484–1546) **70**, 80, 90
Sangallo, Giuliano da (c.1443–1516) 86
Sanmicheli, Michele (c.1484–1559) 77
Sansovino, Jacopo (1486–1570) 81, 82–4
sarcophagi
  S. Francesco in Rimini, **71**
  S. Pancras church, London **150**
  'Weepers from Sidon' **67**
Savile, Sir Henry (1549–1622) **96**
Sayer, Robert 147
Scamozzi, Vincenzo (1552–1616) 82, 84, 103
  Classical Orders description 17
  Roman Orders, Ionic **40**
Scandinavia, Classical Architecture preference 168, 169, 170
Schinkel, Karl Friedrich (1781–1841)
  Altes Museum, Berlin **30**
  Egyptian influences 56
  Neoclassicism 151, 168
  Neue Wache, Berlin **22**
  Schauspielhaus, Berlin **32**
Schlüter, Andreas (c.1659–1714) 132
schools, Greek Doric High School, Edinburgh 155
Schools, Classical Architecture 56–8
Schools Quadrangle gate-tower, Oxford **96**
Schwanthaler, Ludwig (1802–1848) **20–1**
Scott, Sir George Gilbert (1811–1878) 12, 163
Selfridge's, Oxford St, London **167**
Sellars, James (1843–1888) 166
Serliana 77, 127, **128**, 129
Serlio, Sebastiano (1475–1554) 94
  Classical Orders description 16–17
  Roman Orders
    Corinthian 48
    Doric 38
    Ionic 41
    Tuscan Order **34–5**

Servandoni, G.-N. (1695–1766) 122
shafts
  Greek Orders
    Corinthian 33–4
    Doric 18, 22
    Ionic 24, 28, 31
  Roman Orders
    Composite 49
    Corinthian 43, 46
    Doric 36–7
    Ionic 38
    Tuscan 34
Shanahan, Michael **159**
Shaw, R. Norman (1831–1912) 166, 167
Shchusev, Alexei (1873–1949) 168, 169
Simpson, J. (b. 1954) 170n
Smirke, Sydney (1798–1877) 151, 163, **164**
Smith, A. D. (1866–1933) 167
Smith, A., Army and Navy Club, London 163
Soane, (Sir) John (1753–1837), Neoclassicism 147, 151, **153**, 155
Socialism, Classical Architecture and 170
Solari, Santino (1576–1646) 116
Somerset House, London 123, 140
Soufflot, J.-G. (1713–1780) 122–3, 147
Speer, Albert (1905–1981) 56, 168, 169
Statham, H. Heathcote (1839–1924) 17
statues **95**, **157**
Stern, R. A. M. (b. 1939) 170n
Strack, J. H. (1805–1880) **161**
Stuart, J. (1713–1788) 34, 147, **148**
Stüler, F. A. (1800–1865) **161**
stylobate 66
Summerson, Sir John (1904–1992) 13
Swales, Francis S. (1878–1962) 167

taenia, Greek Orders, Doric 24
Tait, Thomas S. (1882–1954) 170
Talman, William (1650–1719) 127
Taylorian Institution, Oxford 159
Tegae, Corinthian designs 57
temples
  see also churches and chapels
  Acropolis, Athens 57
  Apollo Didymaeus, Miletus **28**, 57
  Apollo Epicurius, Bassae 24, 28, **29**, 33
  Artemis, Ephesus 24, 57
  Athena Alea, Tegea 49
  Athena Pronaia, Delphi 17–18
  Bacchus, Baalbeck 53
  Bassae, Corinthia designs 57
  Castor and Pollux, Rome **44**
  circular 156–9
  Cori **36**, 53, 58
  Corinthian designs 57
  Doric Temple, Hagley, Worcs. **48**
  Elephantine, Egypt 56
  Erechtheion, Athens **26–8**, 31, 57, **63**
  Etruscan 58
  Fortuna Virilis, Rome 38–40, 58
  Four Winds, Castle Howard **128**
  Hephaestus, Athens **20**
  Ilissus, Athens 26, 57
  Jupiter, Rome 57
  Jupiter Stator, Rome **44**
  Maison Carrée, Nîmes **48**, 58
  Mars Ultor **58**
  Minerva Medica, Rome 86, **87**
  Minerva Polias, Athens **26**
  Mussenden, Downhill, Co. Londonderry **159**
  Neandria **25**, 26

Olympieion *see* Zeus Olympios
Pestum
  capitals **20**, 23
  Composite Order 49
  entasis 22
  Neoclassicism influence 147, 151
Pantheon, Rome 43, **46**, 59, **60**, 86, **87**
  architraves **63**
  Neoclassicism influence 159
Parthenon, Athens **18**, 57
  architraves **63**
  models 20–1
Poseidon Hippios, wooden columns 18
Queen Hatshepsut, Dêr el-Bahari 56
Roman Architecture revival 155–9
round, Baalbeck 54
Tempietto, S. Pietro in Montorio, Rome 86,
   88, **89**, 90, 92, 155, 159
Termessus, Pisidia 54
Theseum, Athens **20**
Venus, Baalbek **54**
Vesta, Tivoli **44**, **63**, 86, **88**
Zeus, Cilicia 57
Zeus, Olbios, Cilicia 57
Zeus, Olympia 18
Zeus Olympios, Athens **43**, 57
Tengbom, I. J. (1878–1968) 168
Terry, Q. (b. 1937) 170n
theatres
  Marcellus, Rome **36–7**, **51**
  Opera House, Berlin 133, **134**, 140
  Schauspielhaus, Berlin **32**
  Teatro Olimpico, vicenza **101**, 103
  Theatre of Marcellus, Rome 82, 84
Thermae
  Caracalla, Rome 59, **61**, 146, 159, 163
  Diocletian, Rome **61**, 146
Thibierge, Habert **23**
Thomas, Grand Palais, Paris **60**
Thomas, Sir Alfred Brumwell *see* Brumwell
   Thomas
Thomson, Alexander (1817–1875) **32**
  Egyptian influences 56
  Neoclassicism 151, 166
Thorvaldsen, Bertel (1770–1844) 23
timber, Doric Order origins 17–18
tombs
  Beni-Hasan, Egypt 56
  David Hume, Edinburgh **157**
  Lion tomb, Cnidos 19, 57

torus
  Greek Orders 24, 33
  Roman Orders 34, 49
Tower of the Winds, Athens 33, **34**
town halls
  Belfast City Hall 167
  Birmingham 159, **161**
  Chelsea **165**
  Leeds 166–7
  Stockport **166**, 167
  Todmorden 159, **162**
  Vicenza **99**, 100
trabeation 51, 53, 56, 62–3
Travellers' Club, London 163
triglyphs
  Greek Orders, Doric **19**, 24
  Hellenistic modifications 57
  Roman Orders, Doric 36–8
  wooden origins 18
Trinity College Library, Cambridge 125, **126**
triumphal arches 58–61
  see also arches
Troost, Paul Ludwig (1878–1934) 169
  Haus der Kunst, Munilh **31**, 168
Tuscan Order 16, 34–6
  derivations 57
  pilasters 77

Üblhör, J. G. (1700–1763) 118–9

Vanbrugh, Sir John (1664–1726) 127–8, 129
Vasari, Giorgio (1511–1574) 93
Vatican 86, 116
vaulting 53–4, 58, 59, 62
Venice
  Biblioteca Marciana 82–3, **84**
  La Zecca (The Mint) 83
  palazzi 81–3
Vestier, Nicolas-Jacques-Antoine (1765–1816) **23**
Vignola, Giacomo Barozzi da (1507–1573) 17,
   94, 97–8
  Roman Orders
    Composite **49**
    Corinthian **46**
    Doric **37**, 38
    Ionic **40**
    Tuscan **35**
Vignon, A.-P. (1762–1828) 159, **160–1**
villas
  see also country houses

Adriana, Tivoli 59
Chiswick House, London **136**
Heathcote, nr Ilkley, Yorkshire 167
Villa Capra, nr Vicenza 100, **101**, 103, **136**, 137
Villa Madama, Rome 77
Villa Malcontenta, near Mestre 103
Villa Rotonda *see* Villa Capra
Viscardi, Giovanni (1647–1713) 133
Vitruvius (Marcus Vitruvius Pollio)
  Architecture definition 12
  Etruscan temple description **58**
  Orders, early descriptions 16
  Roman Orders, Ionic 41
volutes
  Greek Orders, Ionic 24–8
  Roman Orders
    Composite 49
    Corinthian 44, **47**, 48
    Ionic 38–43

Wagner, Otto (1841–1918) 170
Walhalla, Bavaria 20–1
War Office, Whitehall, London **166**
Webb, John (1611–1672) 123
Weinbrenner, Friedrich (1766–1826),
   Neoclassicism 155
Welch, Edward (1806–1868) 159, **161**
Wilkins, William (1778–1839) 151, 155
Winckelmann, J. J. (1717–1768) 147
windows
  Diocletian, Vignola variation **97**
  Greek/Roman comparison 63
  Palazzo Medici, Florence **72**
  Venetian type 81
Wood, John, the Elder (1704–1754) 144
Wood, John, the Younger (1728–1781) 144
Wood, Robert (*c.*1717–1771) 147
Woolfe, John (*ob.*1793) 144
Wotton, Sir Henry (1568–1639) 12
Wren, Sir Christopher (1632–1723) 12, 123,
   125–7
Wrenaissance **165**, 167
Wyatt, James (1746–1813) **157**

Young, William (1843–1900) **165–6**

Zeughaus, Berlin 132
Zimmermann, Dominikus (1685–1766) 118–
   19
Zuccalli, Enrico (1642–1724) 114, 116